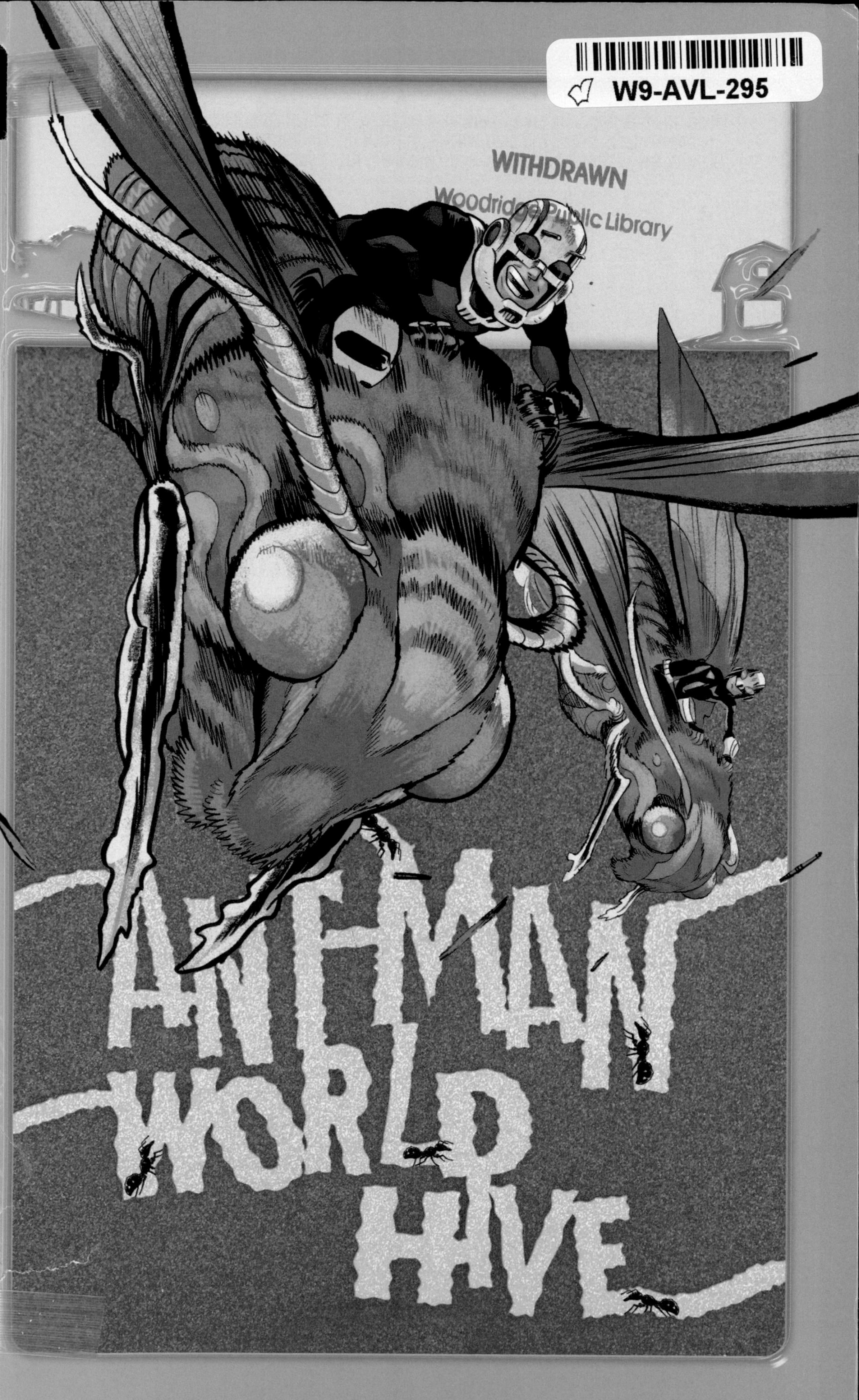
ANT-MAN
WORLD
HIVE

WHEN THE ORIGINAL ANT-MAN, HANK PYM, RETIRED, ANOTHER MAN ROSE/SHRANK TO THE OCCASION (ERR, STOLE THE COSTUME)—SCOTT LANG! WITH HIS SORDID PAST SOMEWHAT BEHIND HIM, SCOTT TOOK ON THE SIZE-CHANGING, ANT-COMMUNICATING ABILITIES OF...

ANT-MAN

WORLD HIVE

ZEB WELLS WRITER

DYLAN BURNETT ARTIST

MIKE SPICER COLORIST

VC's CORY PETIT LETTERER

EDUARD PETROVICH COVER ARTIST

LAUREN AMARO ASSISTANT EDITOR

DARREN SHAN EDITOR

ANT-MAN CREATED BY STAN LEE, LARRY LIEBER & JACK KIRBY

JENNIFER GRÜNWALD COLLECTION EDITOR
MAIA LOY ASSISTANT MANAGING EDITOR
LISA MONTALBANO ASSISTANT MANAGING EDITOR
MARK D. BEAZLEY EDITOR, SPECIAL PROJECTS
JEFF YOUNGQUIST VP PRODUCTION & SPECIAL PROJECTS
JAY BOWEN BOOK DESIGNER
DAVID GABRIEL SVP PRINT, SALES & MARKETING
C.B. CEBULSKI EDITOR IN CHIEF

ANT-MAN: WORLD HIVE. Contains material originally published in magazine form as ANT-MAN (2020) #1-5. First printing 2020. ISBN 978-1-302-92258-0. Published by MARVEL WORLDWIDE, INC., a subsidiary of MARVEL ENTERTAINMENT, LLC. OFFICE OF PUBLICATION: 1290 Avenue of the Americas, New York, NY 10104. © 2020 MARVEL No similarity between any of the names, characters, persons, and/or institutions in this magazine with those of any living or dead person or institution is intended, and any such similarity which may exist is purely coincidental. **Printed in Canada.** KEVIN FEIGE, Chief Creative Officer; DAN BUCKLEY, President, Marvel Entertainment; JOHN NEE, Publisher; JOE QUESADA, EVP & Creative Director; TOM BREVOORT, SVP of Publishing; DAVID BOGART, Associate Publisher & SVP of Talent Affairs; Publishing & Partnership; DAVID GABRIEL, VP of Print & Digital Publishing; JEFF YOUNGQUIST, VP of Production & Special Projects; DAN CARR, Executive Director of Publishing Technology; ALEX MORALES, Director of Publishing Operations; DAN EDINGTON, Managing Editor; SUSAN CRESPI, Production Manager; STAN LEE, Chairman Emeritus. For information regarding advertising in Marvel Comics or on Marvel.com, please contact Vit DeBellis, Custom Solutions & Integrated Advertising Manager, at vdebellis@marvel.com. For Marvel subscription inquiries, please call 888-511-5480. **Manufactured between 7/3/2020 and 8/4/2020 by SOLISCO PRINTERS, SCOTT, QC, CANADA.**

10 9 8 7 6 5 4 3 2 1

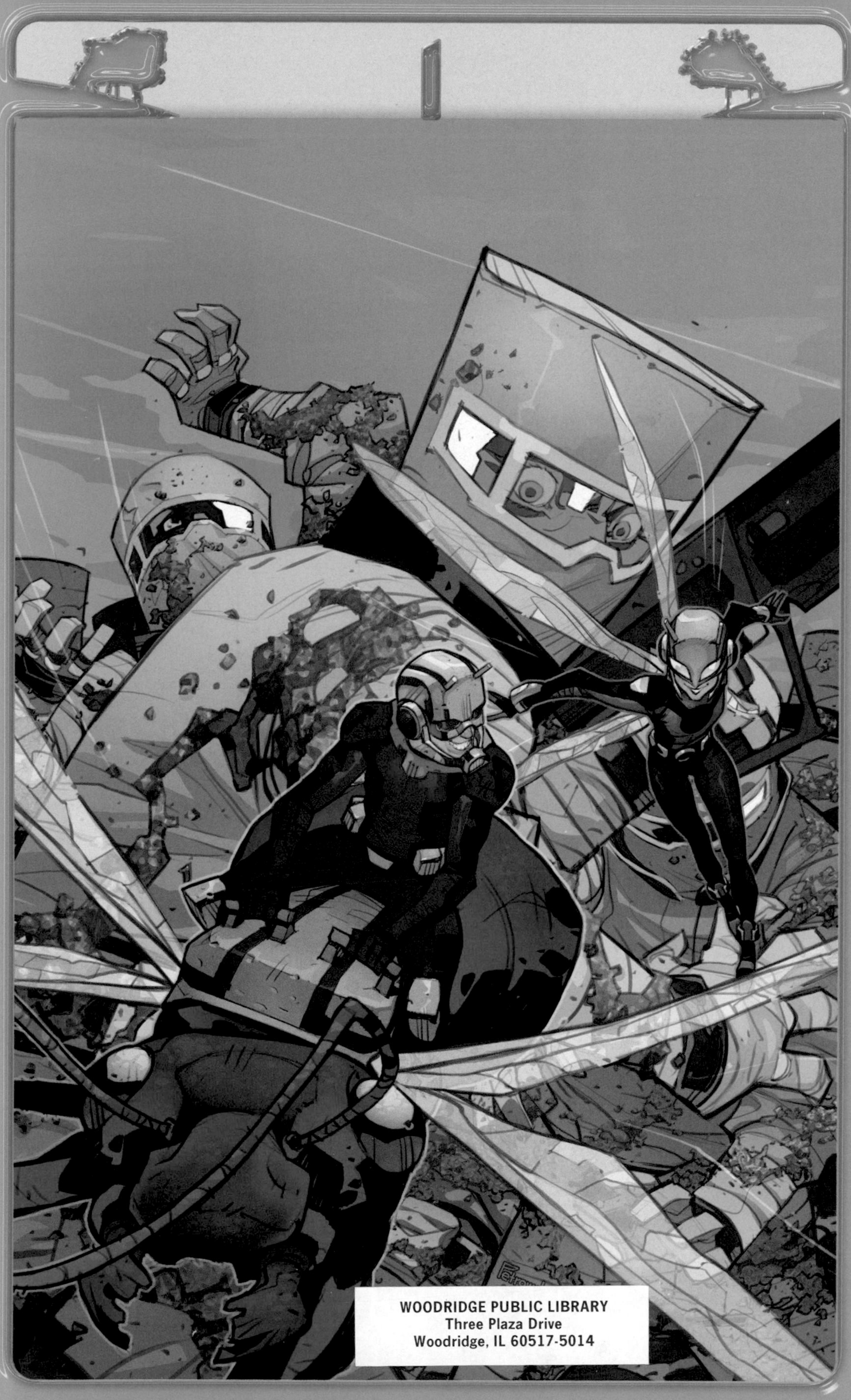

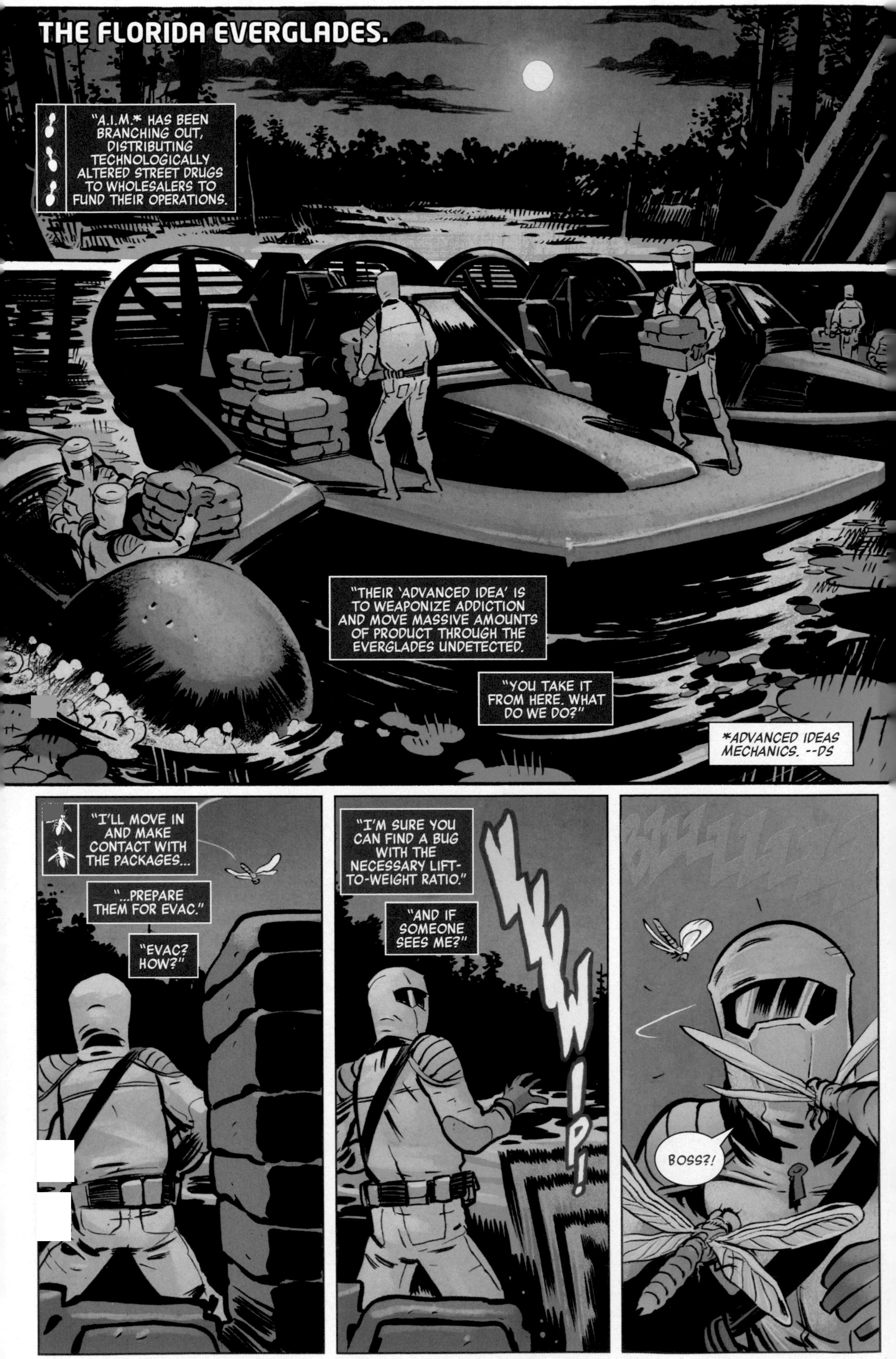
THE FLORIDA EVERGLADES.
"A.I.M.* HAS BEEN BRANCHING OUT, DISTRIBUTING TECHNOLOGICALLY ALTERED STREET DRUGS TO WHOLESALERS TO FUND THEIR OPERATIONS.
"THEIR 'ADVANCED IDEA' IS TO WEAPONIZE ADDICTION AND MOVE MASSIVE AMOUNTS OF PRODUCT THROUGH THE EVERGLADES UNDETECTED.
"YOU TAKE IT FROM HERE. WHAT DO WE DO?"
*ADVANCED IDEAS MECHANICS. --DS
"I'LL MOVE IN AND MAKE CONTACT WITH THE PACKAGES...
"...PREPARE THEM FOR EVAC."
"EVAC? HOW?"
"I'M SURE YOU CAN FIND A BUG WITH THE NECESSARY LIFT-TO-WEIGHT RATIO."
"AND IF SOMEONE SEES ME?"
WHWIP!
BOSS?!

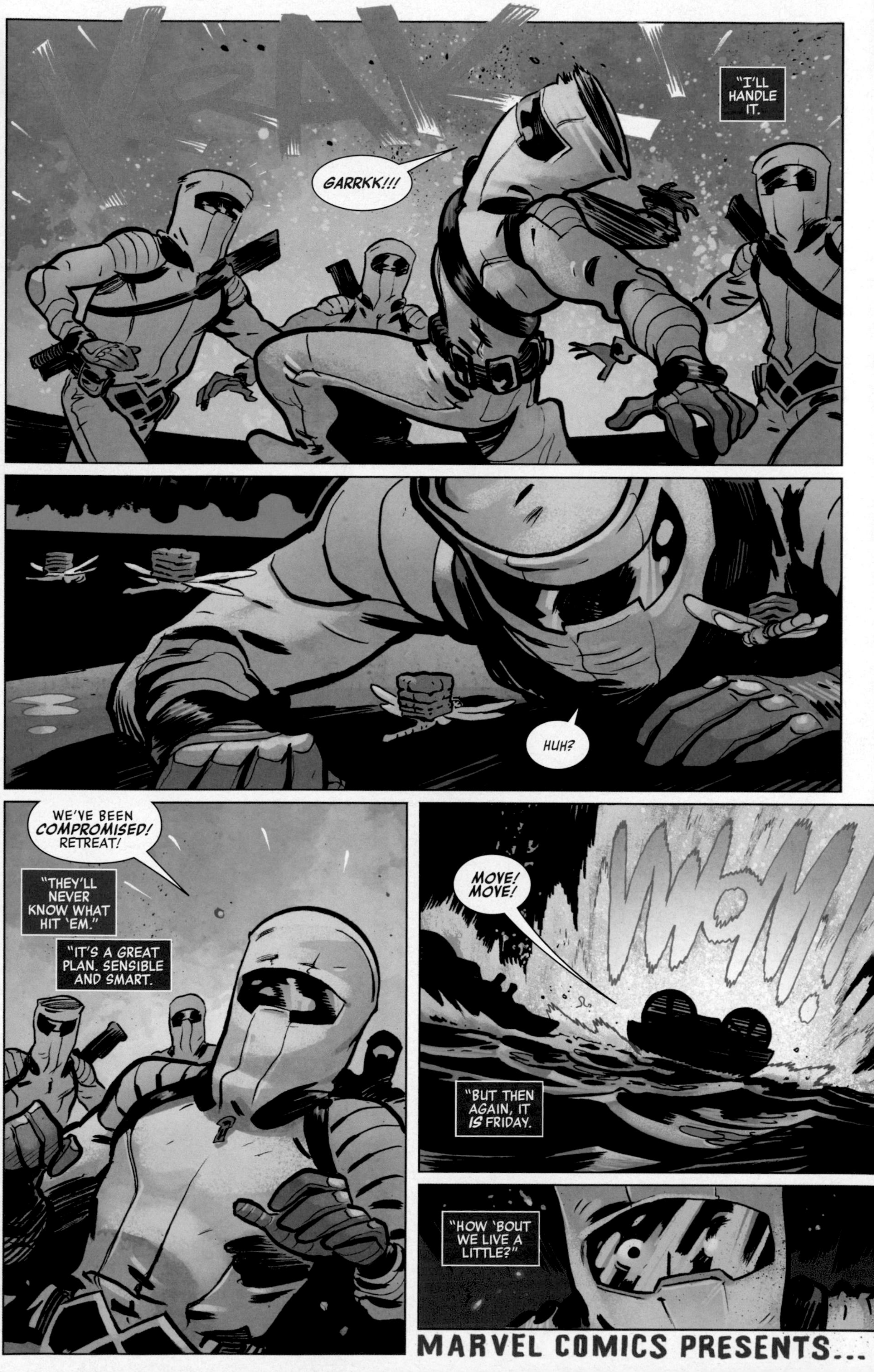
"I'LL HANDLE IT.
GARRKK!!!
HUH?
WE'VE BEEN COMPROMISED! RETREAT!
"THEY'LL NEVER KNOW WHAT HIT 'EM."
"IT'S A GREAT PLAN. SENSIBLE AND SMART.
MOVE! MOVE!
"BUT THEN AGAIN, IT IS FRIDAY.
"HOW 'BOUT WE LIVE A LITTLE?"
MARVEL COMICS PRESENTS...

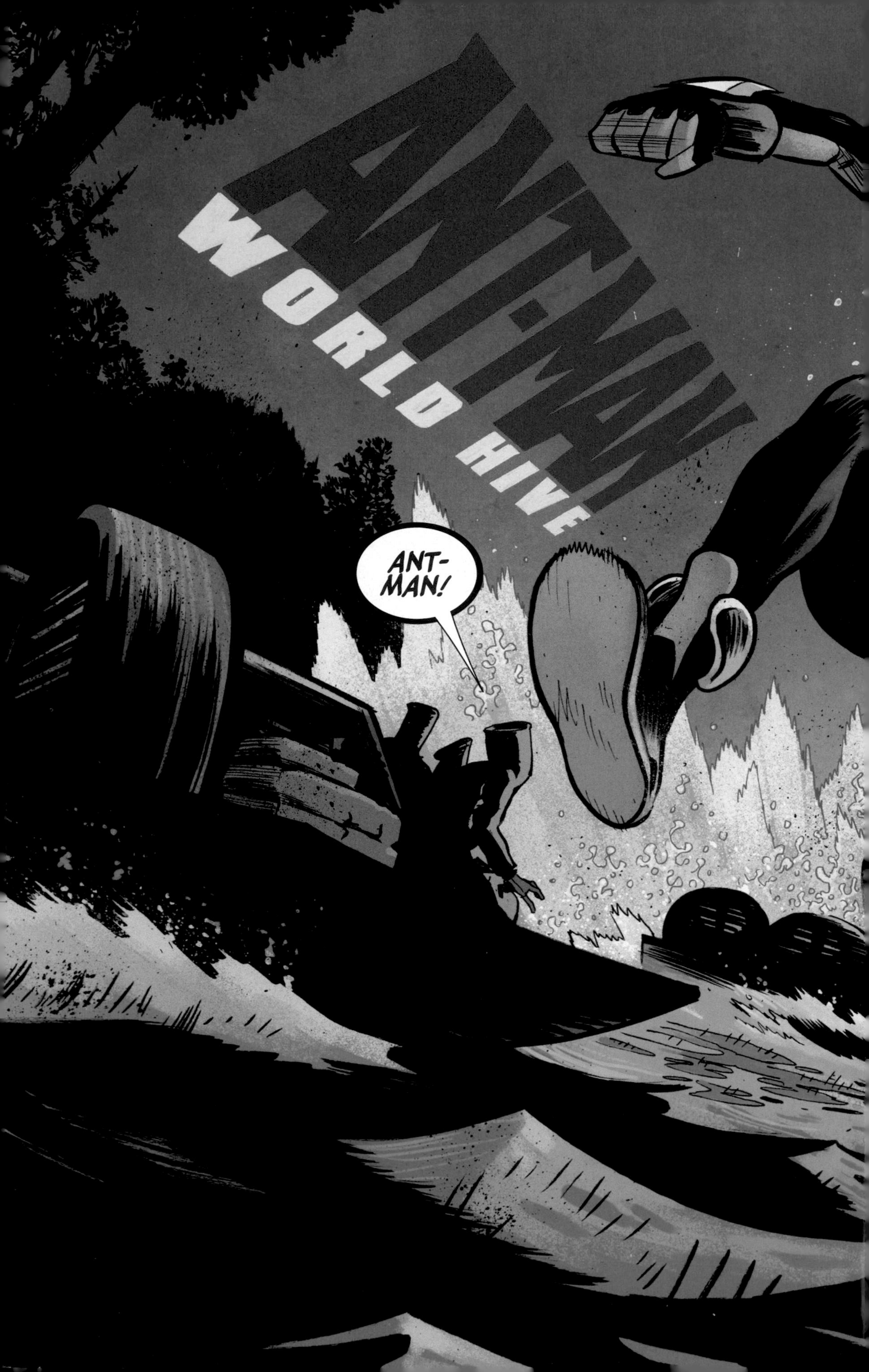
ANT-MAN
WORLD HIVE
ANT-MAN!

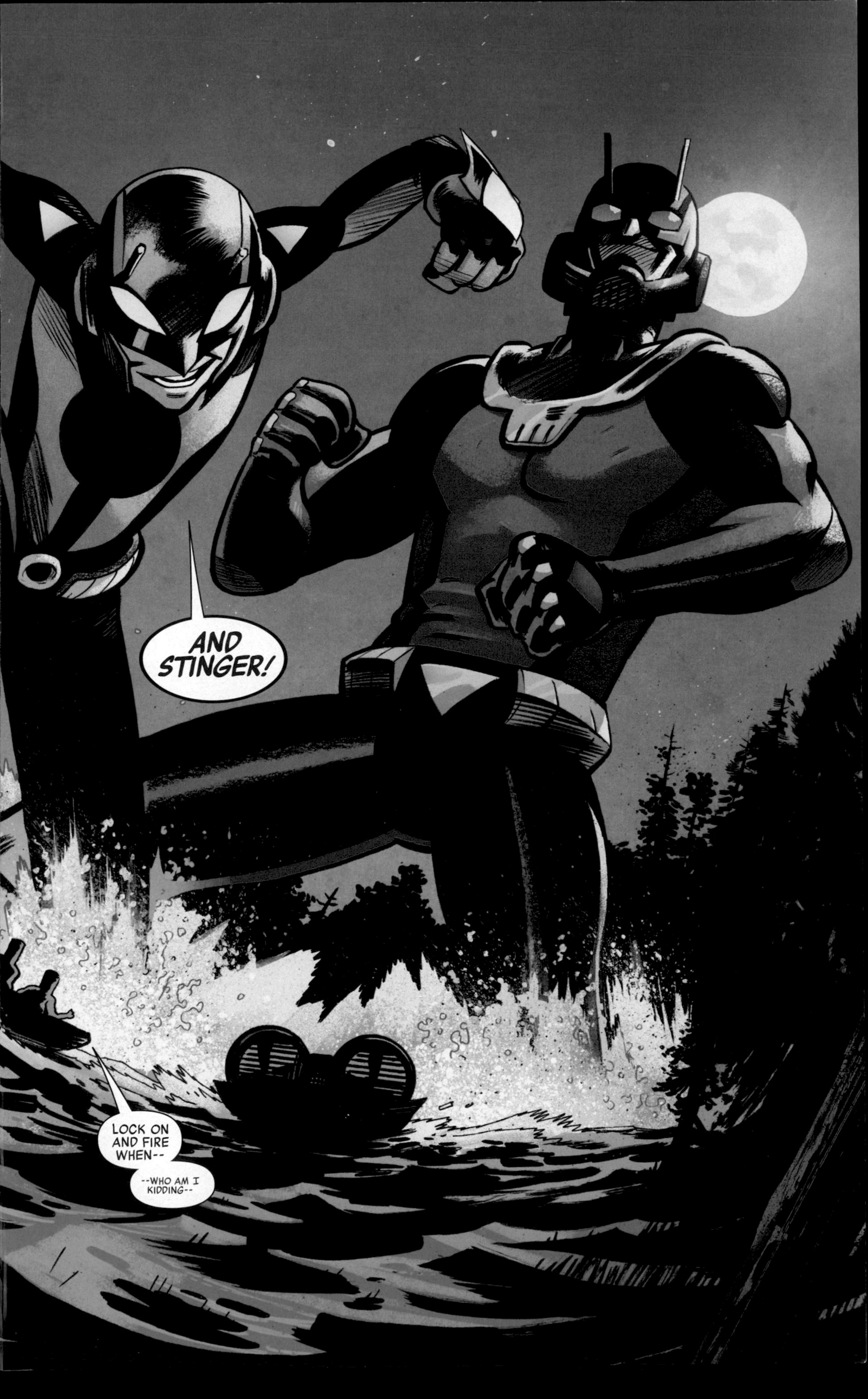
AND STINGER!
LOCK ON AND FIRE WHEN--
--WHO AM I KIDDING--

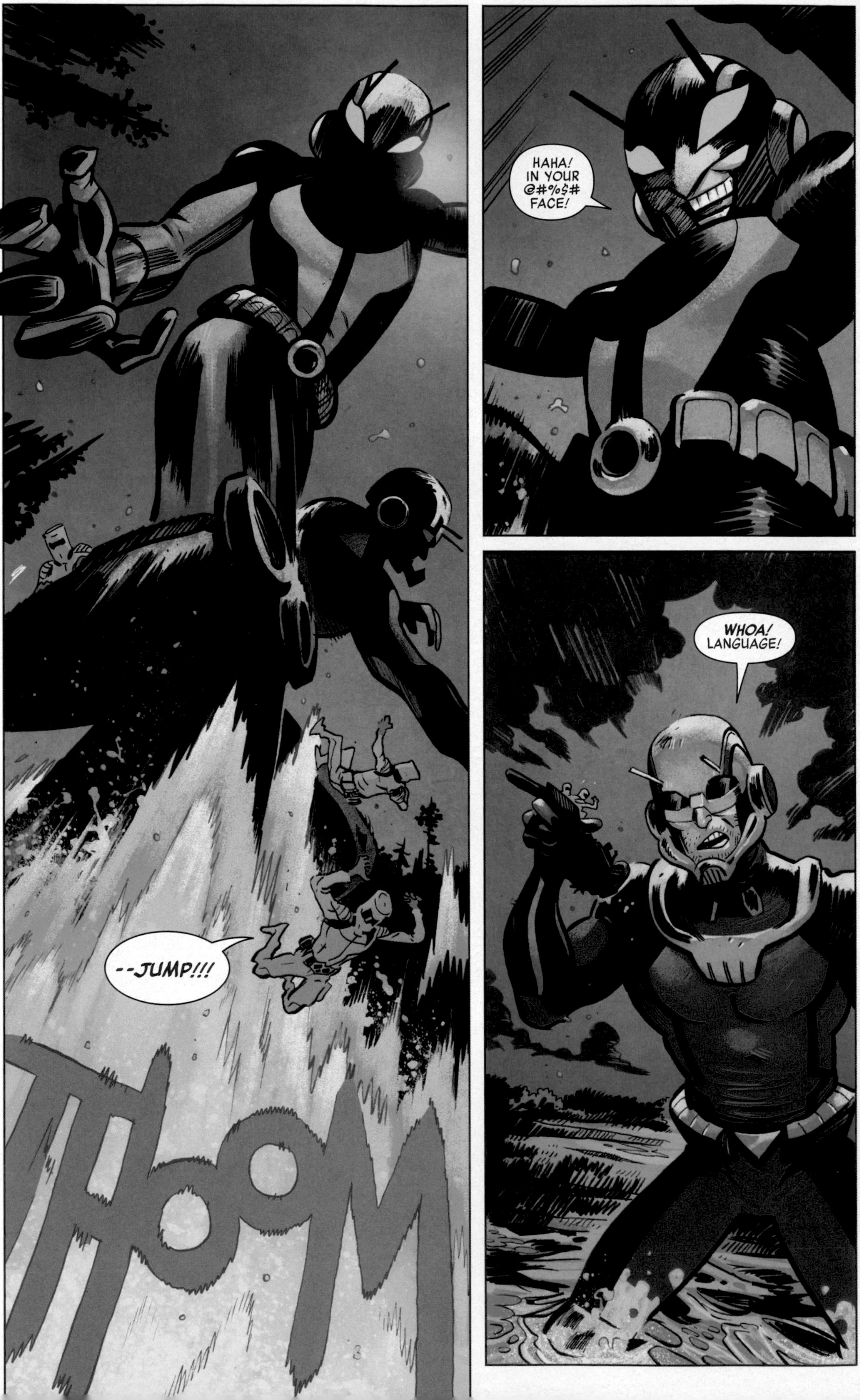
--JUMP!!!
THOOM
HAHA! IN YOUR @#%$# FACE!
WHOA! LANGUAGE!

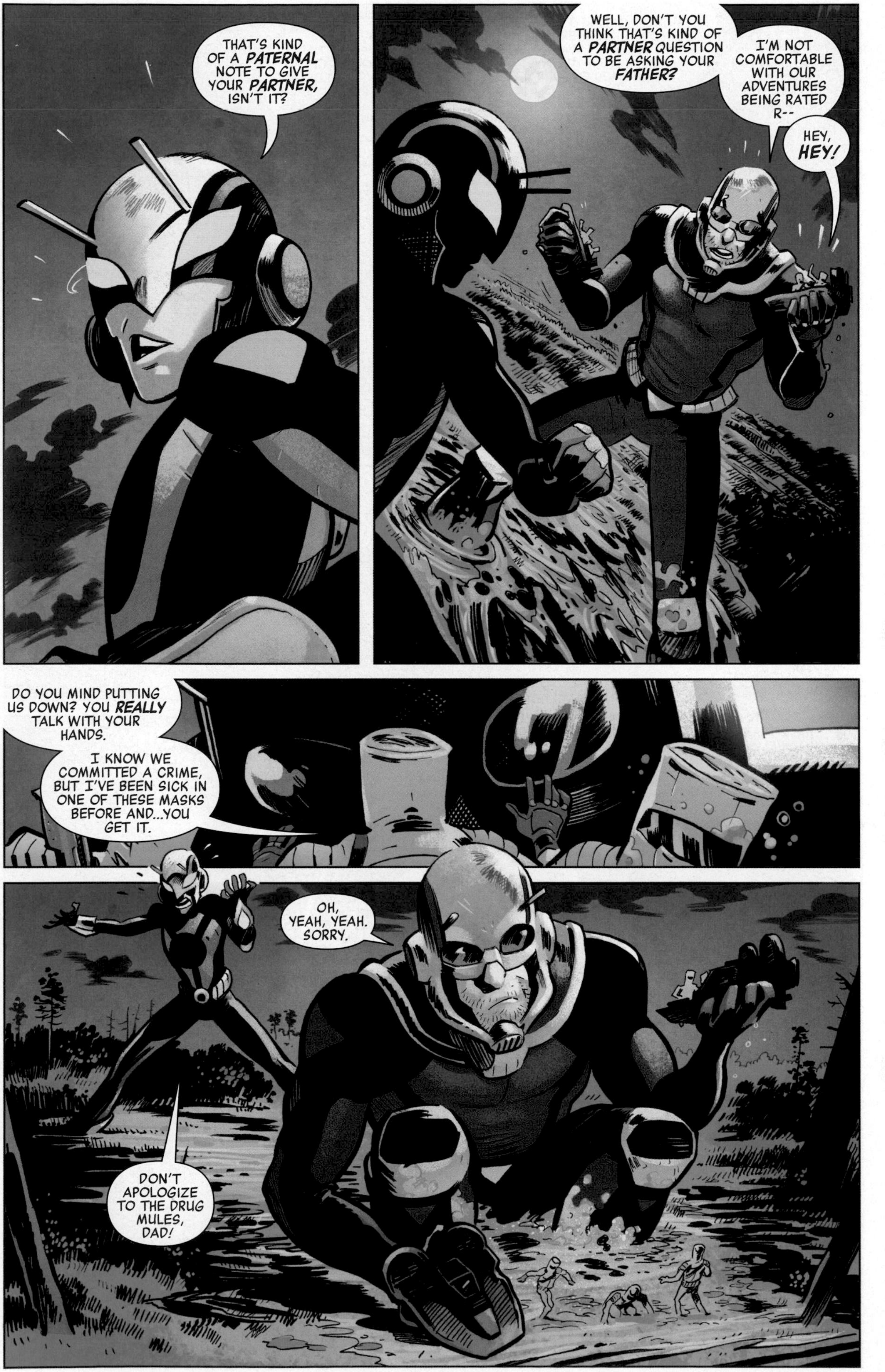

THAT'S KIND OF A PATERNAL NOTE TO GIVE YOUR PARTNER, ISN'T IT?
WELL, DON'T YOU THINK THAT'S KIND OF A PARTNER QUESTION TO BE ASKING YOUR FATHER?
I'M NOT COMFORTABLE WITH OUR ADVENTURES BEING RATED R--
HEY, HEY!
DO YOU MIND PUTTING US DOWN? YOU REALLY TALK WITH YOUR HANDS.
I KNOW WE COMMITTED A CRIME, BUT I'VE BEEN SICK IN ONE OF THESE MASKS BEFORE AND...YOU GET IT.
OH, YEAH, YEAH. SORRY.
DON'T APOLOGIZE TO THE DRUG MULES, DAD!

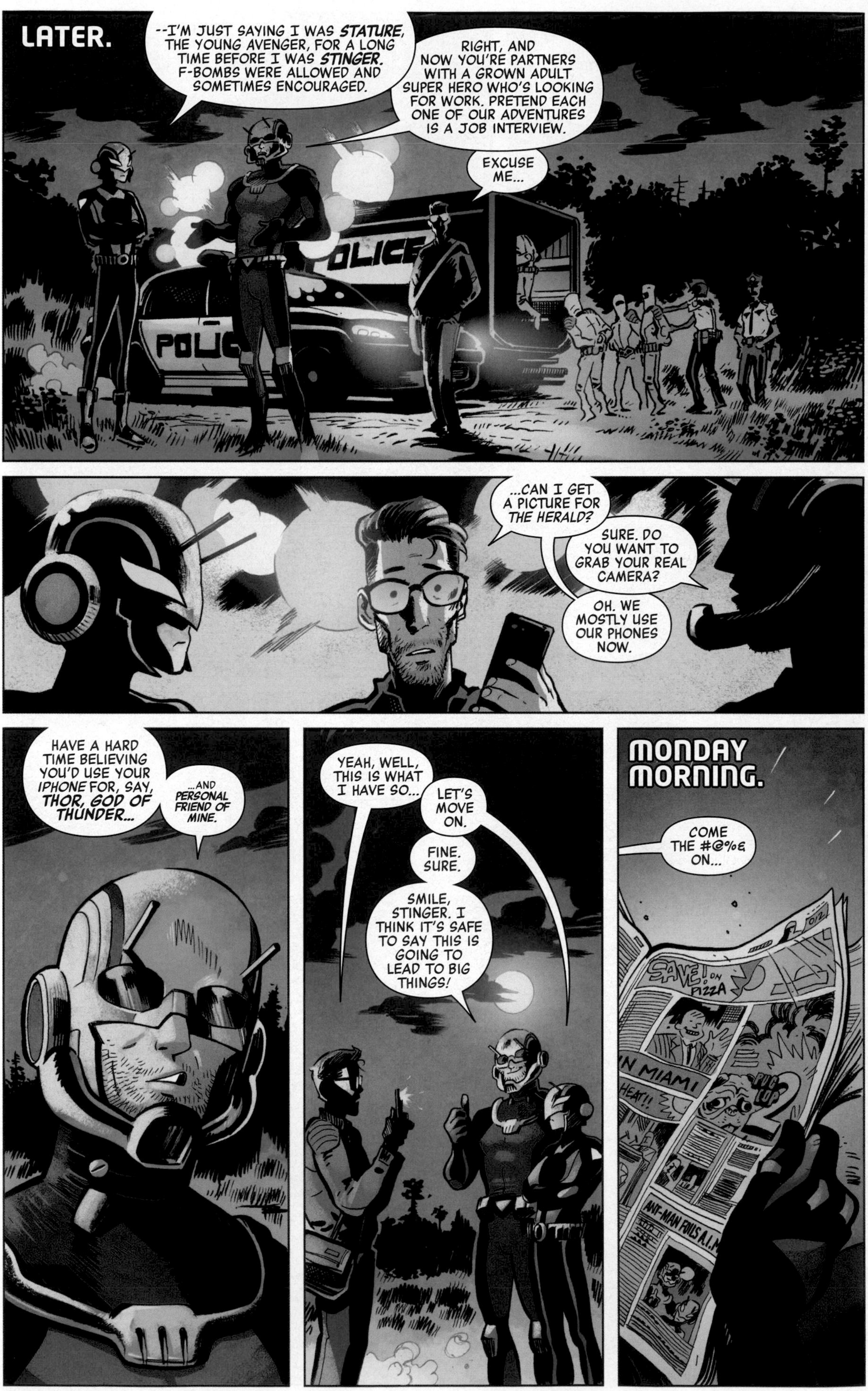
LATER.
--I'M JUST SAYING I WAS STATURE, THE YOUNG AVENGER, FOR A LONG TIME BEFORE I WAS STINGER. F-BOMBS WERE ALLOWED AND SOMETIMES ENCOURAGED.
RIGHT, AND NOW YOU'RE PARTNERS WITH A GROWN ADULT SUPER HERO WHO'S LOOKING FOR WORK. PRETEND EACH ONE OF OUR ADVENTURES IS A JOB INTERVIEW.
EXCUSE ME...
POLICE
POLICE
...CAN I GET A PICTURE FOR THE HERALD?
SURE. DO YOU WANT TO GRAB YOUR REAL CAMERA?
OH. WE MOSTLY USE OUR PHONES NOW.
HAVE A HARD TIME BELIEVING YOU'D USE YOUR IPHONE FOR, SAY, THOR, GOD OF THUNDER...
...AND PERSONAL FRIEND OF MINE.
YEAH, WELL, THIS IS WHAT I HAVE SO...
LET'S MOVE ON.
FINE. SURE.
SMILE, STINGER. I THINK IT'S SAFE TO SAY THIS IS GOING TO LEAD TO BIG THINGS!
MONDAY MORNING.
COME THE #@%& ON...
SAVE! ON PIZZA
ANT-MAN FOILS A.I.M.

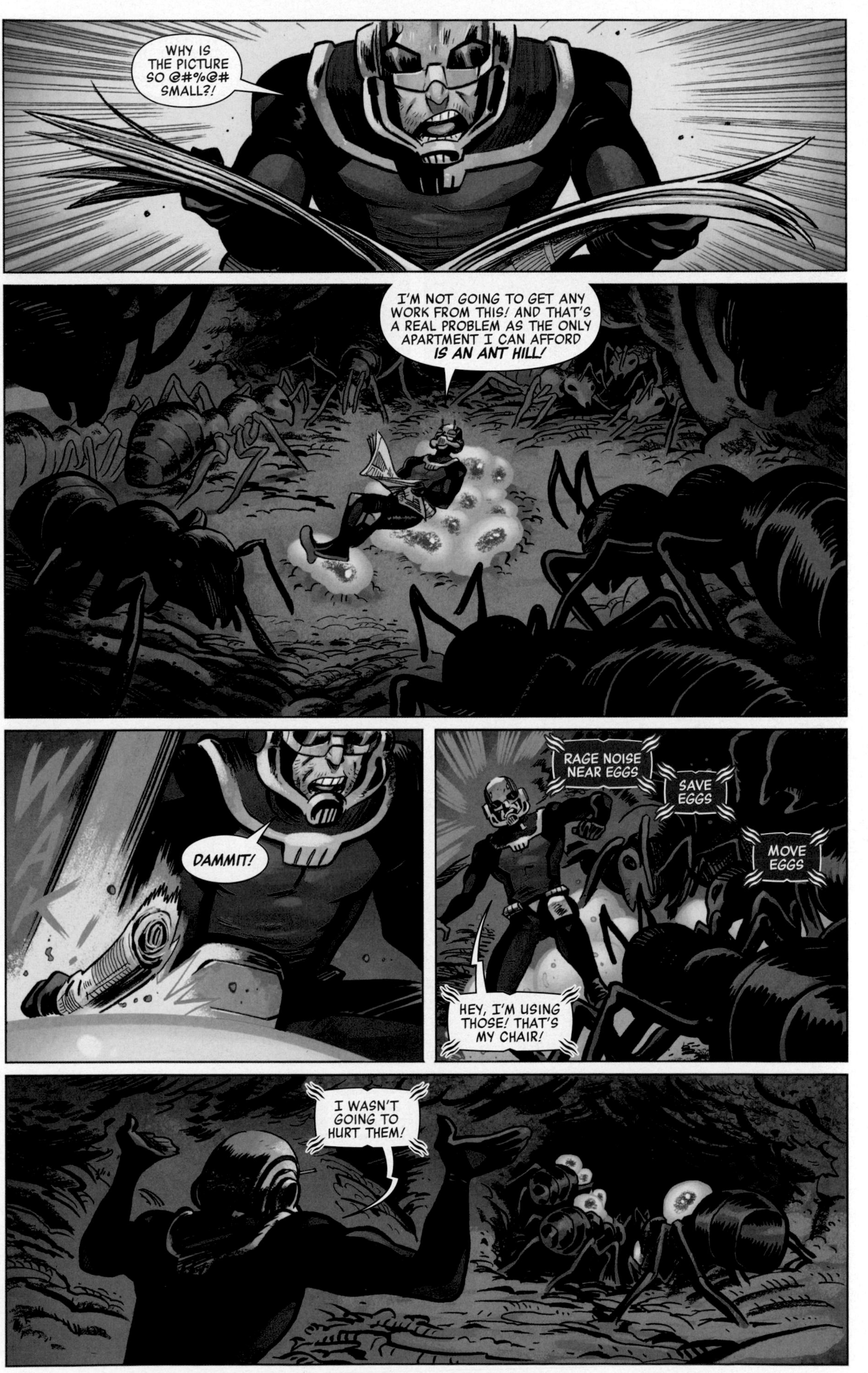
WHY IS THE PICTURE SO @#%@# SMALL?!
I'M NOT GOING TO GET ANY WORK FROM THIS! AND THAT'S A REAL PROBLEM AS THE ONLY APARTMENT I CAN AFFORD IS AN ANT HILL!
DAMMIT!
RAGE NOISE NEAR EGGS
SAVE EGGS
MOVE EGGS
HEY, I'M USING THOSE! THAT'S MY CHAIR!
I WASN'T GOING TO HURT THEM!

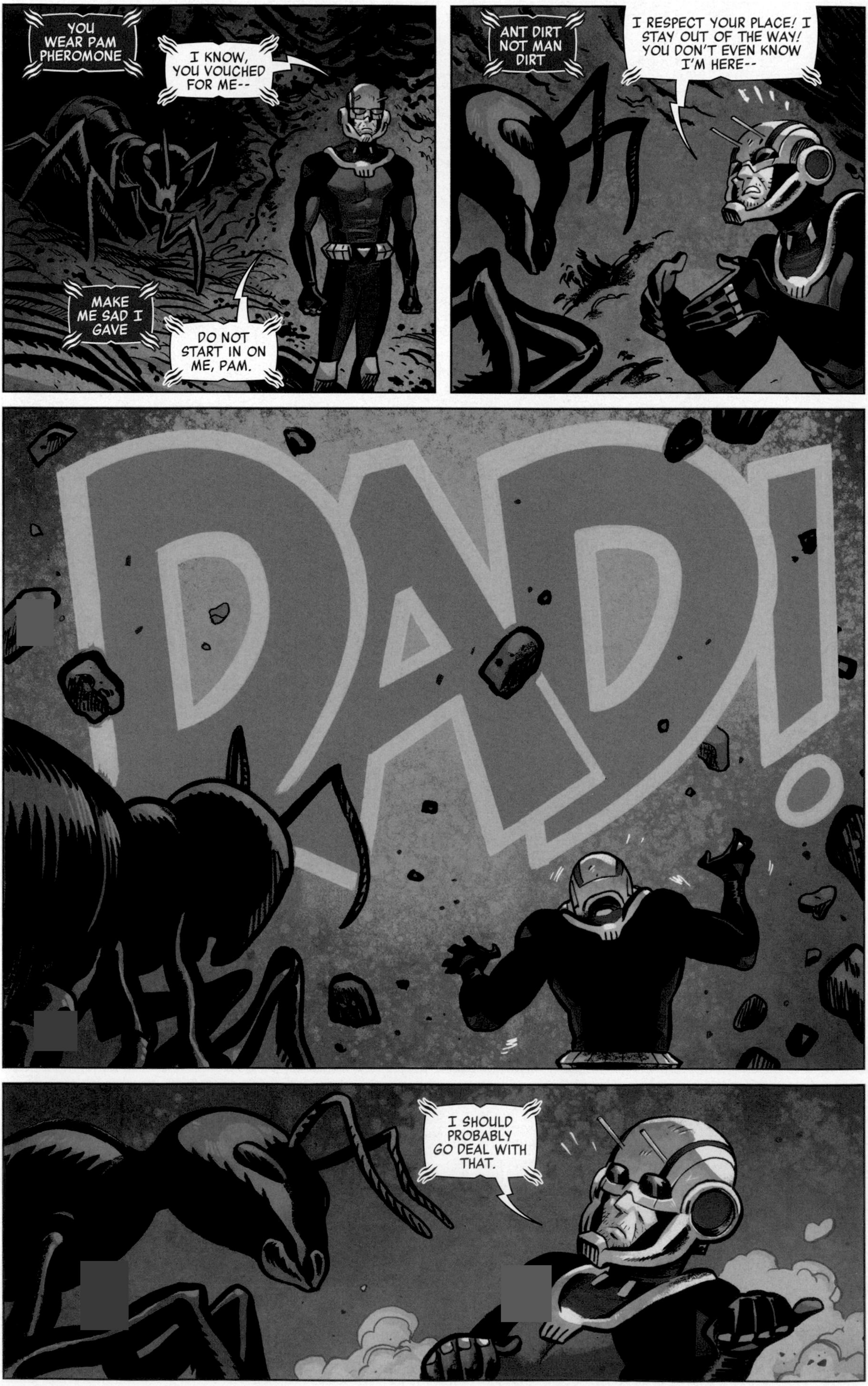
YOU WEAR PAM PHEROMONE
I KNOW, YOU VOUCHED FOR ME--
MAKE ME SAD I GAVE
DO NOT START IN ON ME, PAM.
ANT DIRT NOT MAN DIRT
I RESPECT YOUR PLACE! I STAY OUT OF THE WAY! YOU DON'T EVEN KNOW I'M HERE--
DAD!
I SHOULD PROBABLY GO DEAL WITH THAT.

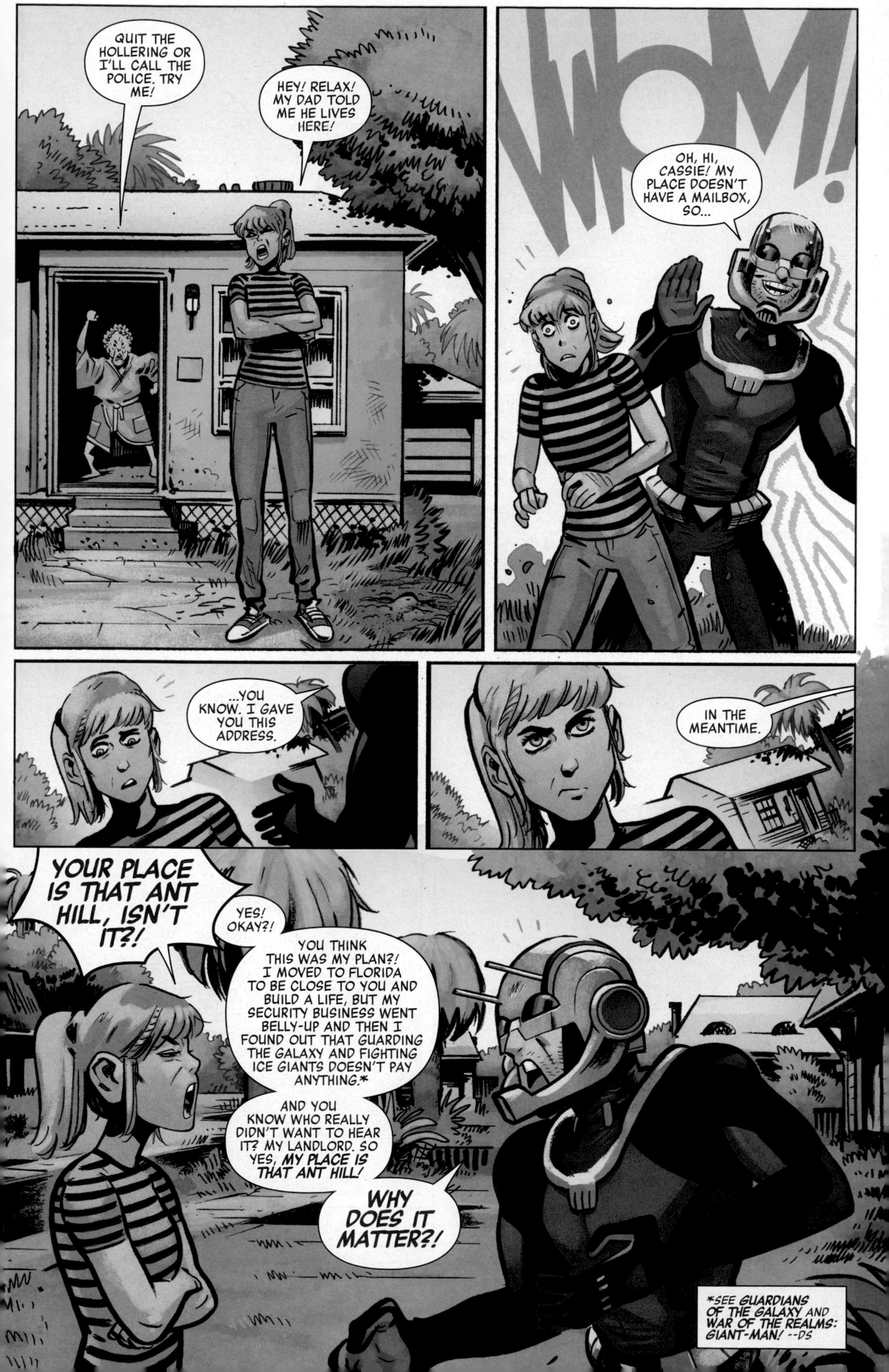
QUIT THE HOLLERING OR I'LL CALL THE POLICE. TRY ME!
HEY! RELAX! MY DAD TOLD ME HE LIVES HERE!
WOM!
OH, HI, CASSIE! MY PLACE DOESN'T HAVE A MAILBOX, SO...
...YOU KNOW. I GAVE YOU THIS ADDRESS.
IN THE MEANTIME.
YOUR PLACE IS THAT ANT HILL, ISN'T IT?!
YES! OKAY?!
YOU THINK THIS WAS MY PLAN?! I MOVED TO FLORIDA TO BE CLOSE TO YOU AND BUILD A LIFE, BUT MY SECURITY BUSINESS WENT BELLY-UP AND THEN I FOUND OUT THAT GUARDING THE GALAXY AND FIGHTING ICE GIANTS DOESN'T PAY ANYTHING.*
AND YOU KNOW WHO REALLY DIDN'T WANT TO HEAR IT? MY LANDLORD. SO YES, MY PLACE IS THAT ANT HILL!
WHY DOES IT MATTER?!
*SEE GUARDIANS OF THE GALAXY AND WAR OF THE REALMS: GIANT-MAN! --DS

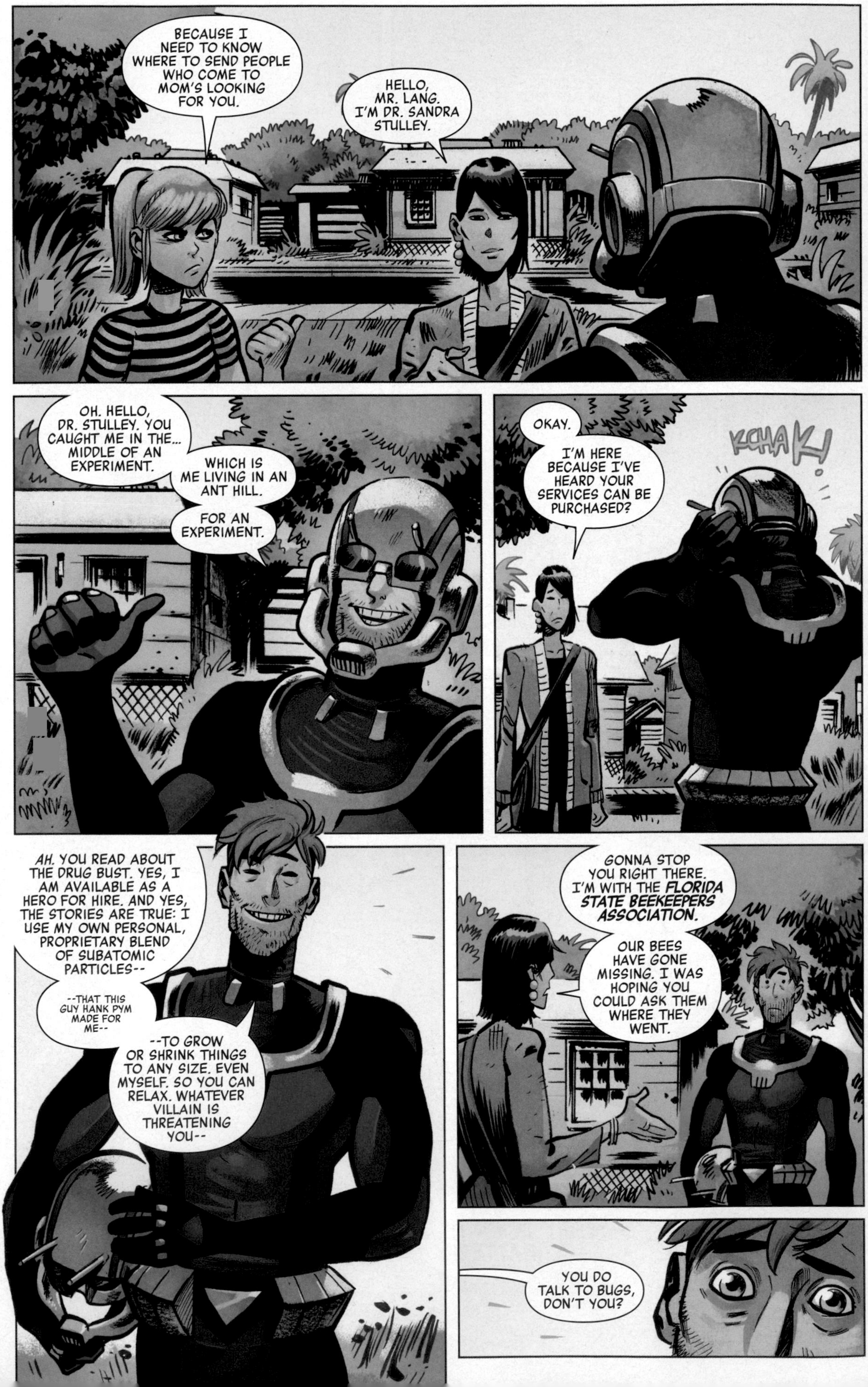

BECAUSE I NEED TO KNOW WHERE TO SEND PEOPLE WHO COME TO MOM'S LOOKING FOR YOU.
HELLO, MR. LANG. I'M DR. SANDRA STULLEY.
OH. HELLO, DR. STULLEY. YOU CAUGHT ME IN THE... MIDDLE OF AN EXPERIMENT.
WHICH IS ME LIVING IN AN ANT HILL.
FOR AN EXPERIMENT.
OKAY.
I'M HERE BECAUSE I'VE HEARD YOUR SERVICES CAN BE PURCHASED?
KCHAK!
AH. YOU READ ABOUT THE DRUG BUST. YES, I AM AVAILABLE AS A HERO FOR HIRE. AND YES, THE STORIES ARE TRUE: I USE MY OWN PERSONAL, PROPRIETARY BLEND OF SUBATOMIC PARTICLES--
--THAT THIS GUY HANK PYM MADE FOR ME--
--TO GROW OR SHRINK THINGS TO ANY SIZE. EVEN MYSELF. SO YOU CAN RELAX. WHATEVER VILLAIN IS THREATENING YOU--
GONNA STOP YOU RIGHT THERE. I'M WITH THE FLORIDA STATE BEEKEEPERS ASSOCIATION.
OUR BEES HAVE GONE MISSING. I WAS HOPING YOU COULD ASK THEM WHERE THEY WENT.
YOU DO TALK TO BUGS, DON'T YOU?

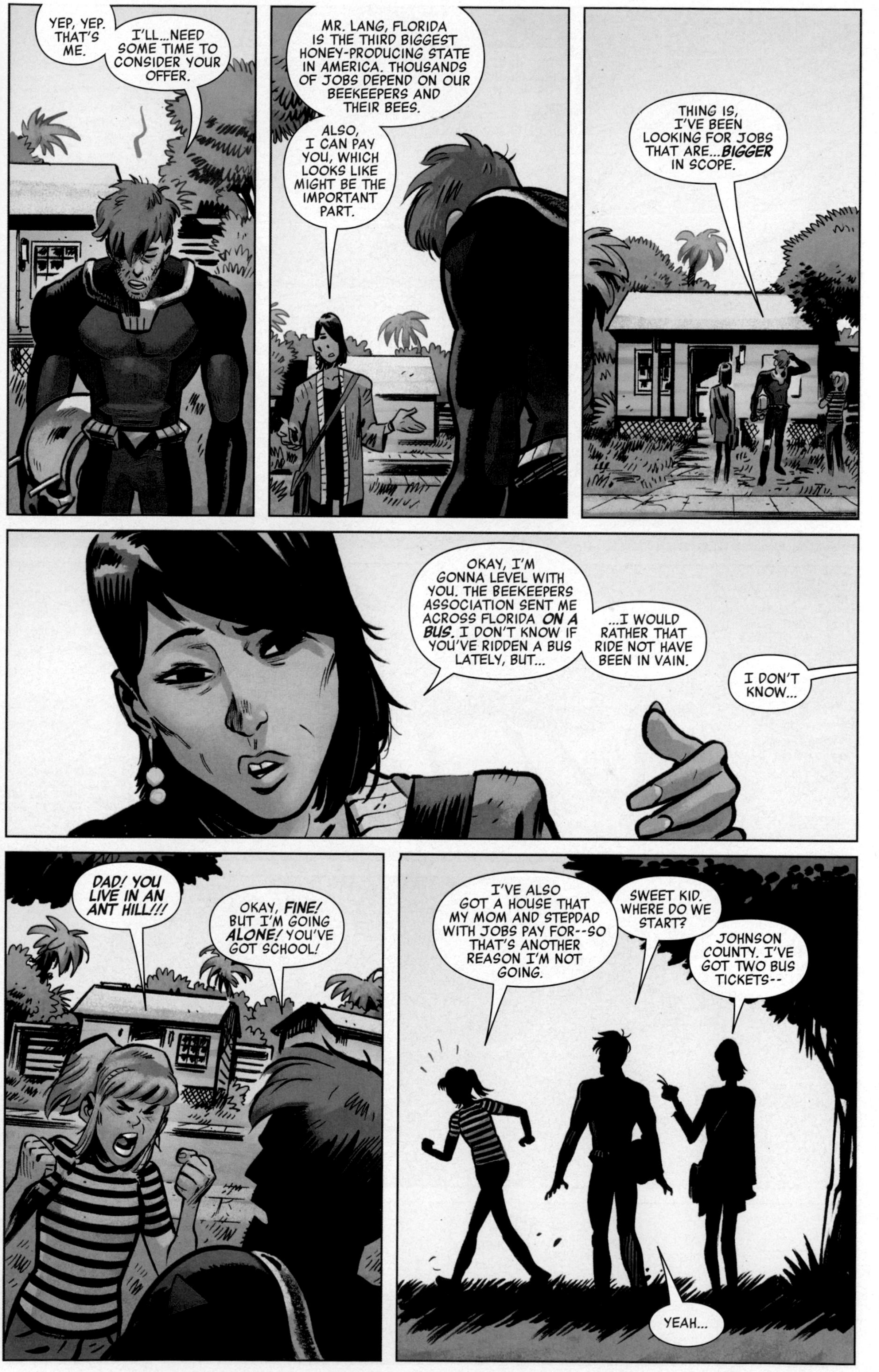
YEP, YEP. THAT'S ME.
I'LL...NEED SOME TIME TO CONSIDER YOUR OFFER.
MR. LANG, FLORIDA IS THE THIRD BIGGEST HONEY-PRODUCING STATE IN AMERICA. THOUSANDS OF JOBS DEPEND ON OUR BEEKEEPERS AND THEIR BEES.
ALSO, I CAN PAY YOU, WHICH LOOKS LIKE MIGHT BE THE IMPORTANT PART.
THING IS, I'VE BEEN LOOKING FOR JOBS THAT ARE...BIGGER IN SCOPE.
OKAY, I'M GONNA LEVEL WITH YOU. THE BEEKEEPERS ASSOCIATION SENT ME ACROSS FLORIDA ON A BUS. I DON'T KNOW IF YOU'VE RIDDEN A BUS LATELY, BUT...
...I WOULD RATHER THAT RIDE NOT HAVE BEEN IN VAIN.
I DON'T KNOW...
DAD! YOU LIVE IN AN ANT HILL!!!
OKAY, FINE! BUT I'M GOING ALONE! YOU'VE GOT SCHOOL!
I'VE ALSO GOT A HOUSE THAT MY MOM AND STEPDAD WITH JOBS PAY FOR--SO THAT'S ANOTHER REASON I'M NOT GOING.
SWEET KID. WHERE DO WE START?
JOHNSON COUNTY. I'VE GOT TWO BUS TICKETS--
YEAH...

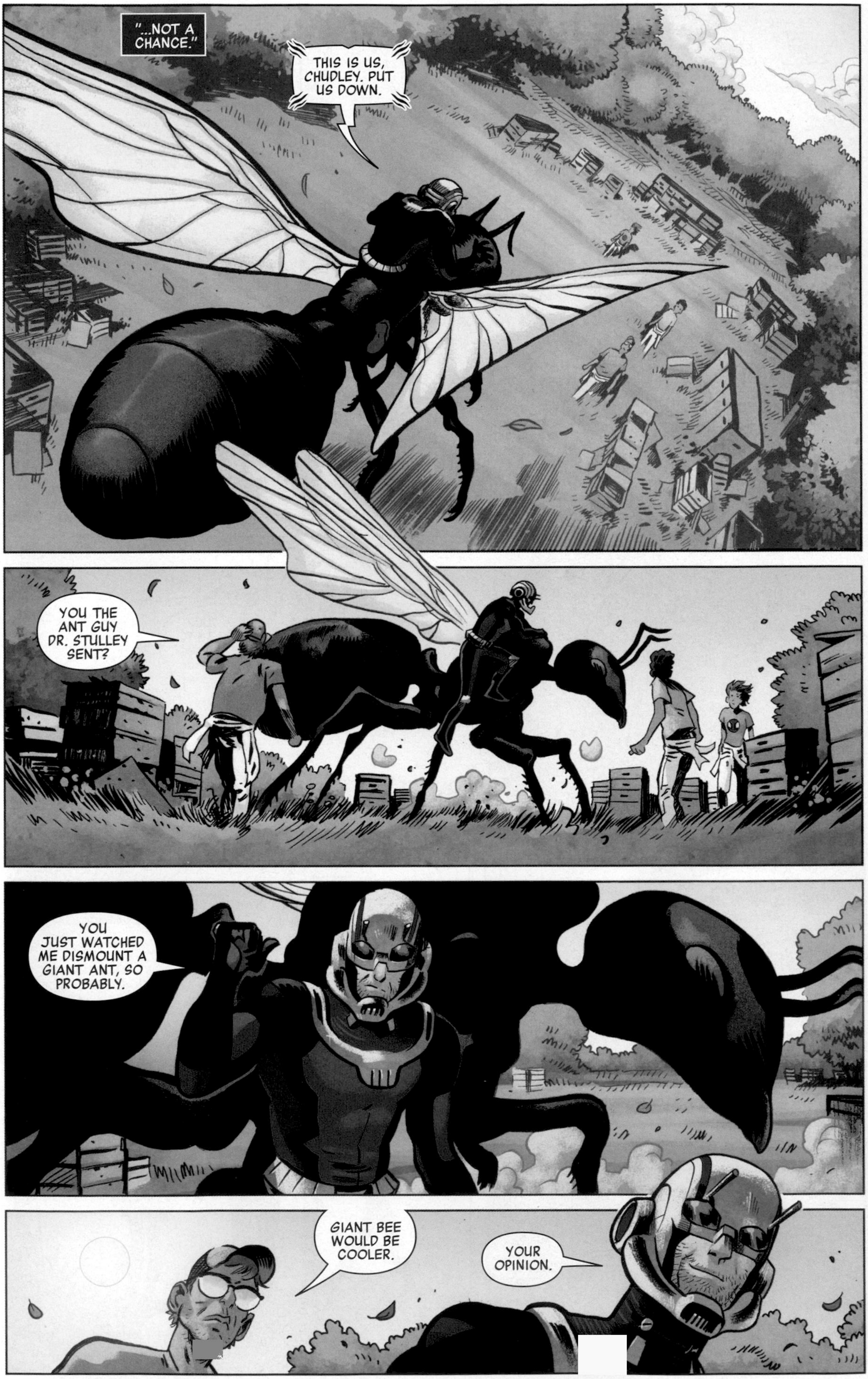
"...NOT A CHANCE."
THIS IS US, CHUDLEY. PUT US DOWN.
YOU THE ANT GUY DR. STULLEY SENT?
YOU JUST WATCHED ME DISMOUNT A GIANT ANT, SO PROBABLY.
GIANT BEE WOULD BE COOLER.
YOUR OPINION.

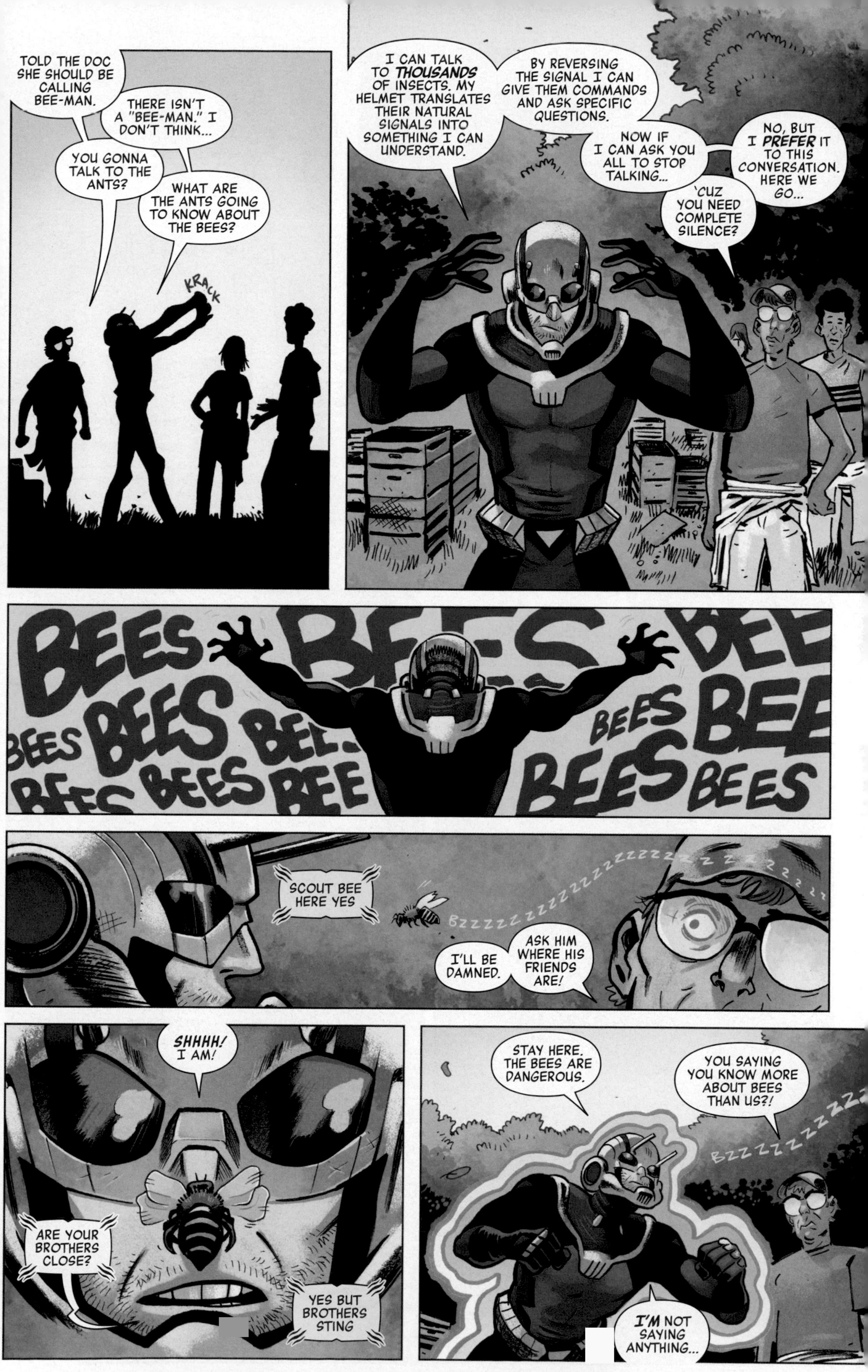

TOLD THE DOC SHE SHOULD BE CALLING BEE-MAN.
THERE ISN'T A "BEE-MAN." I DON'T THINK...
YOU GONNA TALK TO THE ANTS?
WHAT ARE THE ANTS GOING TO KNOW ABOUT THE BEES?
KRACK
I CAN TALK TO THOUSANDS OF INSECTS. MY HELMET TRANSLATES THEIR NATURAL SIGNALS INTO SOMETHING I CAN UNDERSTAND.
BY REVERSING THE SIGNAL I CAN GIVE THEM COMMANDS AND ASK SPECIFIC QUESTIONS.
NOW IF I CAN ASK YOU ALL TO STOP TALKING...
'CUZ YOU NEED COMPLETE SILENCE?
NO, BUT I PREFER IT TO THIS CONVERSATION. HERE WE GO...
BEES BEES BEE BEES BEES BEE BEES BEES BEE BEES BEE BEES BEES
SCOUT BEE HERE YES
BZZZZZ ZZZZZZZZZZZZZZ
I'LL BE DAMNED.
ASK HIM WHERE HIS FRIENDS ARE!
SHHHH! I AM!
ARE YOUR BROTHERS CLOSE?
YES BUT BROTHERS STING
STAY HERE. THE BEES ARE DANGEROUS.
YOU SAYING YOU KNOW MORE ABOUT BEES THAN US?!
BZZZZZZZZZZ
I'M NOT SAYING ANYTHING...

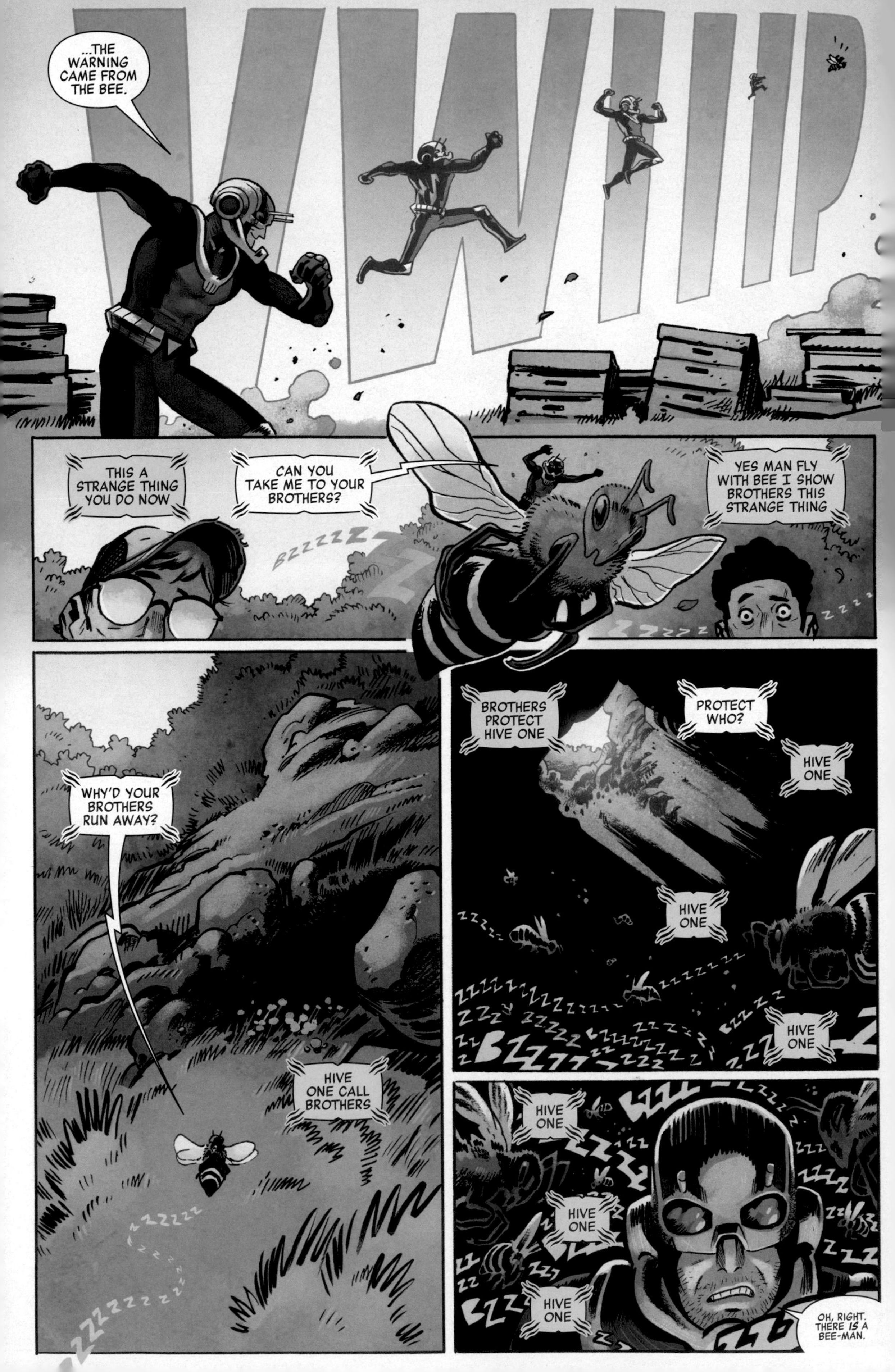

...THE WARNING CAME FROM THE BEE.
VWHIP
THIS A STRANGE THING YOU DO NOW
CAN YOU TAKE ME TO YOUR BROTHERS?
YES MAN FLY WITH BEE I SHOW BROTHERS THIS STRANGE THING
BZZZZZ
WHY'D YOUR BROTHERS RUN AWAY?
HIVE ONE CALL BROTHERS
BROTHERS PROTECT HIVE ONE
PROTECT WHO?
HIVE ONE
HIVE ONE
HIVE ONE
HIVE ONE
HIVE ONE
HIVE ONE
OH, RIGHT. THERE IS A BEE-MAN.

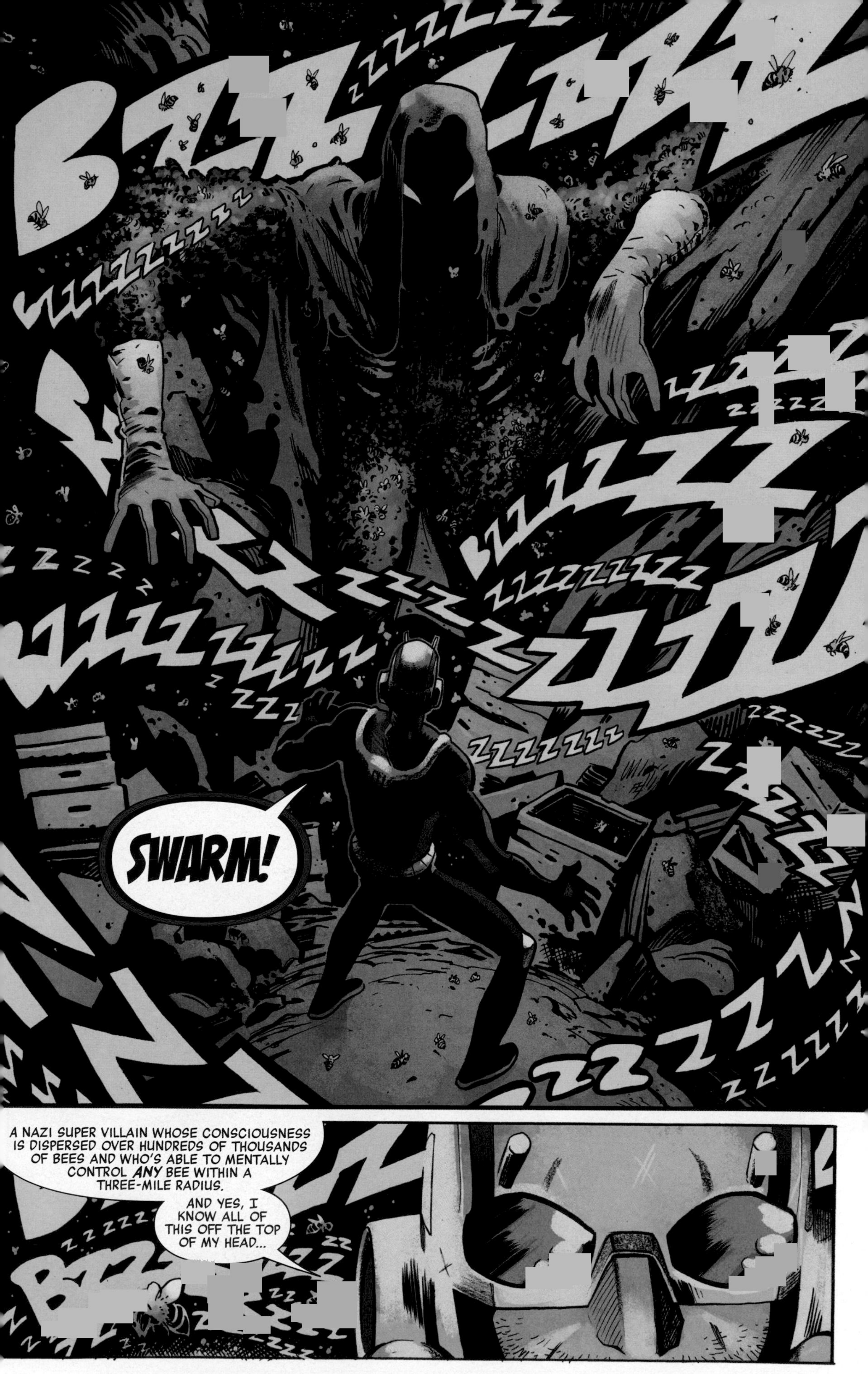
SWARM!
A NAZI SUPER VILLAIN WHOSE CONSCIOUSNESS IS DISPERSED OVER HUNDREDS OF THOUSANDS OF BEES AND WHO'S ABLE TO MENTALLY CONTROL ANY BEE WITHIN A THREE-MILE RADIUS.
AND YES, I KNOW ALL OF THIS OFF THE TOP OF MY HEAD...

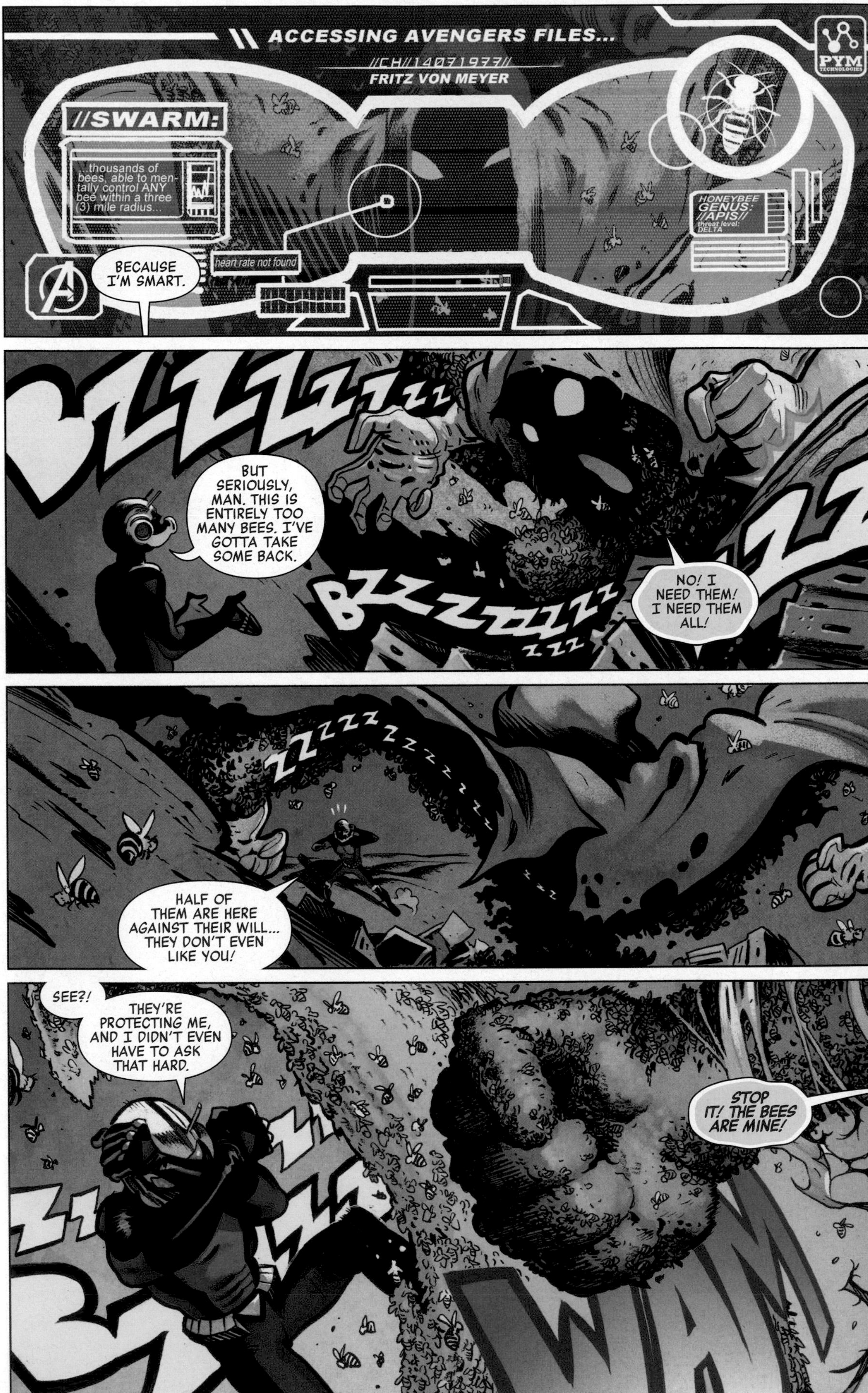

\\ ACCESSING AVENGERS FILES...
//CH//14071977//
FRITZ VON MEYER
//SWARM:
...thousands of bees, able to mentally control ANY bee within a three (3) mile radius...
PYM TECHNOLOGIES
HONEYBEE GENUS: //APIS//
threat level: DELTA
heart rate not found
BECAUSE I'M SMART.
BUT SERIOUSLY, MAN. THIS IS ENTIRELY TOO MANY BEES. I'VE GOTTA TAKE SOME BACK.
BZZZZZZZZ
NO! I NEED THEM! I NEED THEM ALL!
HALF OF THEM ARE HERE AGAINST THEIR WILL... THEY DON'T EVEN LIKE YOU!
SEE?!
THEY'RE PROTECTING ME, AND I DIDN'T EVEN HAVE TO ASK THAT HARD.
STOP IT! THE BEES ARE MINE!

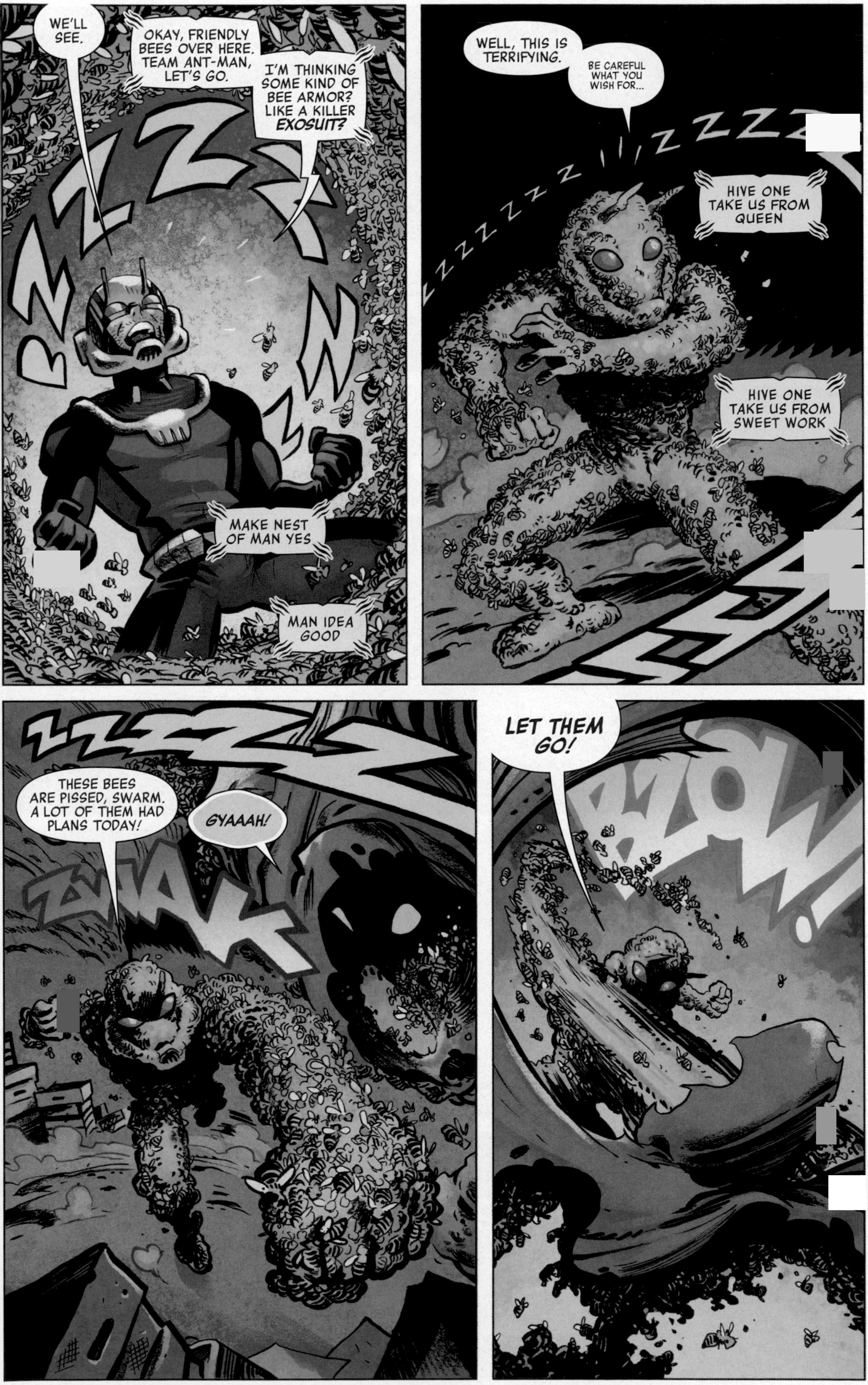
WE'LL SEE.
OKAY, FRIENDLY BEES OVER HERE. TEAM ANT-MAN, LET'S GO.
I'M THINKING SOME KIND OF BEE ARMOR? LIKE A KILLER *EXOSUIT?*
MAKE NEST OF MAN YES
MAN IDEA GOOD
WELL, THIS IS TERRIFYING.
BE CAREFUL WHAT YOU WISH FOR...
HIVE ONE TAKE US FROM QUEEN
HIVE ONE TAKE US FROM SWEET WORK
THESE BEES ARE PISSED, SWARM. A LOT OF THEM HAD PLANS TODAY!
GYAAAH!
LET THEM GO!

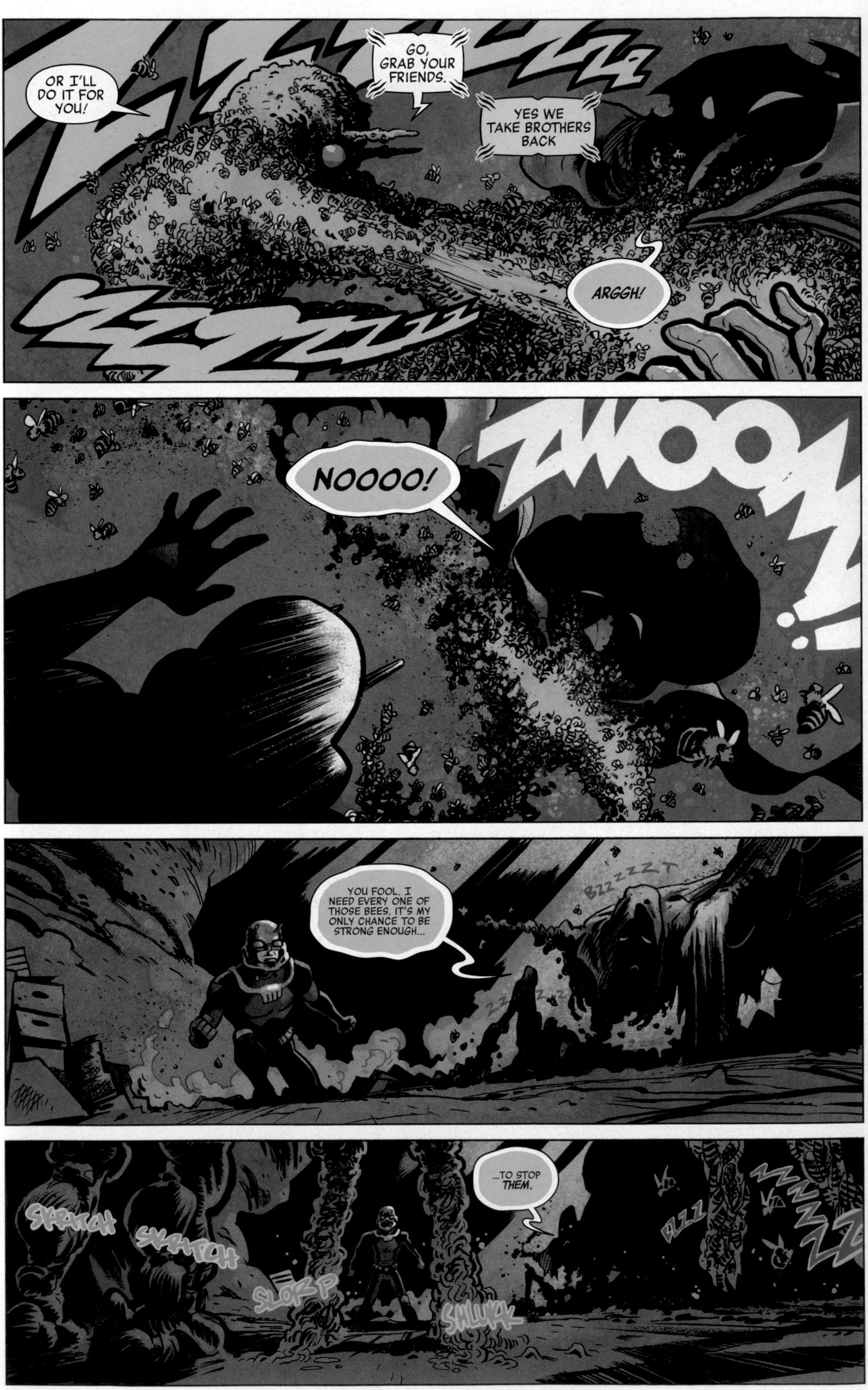
OR I'LL DO IT FOR YOU!
GO, GRAB YOUR FRIENDS.
YES WE TAKE BROTHERS BACK
ARGGH!
NOOOO!
ZWOOM!!
YOU FOOL. I NEED EVERY ONE OF THOSE BEES. IT'S MY ONLY CHANCE TO BE STRONG ENOUGH...
BZZZZZT
...TO STOP THEM.
SKRITCH
SKRITCH
SLORP
SHLUKK
BZZZ

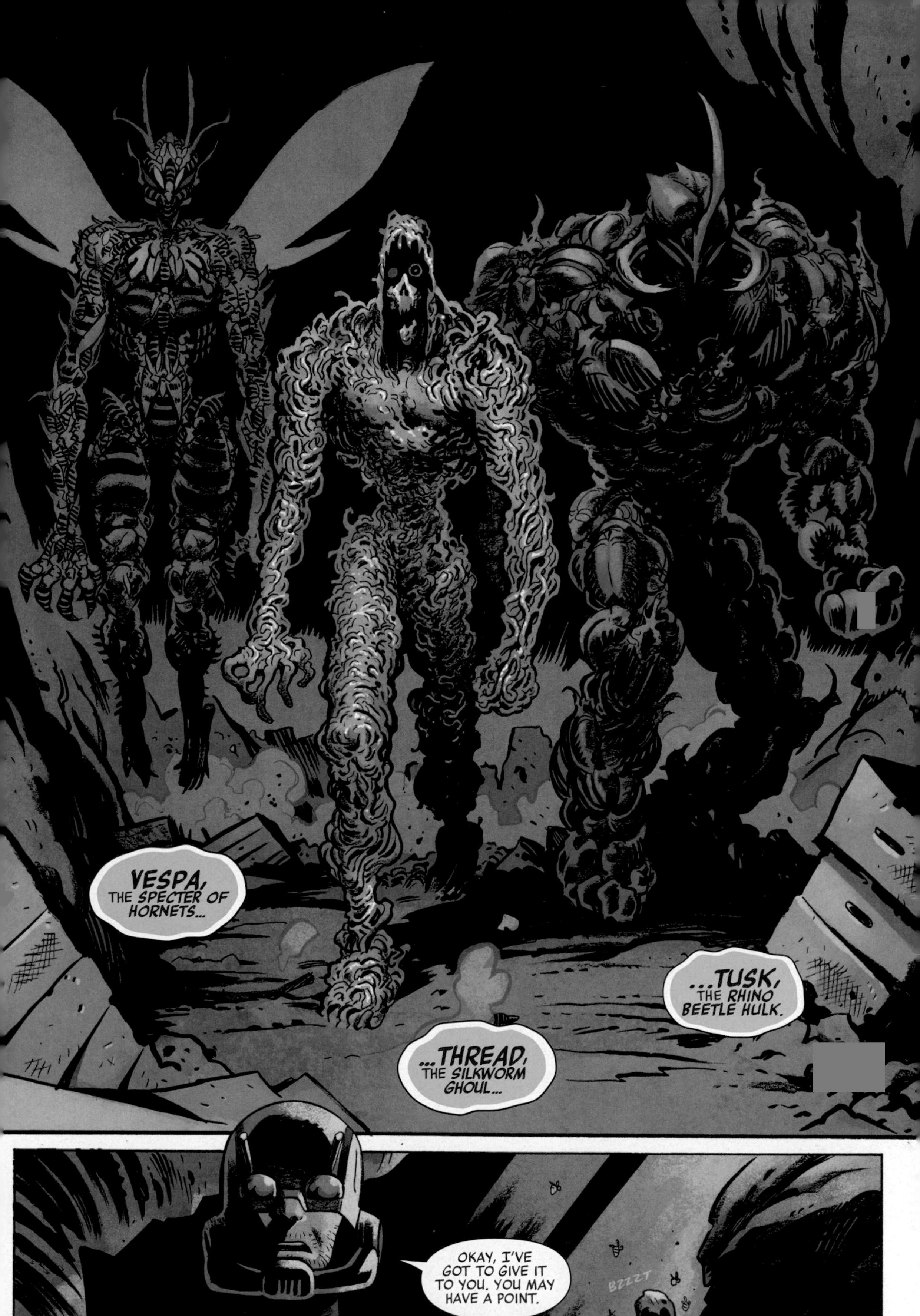
VESPA, THE SPECTER OF HORNETS...
...THREAD, THE SILKWORM GHOUL...
...TUSK, THE RHINO BEETLE HULK.

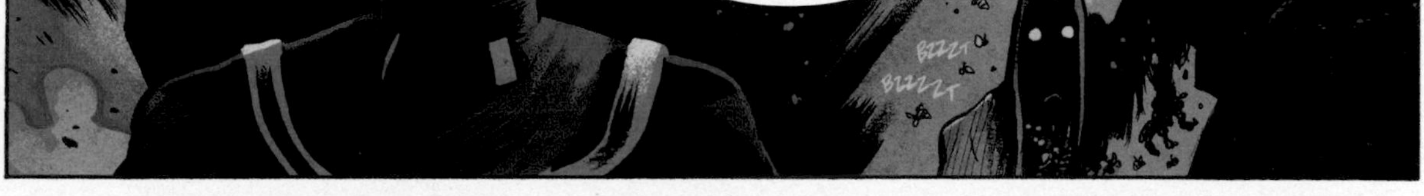
OKAY, I'VE GOT TO GIVE IT TO YOU. YOU MAY HAVE A POINT.
BZZZT
BZZZT
BZZZZT

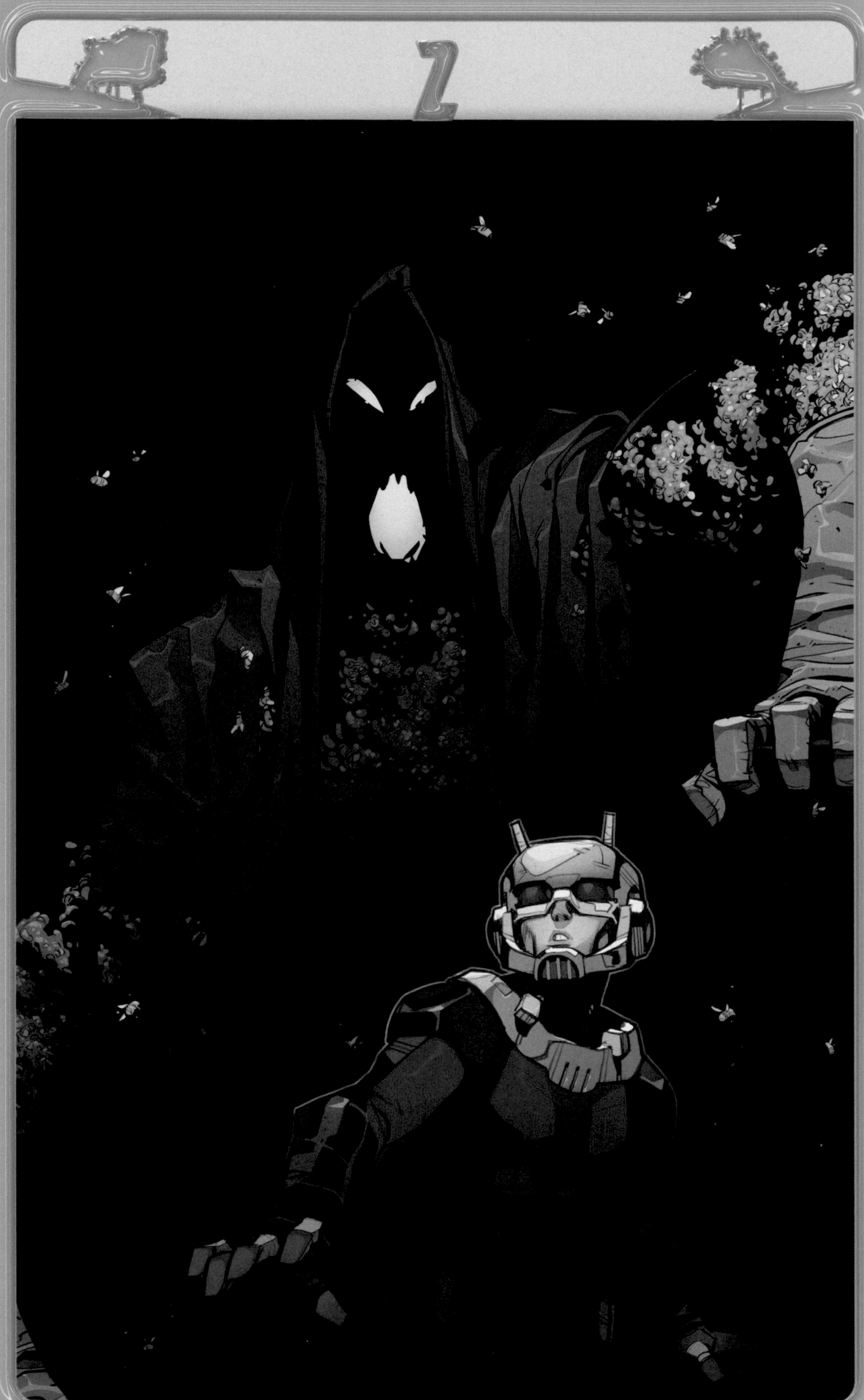
2

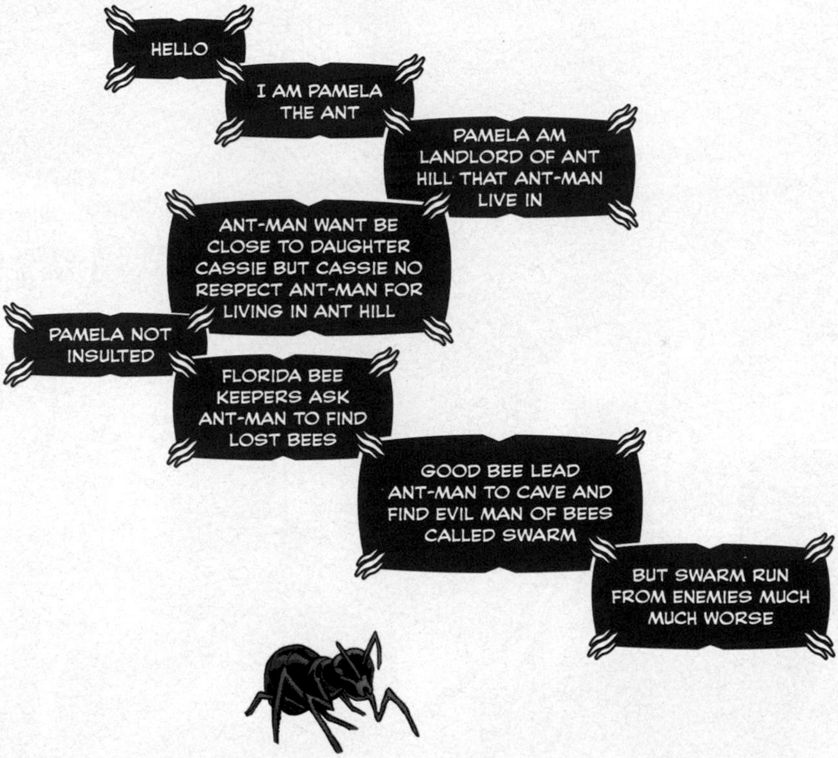
HELLO
I AM PAMELA THE ANT
PAMELA AM LANDLORD OF ANT HILL THAT ANT-MAN LIVE IN
ANT-MAN WANT BE CLOSE TO DAUGHTER CASSIE BUT CASSIE NO RESPECT ANT-MAN FOR LIVING IN ANT HILL
PAMELA NOT INSULTED
FLORIDA BEE KEEPERS ASK ANT-MAN TO FIND LOST BEES
GOOD BEE LEAD ANT-MAN TO CAVE AND FIND EVIL MAN OF BEES CALLED SWARM
BUT SWARM RUN FROM ENEMIES MUCH MUCH WORSE

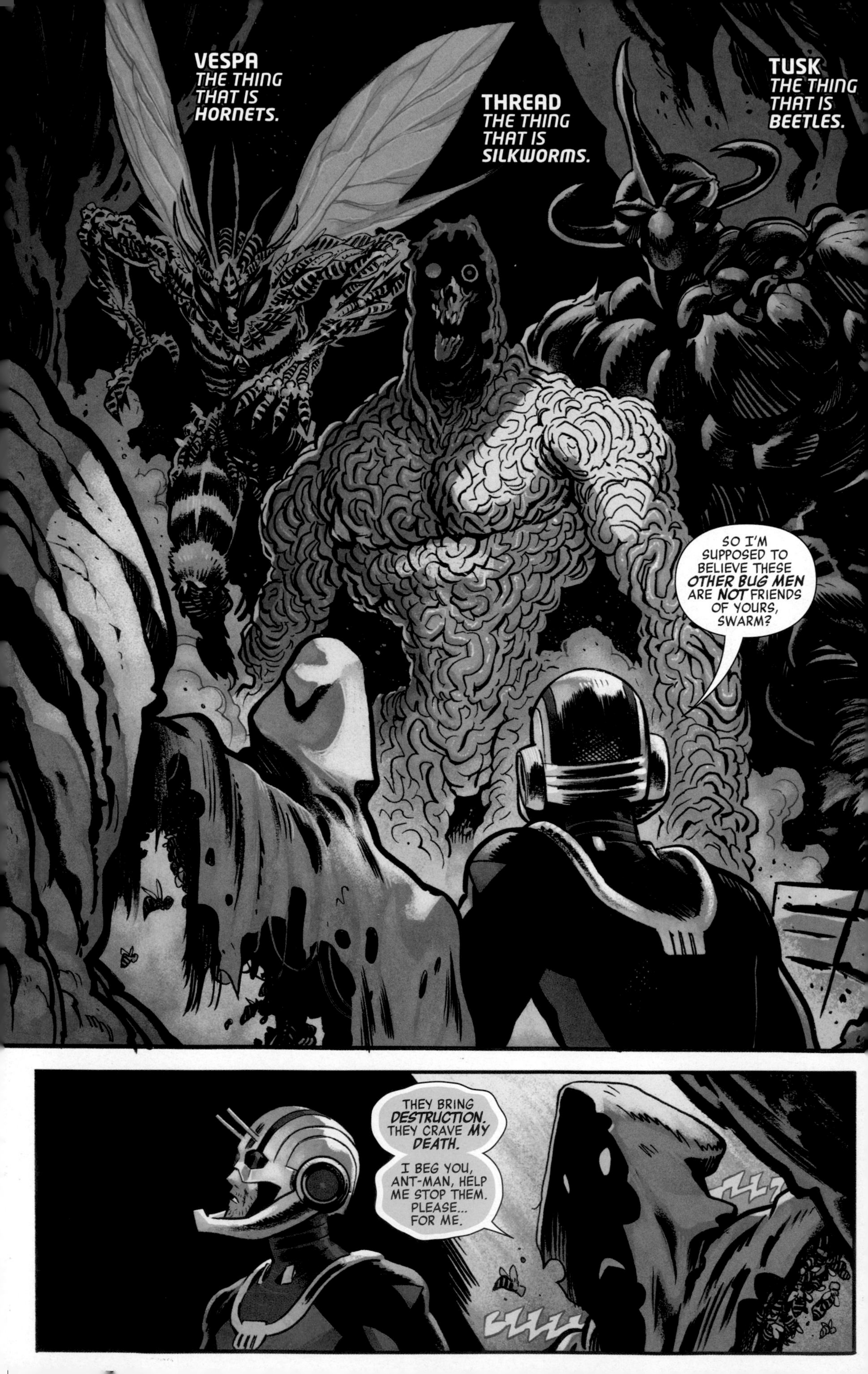
VESPA THE THING THAT IS HORNETS.
THREAD THE THING THAT IS SILKWORMS.
TUSK THE THING THAT IS BEETLES.
SO I'M SUPPOSED TO BELIEVE THESE OTHER BUG MEN ARE NOT FRIENDS OF YOURS, SWARM?
THEY BRING DESTRUCTION. THEY CRAVE MY DEATH.
I BEG YOU, ANT-MAN, HELP ME STOP THEM. PLEASE... FOR ME.

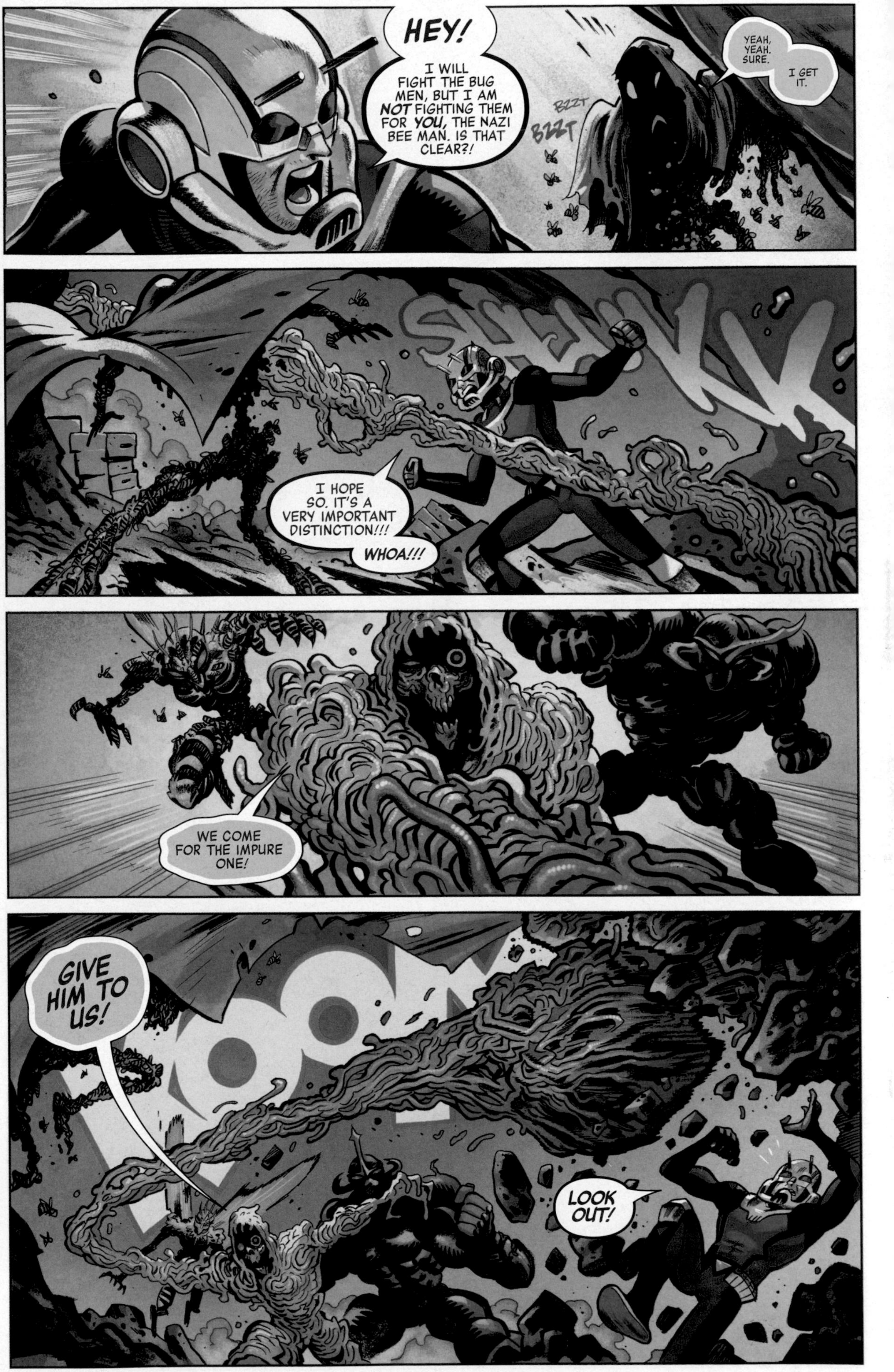
HEY!
I WILL FIGHT THE BUG MEN, BUT I AM NOT FIGHTING THEM FOR YOU, THE NAZI BEE MAN. IS THAT CLEAR?!
BZZT BZZT
YEAH, YEAH. SURE.
I GET IT.
I HOPE SO. IT'S A VERY IMPORTANT DISTINCTION!!!
WHOA!!!
WE COME FOR THE IMPURE ONE!
GIVE HIM TO US!
LOOK OUT!

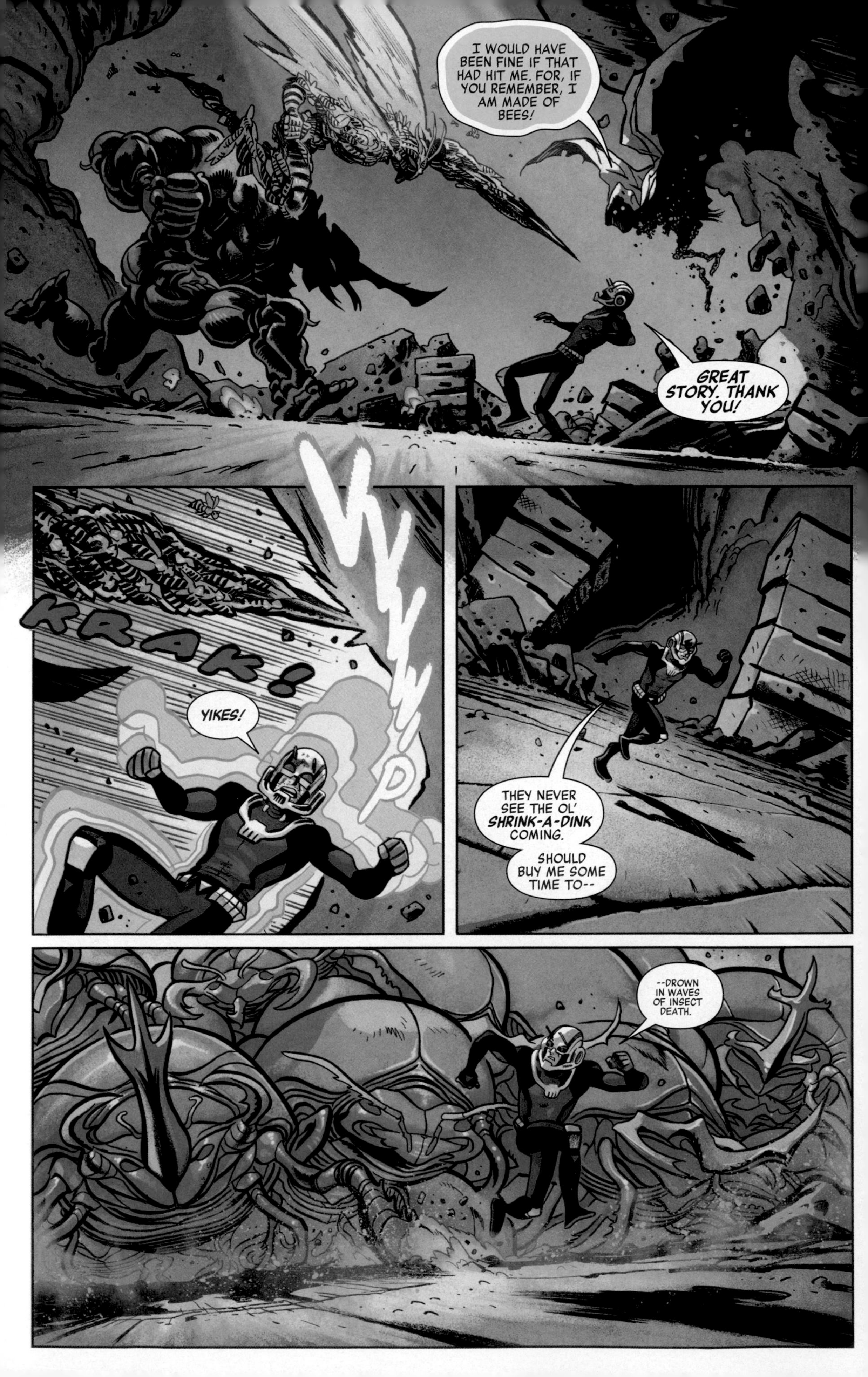
I WOULD HAVE BEEN FINE IF THAT HAD HIT ME. FOR, IF YOU REMEMBER, I AM MADE OF BEES!
GREAT STORY. THANK YOU!
KRAK!
WHIP
YIKES!
THEY NEVER SEE THE OL' SHRINK-A-DINK COMING.
SHOULD BUY ME SOME TIME TO--
--DROWN IN WAVES OF INSECT DEATH.

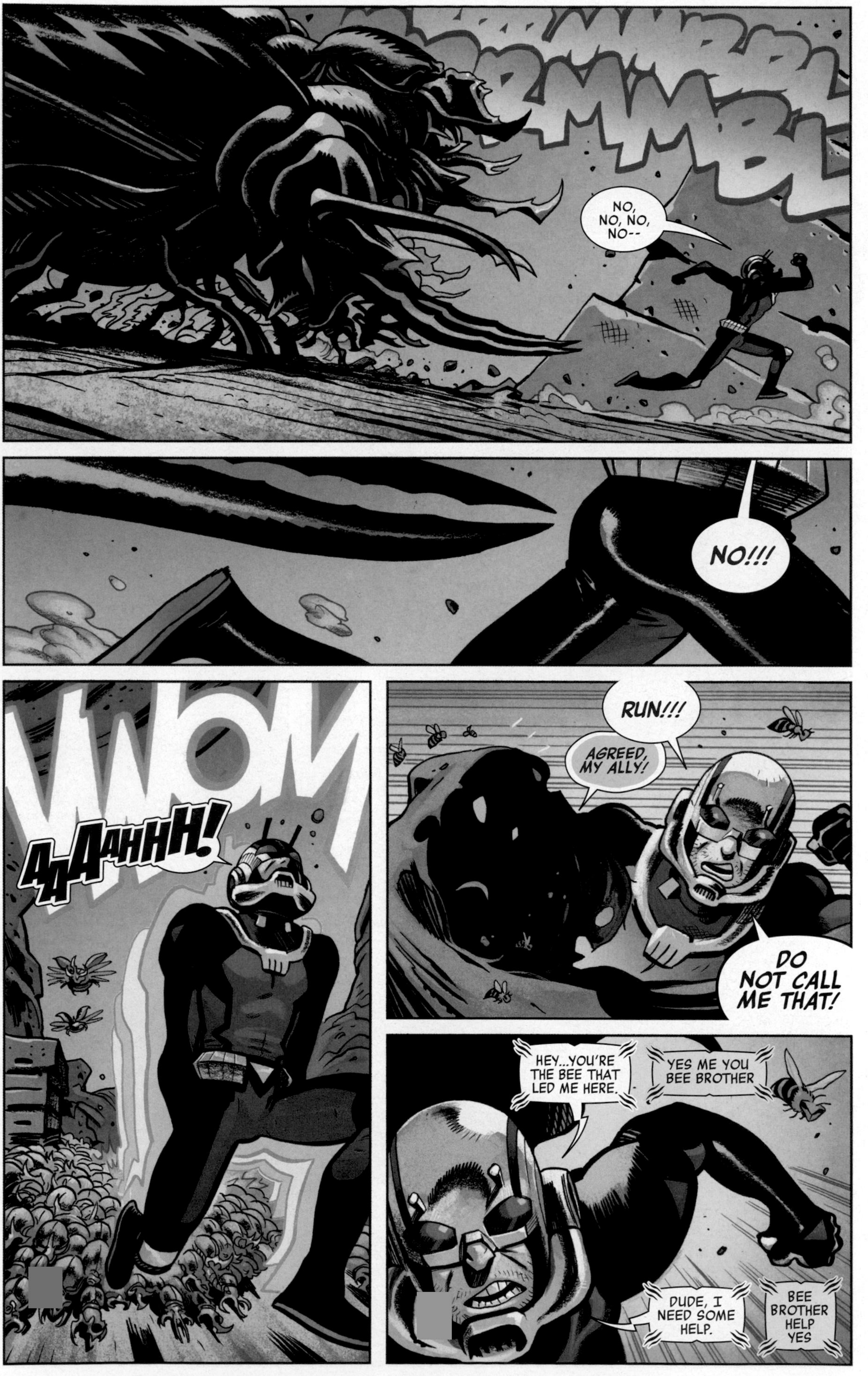
RRMMBL
NO, NO, NO, NO--
NO!!!
VWOM
AAAAHHH!
RUN!!!
AGREED, MY ALLY!
DO NOT CALL ME THAT!
HEY...YOU'RE THE BEE THAT LED ME HERE.
YES ME YOU BEE BROTHER
DUDE, I NEED SOME HELP.
BEE BROTHER HELP YES

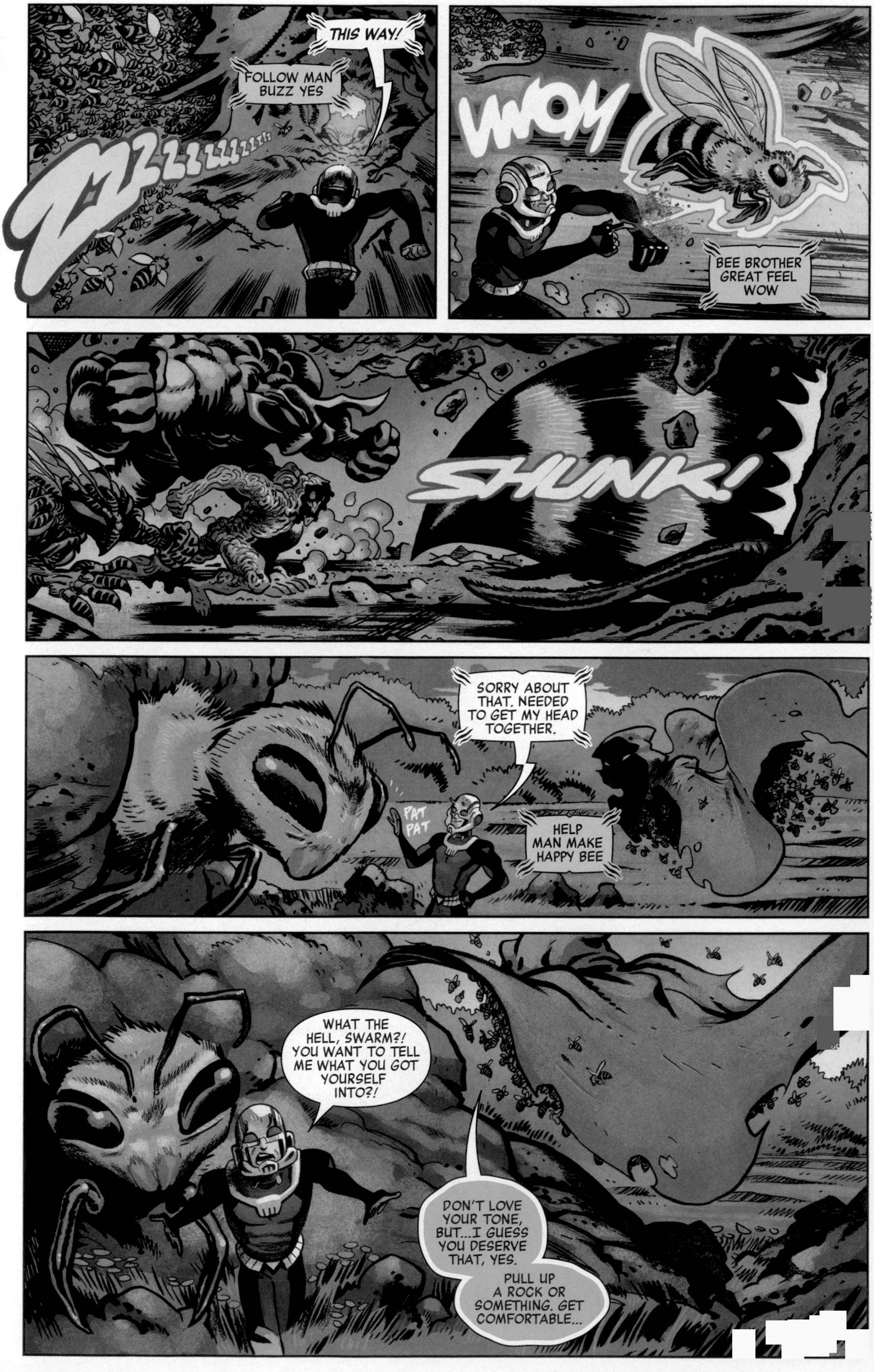
THIS WAY!
FOLLOW MAN BUZZ YES
ZZZzzzzzzzh
VWOM
BEE BROTHER GREAT FEEL WOW
SHUNK!
SORRY ABOUT THAT. NEEDED TO GET MY HEAD TOGETHER.
PAT PAT
HELP MAN MAKE HAPPY BEE
WHAT THE HELL, SWARM?! YOU WANT TO TELL ME WHAT YOU GOT YOURSELF INTO?!
DON'T LOVE YOUR TONE, BUT...I GUESS YOU DESERVE THAT, YES.
PULL UP A ROCK OR SOMETHING. GET COMFORTABLE...

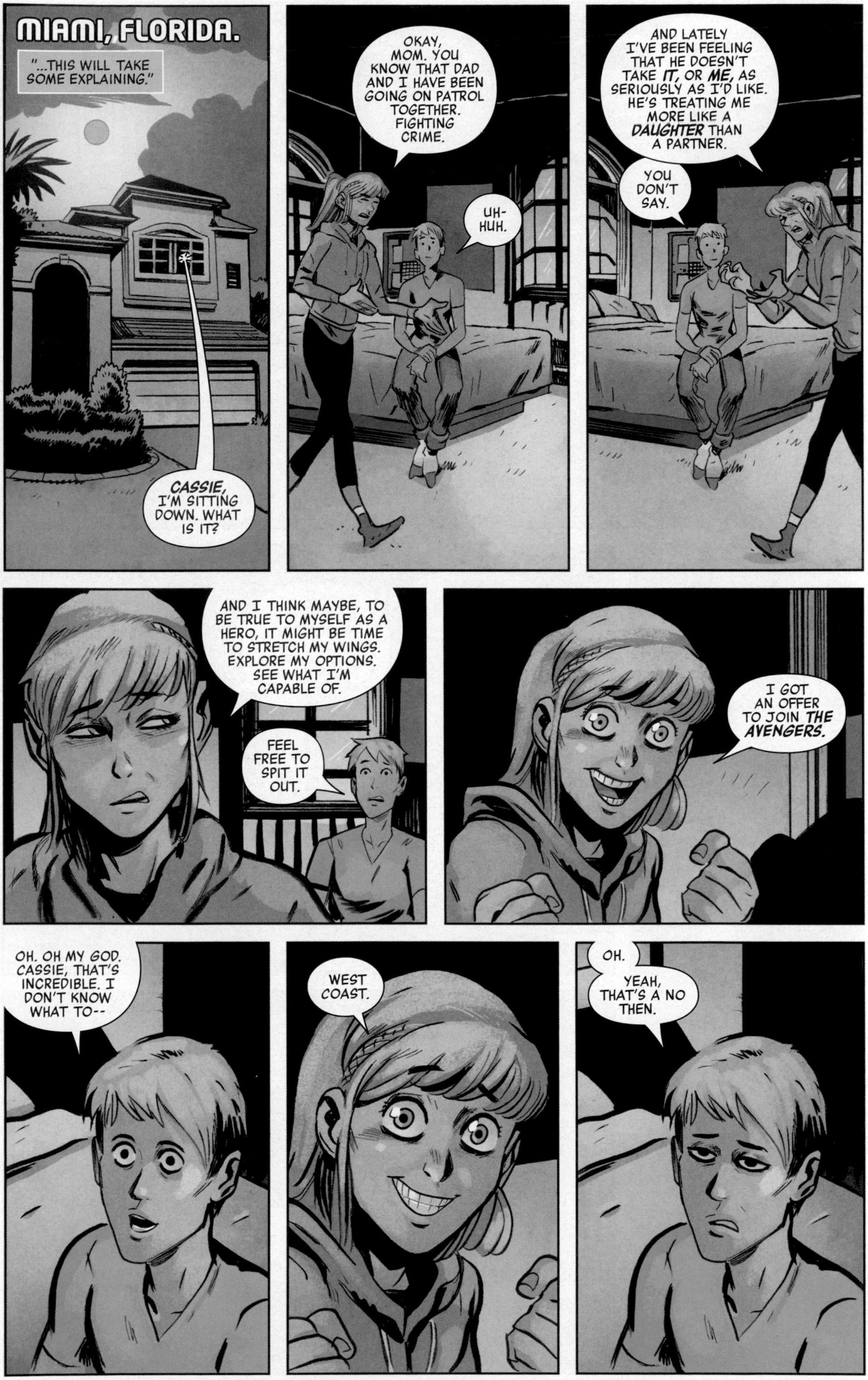
MIAMI, FLORIDA.
"...THIS WILL TAKE SOME EXPLAINING."
CASSIE, I'M SITTING DOWN. WHAT IS IT?
OKAY, MOM. YOU KNOW THAT DAD AND I HAVE BEEN GOING ON PATROL TOGETHER. FIGHTING CRIME.
UH-HUH.
AND LATELY I'VE BEEN FEELING THAT HE DOESN'T TAKE IT, OR ME, AS SERIOUSLY AS I'D LIKE. HE'S TREATING ME MORE LIKE A DAUGHTER THAN A PARTNER.
YOU DON'T SAY.
AND I THINK MAYBE, TO BE TRUE TO MYSELF AS A HERO, IT MIGHT BE TIME TO STRETCH MY WINGS. EXPLORE MY OPTIONS. SEE WHAT I'M CAPABLE OF.
FEEL FREE TO SPIT IT OUT.
I GOT AN OFFER TO JOIN THE AVENGERS.
OH. OH MY GOD. CASSIE, THAT'S INCREDIBLE. I DON'T KNOW WHAT TO--
WEST COAST.
OH.
YEAH, THAT'S A NO THEN.

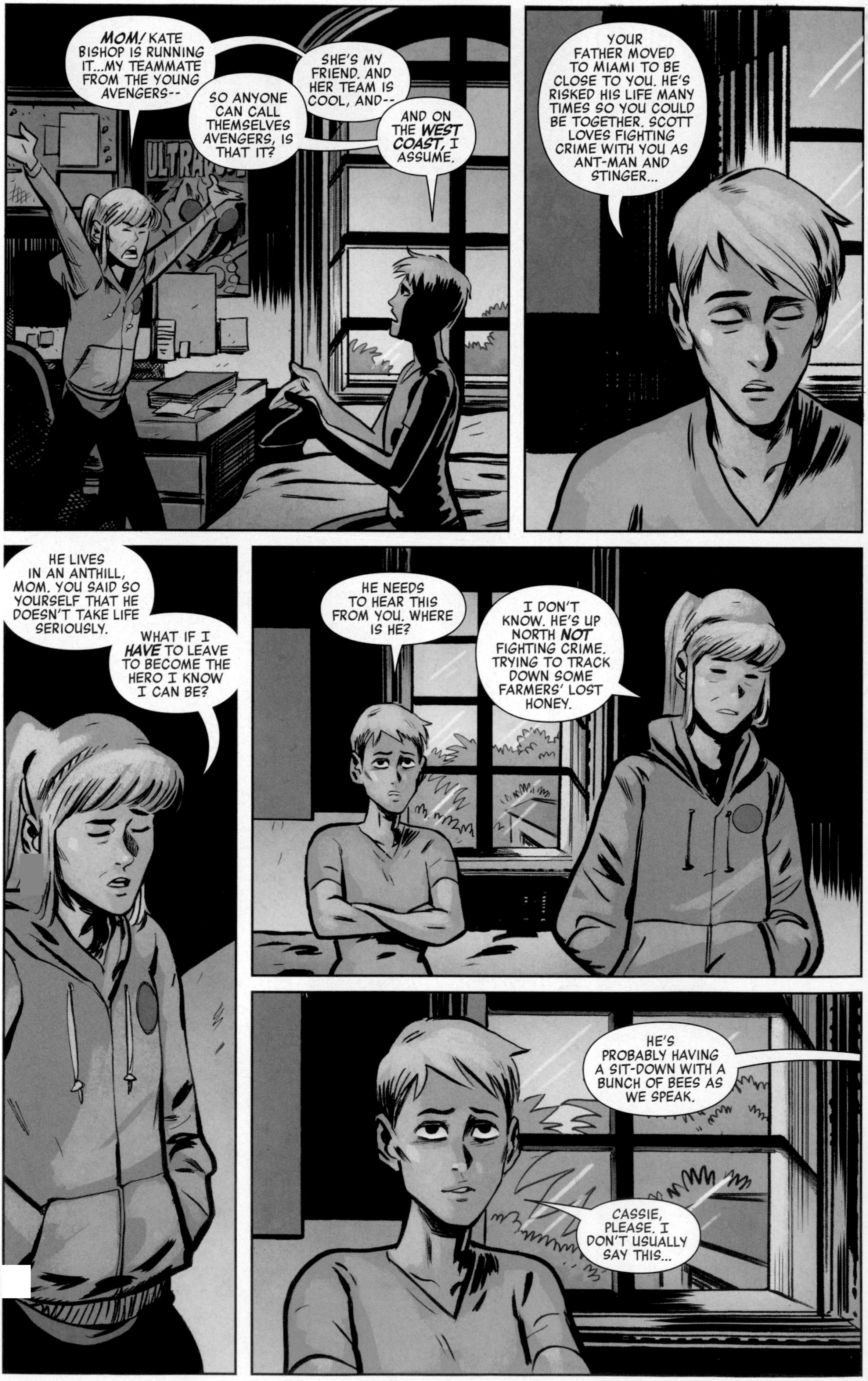
MOM! KATE BISHOP IS RUNNING IT...MY TEAMMATE FROM THE YOUNG AVENGERS--
SO ANYONE CAN CALL THEMSELVES AVENGERS, IS THAT IT?
SHE'S MY FRIEND. AND HER TEAM IS COOL, AND--
AND ON THE WEST COAST, I ASSUME.
YOUR FATHER MOVED TO MIAMI TO BE CLOSE TO YOU. HE'S RISKED HIS LIFE MANY TIMES SO YOU COULD BE TOGETHER. SCOTT LOVES FIGHTING CRIME WITH YOU AS ANT-MAN AND STINGER...
HE LIVES IN AN ANTHILL, MOM. YOU SAID SO YOURSELF THAT HE DOESN'T TAKE LIFE SERIOUSLY.
WHAT IF I HAVE TO LEAVE TO BECOME THE HERO I KNOW I CAN BE?
HE NEEDS TO HEAR THIS FROM YOU. WHERE IS HE?
I DON'T KNOW. HE'S UP NORTH NOT FIGHTING CRIME. TRYING TO TRACK DOWN SOME FARMERS' LOST HONEY.
HE'S PROBABLY HAVING A SIT-DOWN WITH A BUNCH OF BEES AS WE SPEAK.
CASSIE, PLEASE. I DON'T USUALLY SAY THIS...

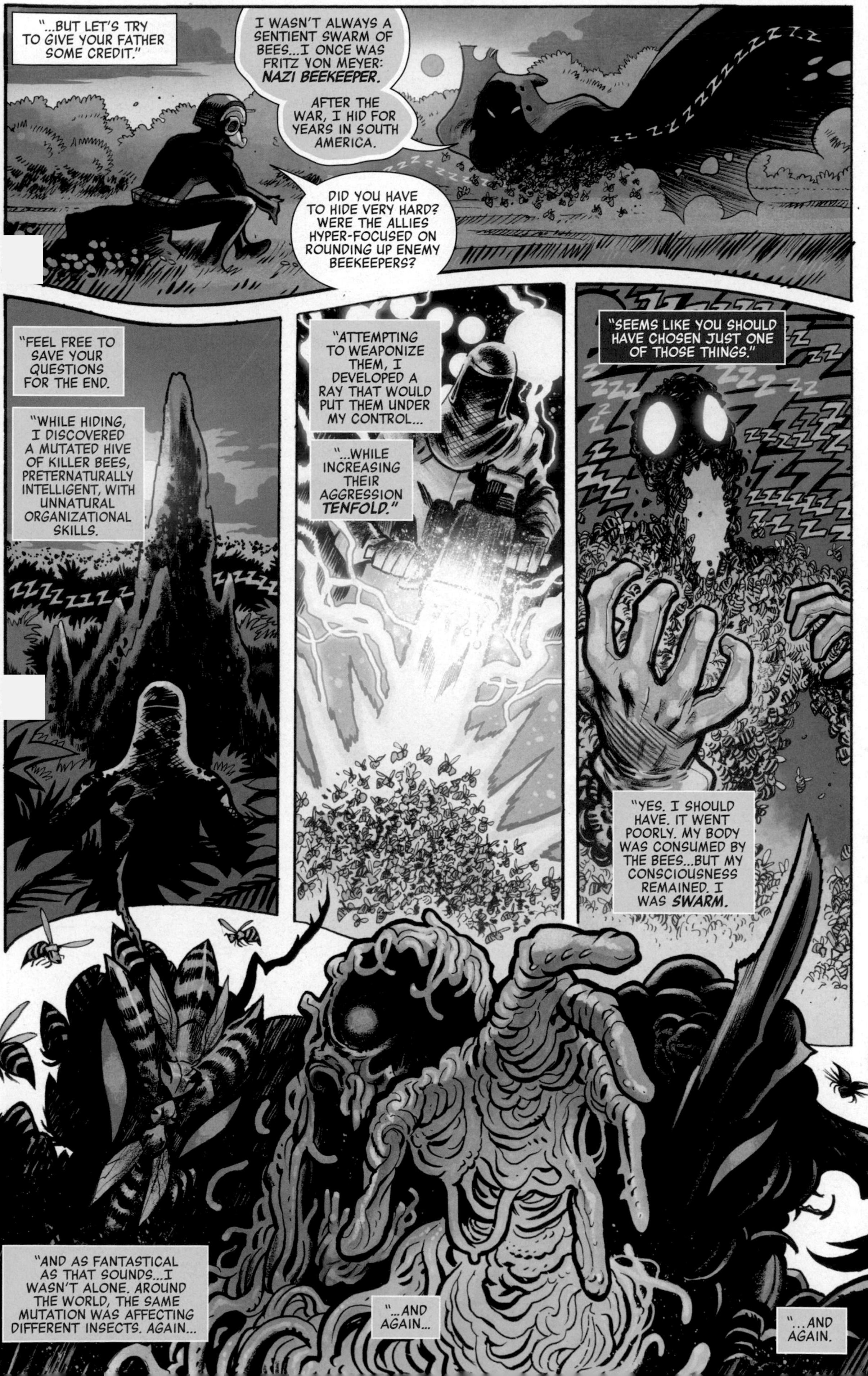
"...BUT LET'S TRY TO GIVE YOUR FATHER SOME CREDIT."
I WASN'T ALWAYS A SENTIENT SWARM OF BEES...I ONCE WAS FRITZ VON MEYER: NAZI BEEKEEPER.
AFTER THE WAR, I HID FOR YEARS IN SOUTH AMERICA.
DID YOU HAVE TO HIDE VERY HARD? WERE THE ALLIES HYPER-FOCUSED ON ROUNDING UP ENEMY BEEKEEPERS?
"FEEL FREE TO SAVE YOUR QUESTIONS FOR THE END.
"WHILE HIDING, I DISCOVERED A MUTATED HIVE OF KILLER BEES, PRETERNATURALLY INTELLIGENT, WITH UNNATURAL ORGANIZATIONAL SKILLS.
"ATTEMPTING TO WEAPONIZE THEM, I DEVELOPED A RAY THAT WOULD PUT THEM UNDER MY CONTROL...
"...WHILE INCREASING THEIR AGGRESSION TENFOLD."
"SEEMS LIKE YOU SHOULD HAVE CHOSEN JUST ONE OF THOSE THINGS."
"YES. I SHOULD HAVE. IT WENT POORLY. MY BODY WAS CONSUMED BY THE BEES...BUT MY CONSCIOUSNESS REMAINED. I WAS SWARM.
"AND AS FANTASTICAL AS THAT SOUNDS...I WASN'T ALONE. AROUND THE WORLD, THE SAME MUTATION WAS AFFECTING DIFFERENT INSECTS. AGAIN...
"...AND AGAIN...
"...AND AGAIN.

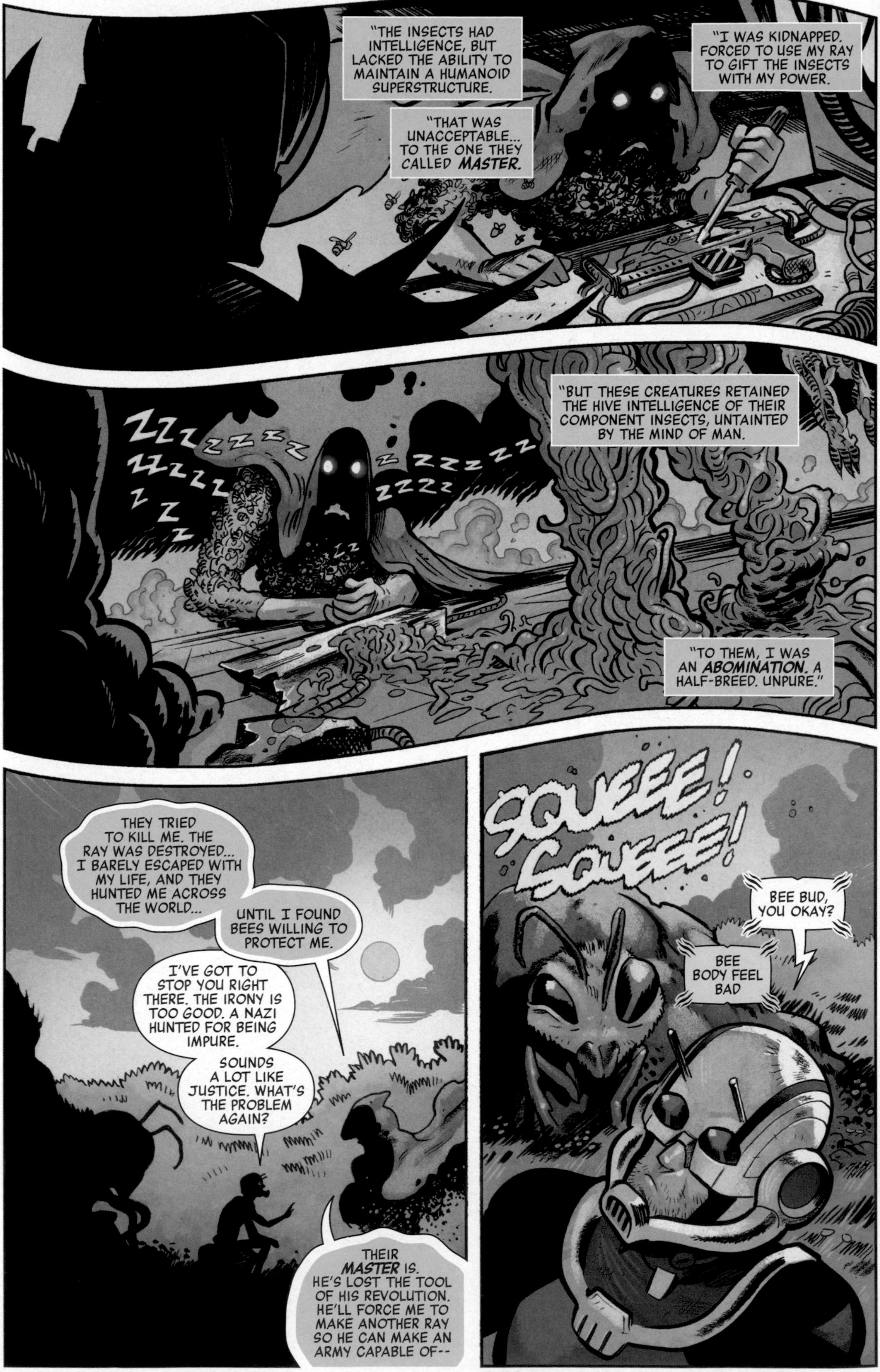
"THE INSECTS HAD INTELLIGENCE, BUT LACKED THE ABILITY TO MAINTAIN A HUMANOID SUPERSTRUCTURE.
"THAT WAS UNACCEPTABLE... TO THE ONE THEY CALLED MASTER.
"I WAS KIDNAPPED. FORCED TO USE MY RAY TO GIFT THE INSECTS WITH MY POWER.
ZZZZZZZZZ
"BUT THESE CREATURES RETAINED THE HIVE INTELLIGENCE OF THEIR COMPONENT INSECTS, UNTAINTED BY THE MIND OF MAN.
"TO THEM, I WAS AN ABOMINATION. A HALF-BREED. UNPURE."
THEY TRIED TO KILL ME. THE RAY WAS DESTROYED... I BARELY ESCAPED WITH MY LIFE, AND THEY HUNTED ME ACROSS THE WORLD...
UNTIL I FOUND BEES WILLING TO PROTECT ME.
I'VE GOT TO STOP YOU RIGHT THERE. THE IRONY IS TOO GOOD. A NAZI HUNTED FOR BEING IMPURE.
SOUNDS A LOT LIKE JUSTICE. WHAT'S THE PROBLEM AGAIN?
THEIR MASTER IS. HE'S LOST THE TOOL OF HIS REVOLUTION. HE'LL FORCE ME TO MAKE ANOTHER RAY SO HE CAN MAKE AN ARMY CAPABLE OF--
SQUEEE! SQUEEE!
BEE BUD, YOU OKAY?
BEE BODY FEEL BAD

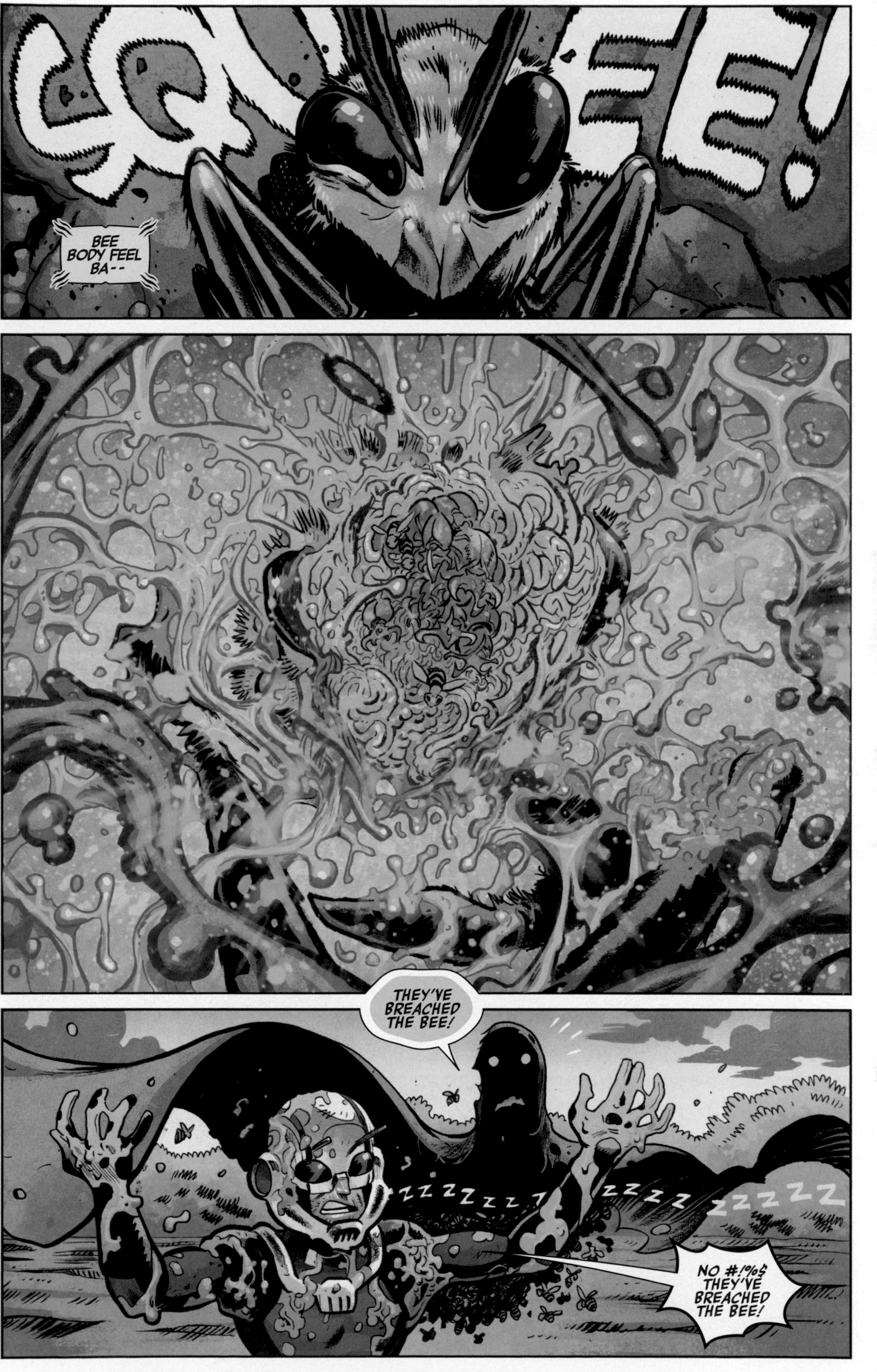
BEE BODY FEEL BA--
THEY'VE BREACHED THE BEE!
NO #!%$ THEY'VE BREACHED THE BEE!

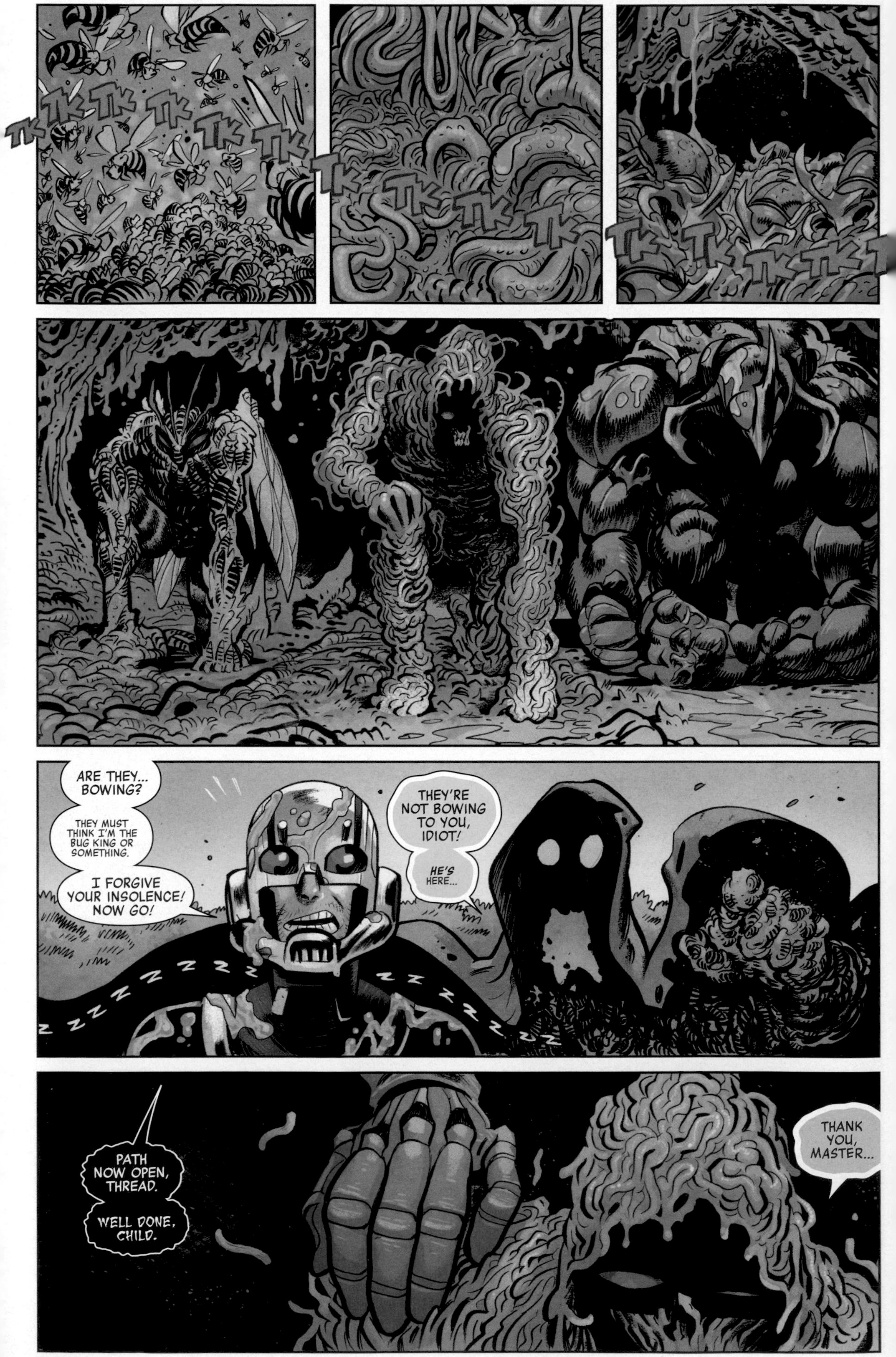
TK TK TK TK TK TK TK
TK TK TK TK TK
TK TK TK TK TK
ARE THEY... BOWING?
THEY MUST THINK I'M THE BUG KING OR SOMETHING.
I FORGIVE YOUR INSOLENCE! NOW GO!
THEY'RE NOT BOWING TO YOU, IDIOT!
HE'S HERE...
PATH NOW OPEN, THREAD.
WELL DONE, CHILD.
THANK YOU, MASTER...

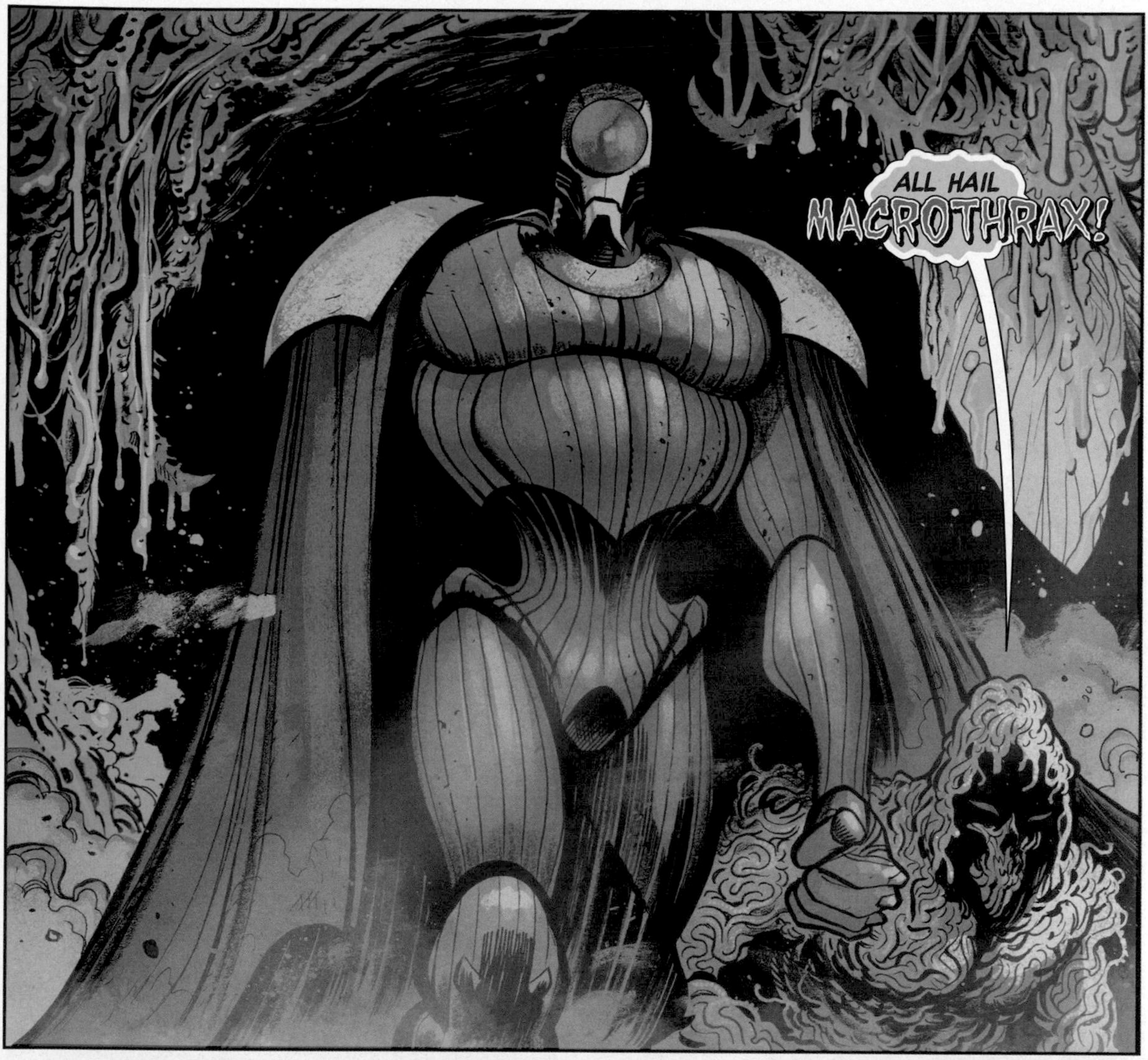
ALL HAIL MACROTHRAX!
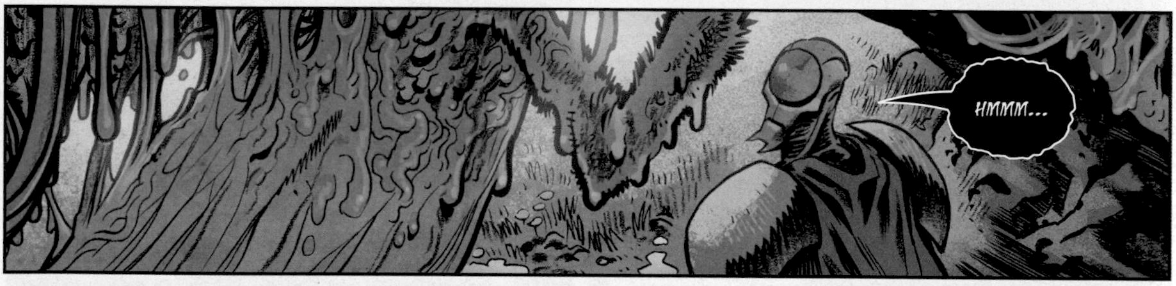
HMMM...
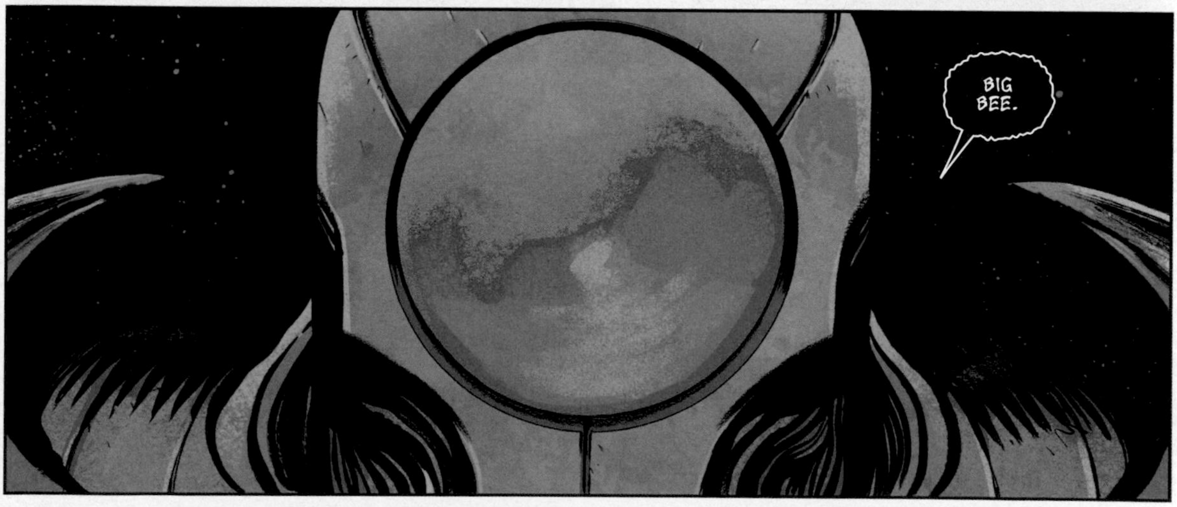
BIG BEE.

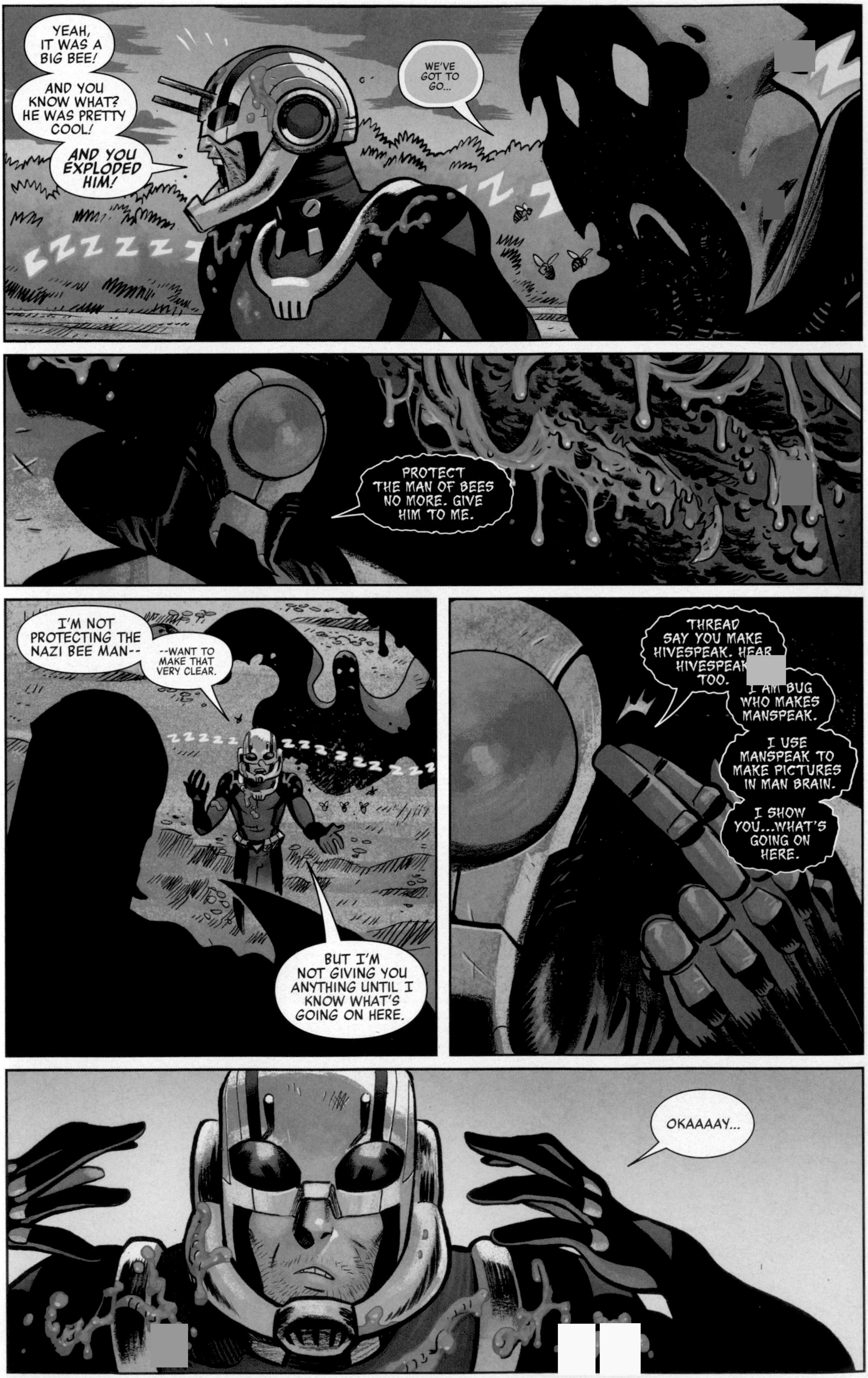

YEAH, IT WAS A BIG BEE!
AND YOU KNOW WHAT? HE WAS PRETTY COOL!
AND YOU EXPLODED HIM!
WE'VE GOT TO GO...
PROTECT THE MAN OF BEES NO MORE. GIVE HIM TO ME.
I'M NOT PROTECTING THE NAZI BEE MAN--
--WANT TO MAKE THAT VERY CLEAR.
BUT I'M NOT GIVING YOU ANYTHING UNTIL I KNOW WHAT'S GOING ON HERE.
THREAD SAY YOU MAKE HIVESPEAK. HEAR HIVESPEAK TOO.
I AM BUG WHO MAKES MANSPEAK.
I USE MANSPEAK TO MAKE PICTURES IN MAN BRAIN.
I SHOW YOU...WHAT'S GOING ON HERE.
OKAAAAY...

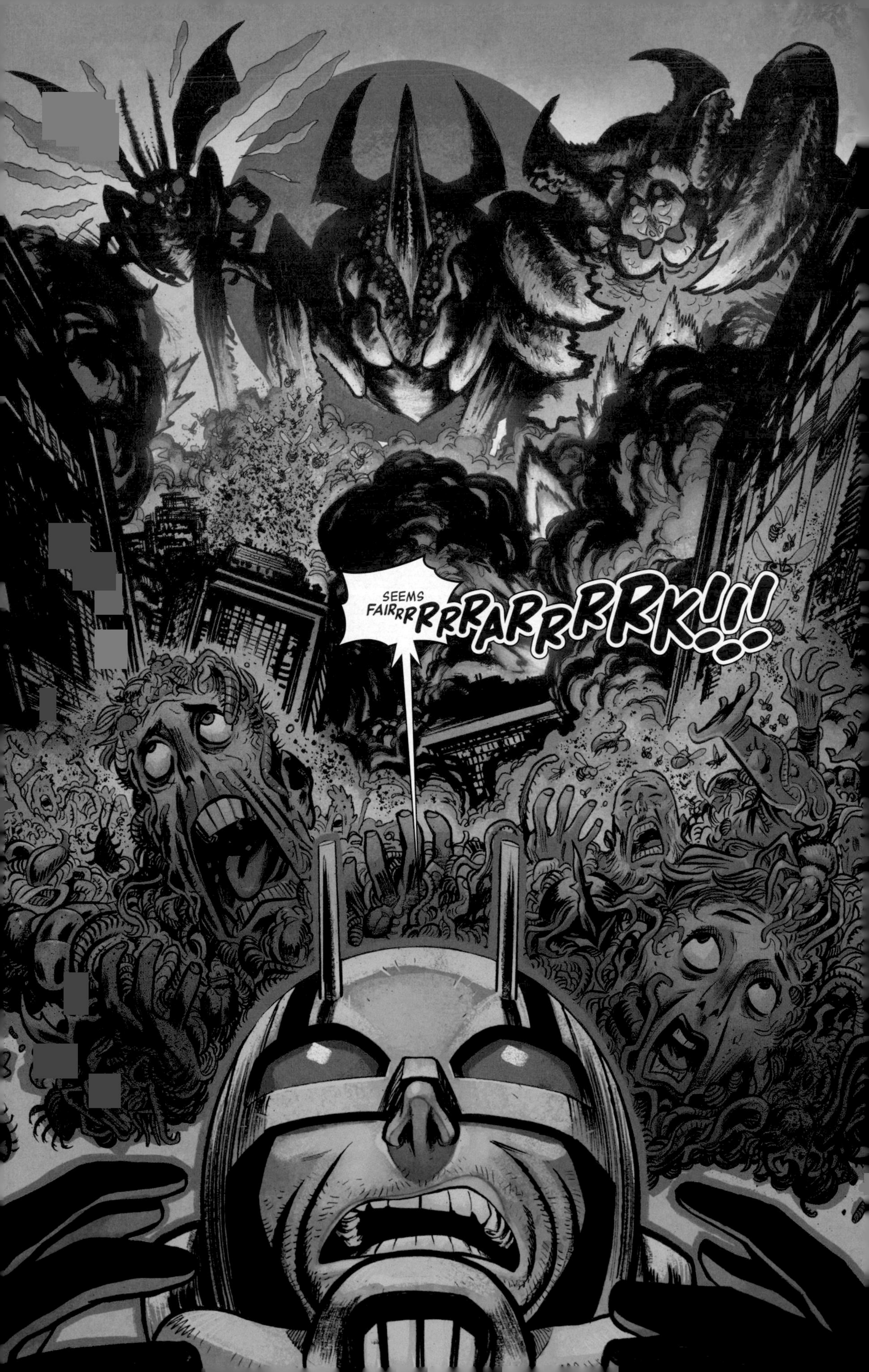
SEEMS FAIRRRRRARRRRRK!!!

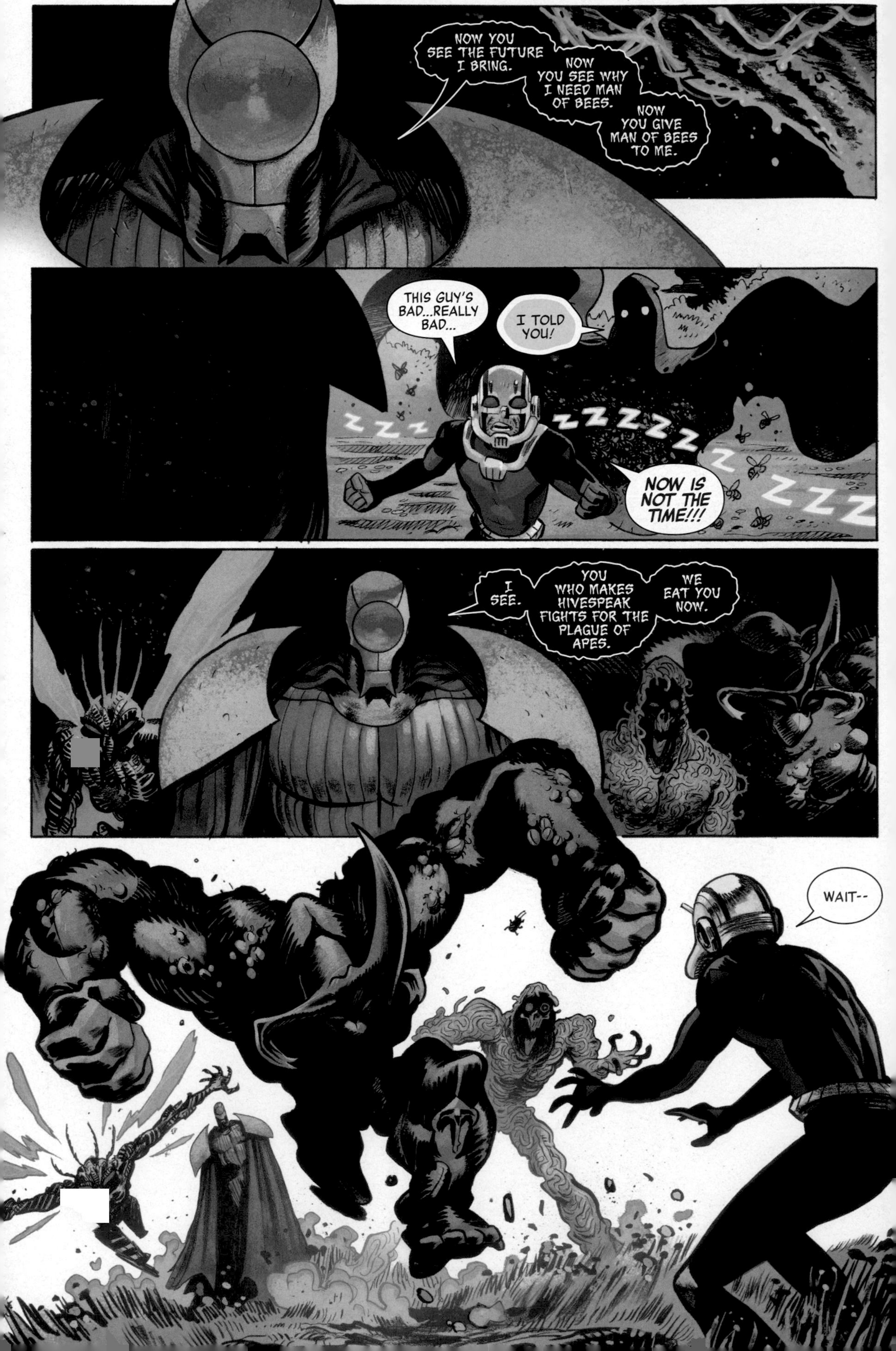
NOW YOU SEE THE FUTURE I BRING.
NOW YOU SEE WHY I NEED MAN OF BEES.
NOW YOU GIVE MAN OF BEES TO ME.
THIS GUY'S BAD...REALLY BAD...
I TOLD YOU!
NOW IS NOT THE TIME!!!
I SEE.
YOU WHO MAKES HIVESPEAK FIGHTS FOR THE PLAGUE OF APES.
WE EAT YOU NOW.
WAIT--

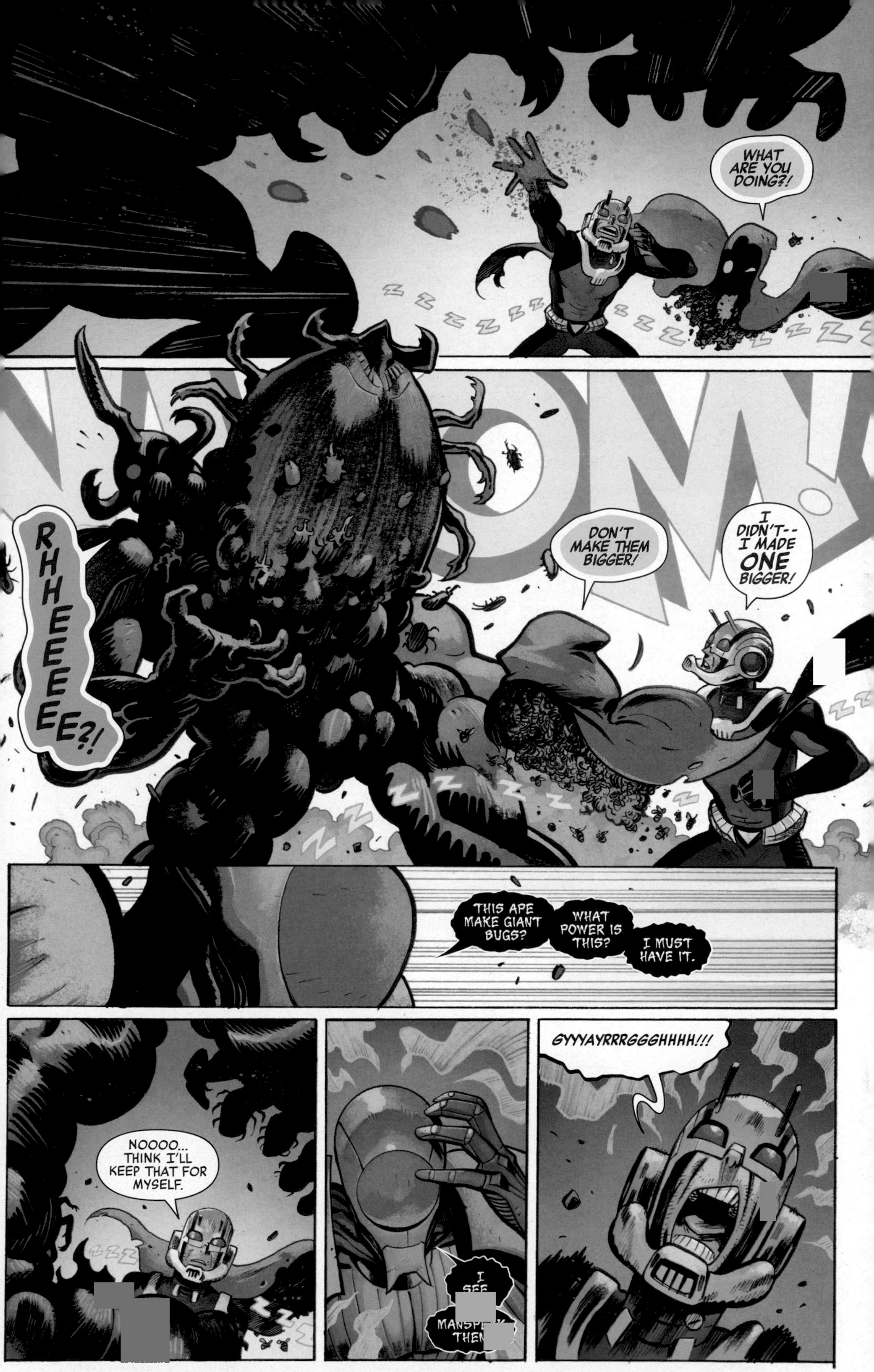
WHAT ARE YOU DOING?!
RHHEEEEEEE?!
DON'T MAKE THEM BIGGER!
I DIDN'T-- I MADE ONE BIGGER!
THIS APE MAKE GIANT BUGS?
WHAT POWER IS THIS?
I MUST HAVE IT.
NOOOO... THINK I'LL KEEP THAT FOR MYSELF.
I SEE
GYYYAYRRRGGGHHHH!!!

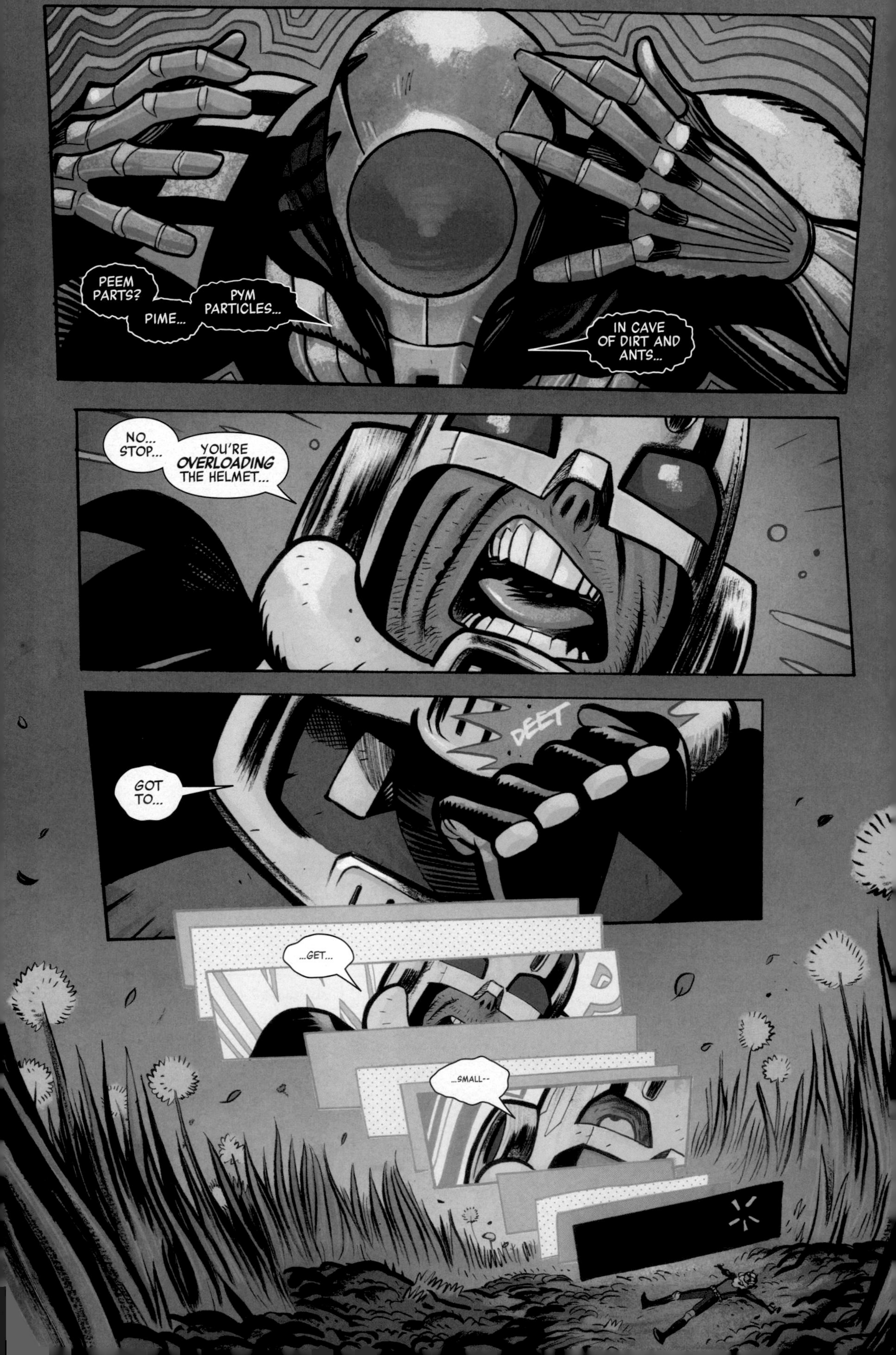

PEEM PARTS?
PIME...
PYM PARTICLES...
IN CAVE OF DIRT AND ANTS...
NO... STOP...
YOU'RE OVERLOADING THE HELMET...
DEET
GOT TO...
...GET...
...SMALL--

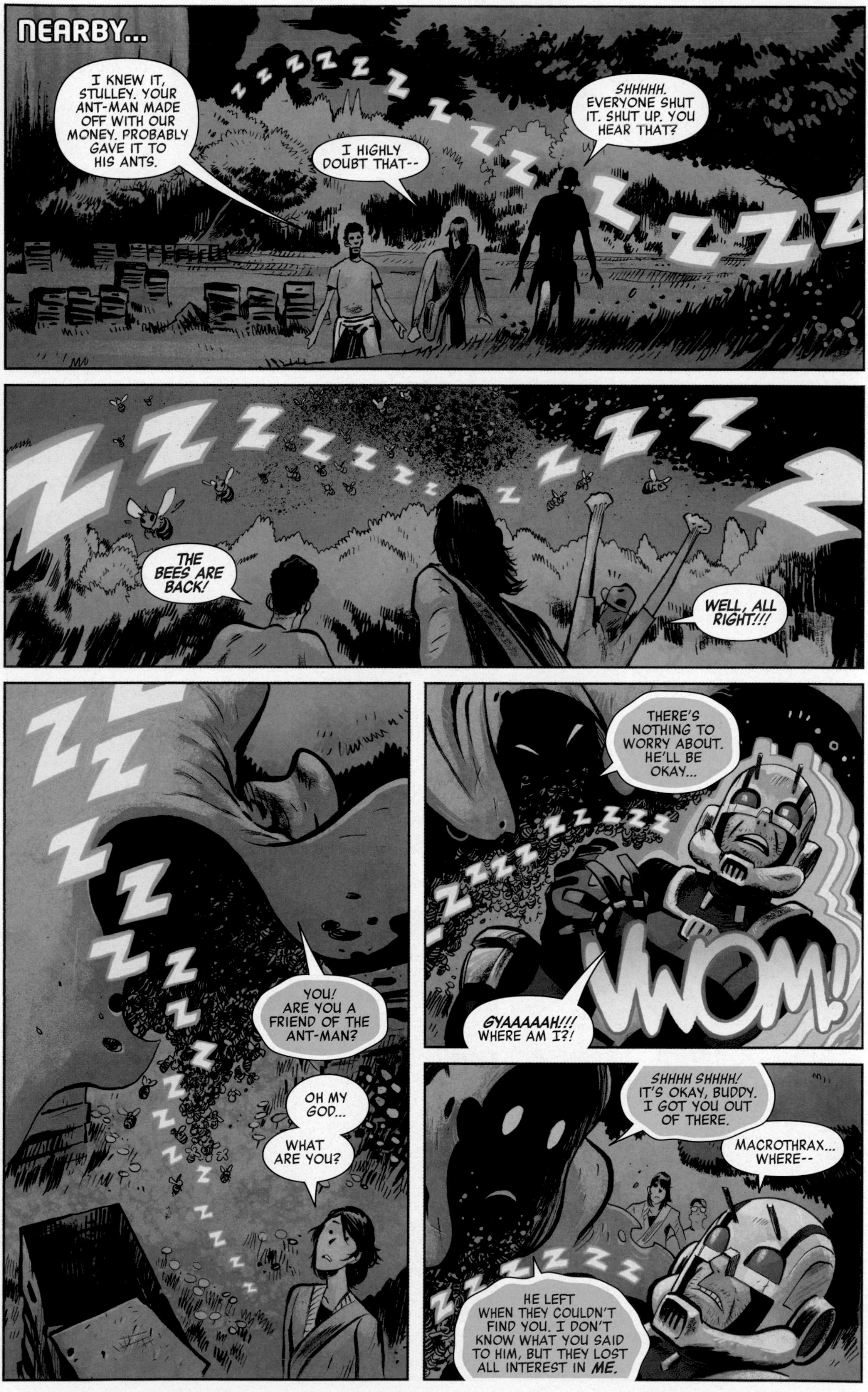
NEARBY...
I KNEW IT, STULLEY. YOUR ANT-MAN MADE OFF WITH OUR MONEY. PROBABLY GAVE IT TO HIS ANTS.
I HIGHLY DOUBT THAT--
SHHHHH. EVERYONE SHUT IT. SHUT UP. YOU HEAR THAT?
THE BEES ARE BACK!
WELL, ALL RIGHT!!!
YOU! ARE YOU A FRIEND OF THE ANT-MAN?
OH MY GOD...
WHAT ARE YOU?
THERE'S NOTHING TO WORRY ABOUT. HE'LL BE OKAY...
VWOM!
GYAAAAAH!!! WHERE AM I?!
SHHHH SHHHH! IT'S OKAY, BUDDY. I GOT YOU OUT OF THERE.
MACROTHRAX... WHERE--
HE LEFT WHEN THEY COULDN'T FIND YOU. I DON'T KNOW WHAT YOU SAID TO HIM, BUT THEY LOST ALL INTEREST IN ME.

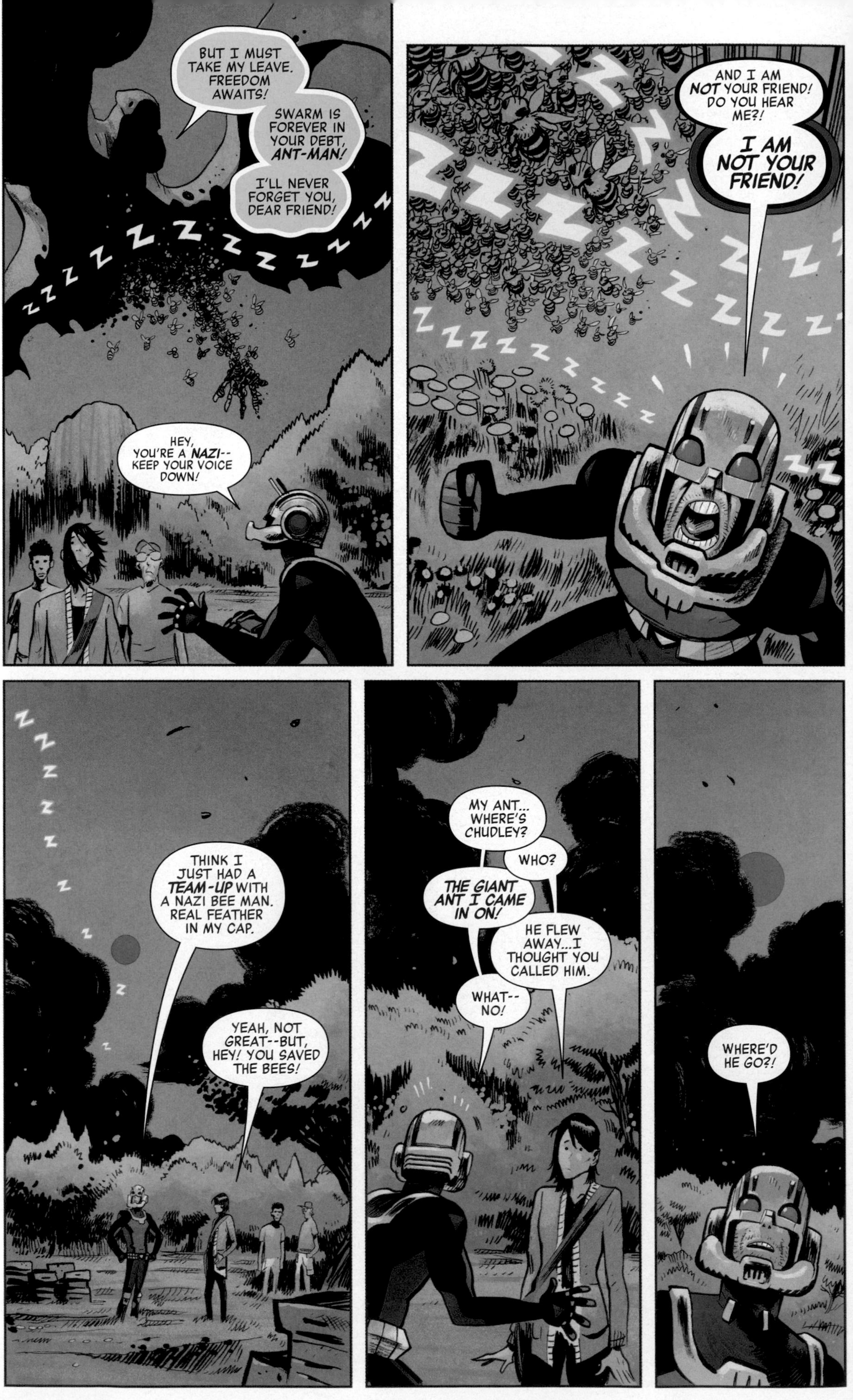
BUT I MUST TAKE MY LEAVE. FREEDOM AWAITS!
SWARM IS FOREVER IN YOUR DEBT, ANT-MAN!
I'LL NEVER FORGET YOU, DEAR FRIEND!
HEY, YOU'RE A NAZI-- KEEP YOUR VOICE DOWN!
AND I AM NOT YOUR FRIEND! DO YOU HEAR ME?!
I AM NOT YOUR FRIEND!
THINK I JUST HAD A TEAM-UP WITH A NAZI BEE MAN. REAL FEATHER IN MY CAP.
YEAH, NOT GREAT--BUT, HEY! YOU SAVED THE BEES!
MY ANT... WHERE'S CHUDLEY?
WHO?
THE GIANT ANT I CAME IN ON!
HE FLEW AWAY...I THOUGHT YOU CALLED HIM.
WHAT-- NO!
WHERE'D HE GO?!

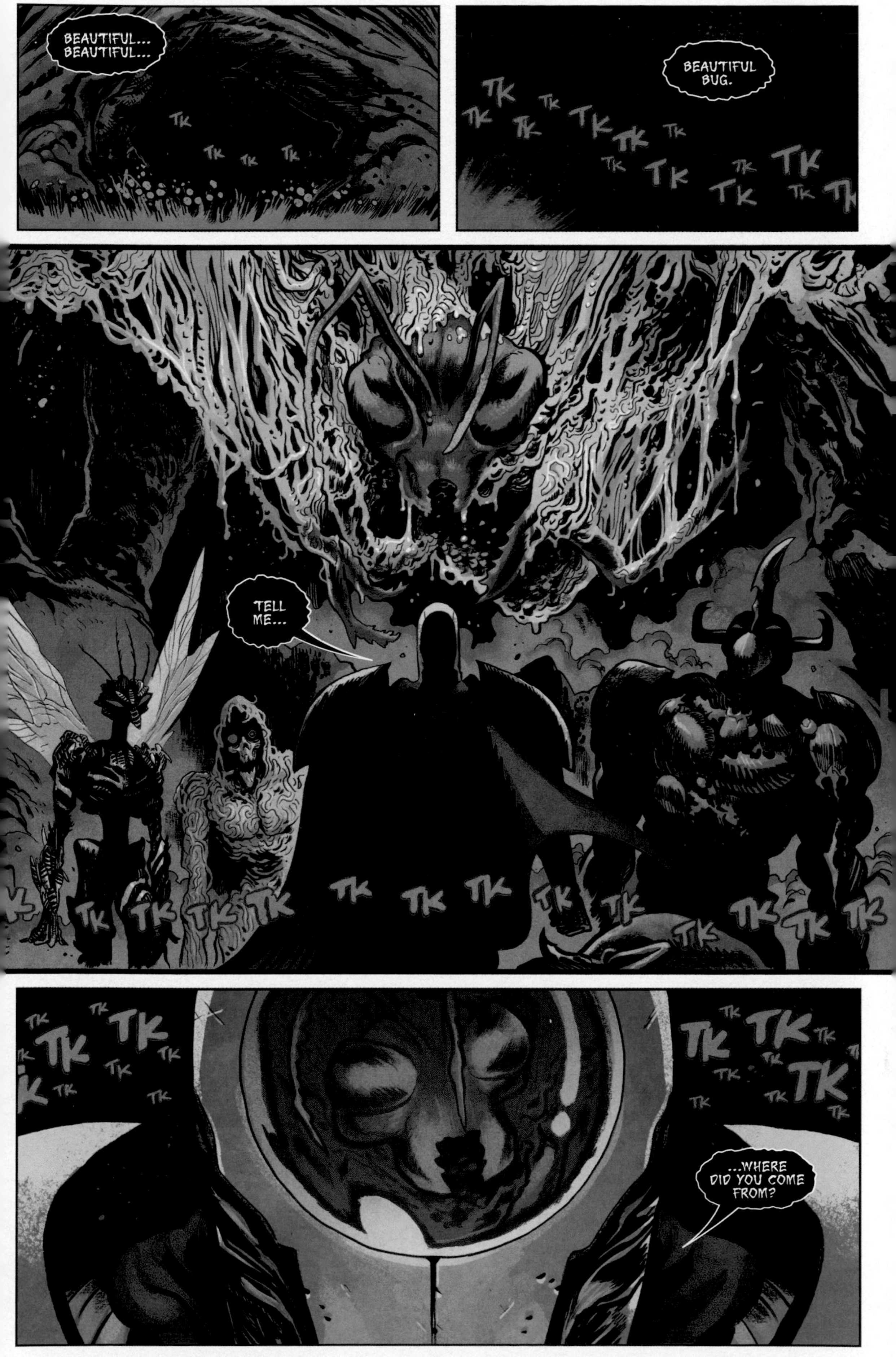
BEAUTIFUL... BEAUTIFUL...
TK TK TK TK
BEAUTIFUL BUG.
TK TK TK TK TK TK TK TK TK TK TK TK TK TK TK
TELL ME...
TK TK TK TK TK TK TK TK TK TK TK TK TK TK
TK TK TK TK TK TK TK TK TK TK TK TK TK TK TK TK TK
...WHERE DID YOU COME FROM?

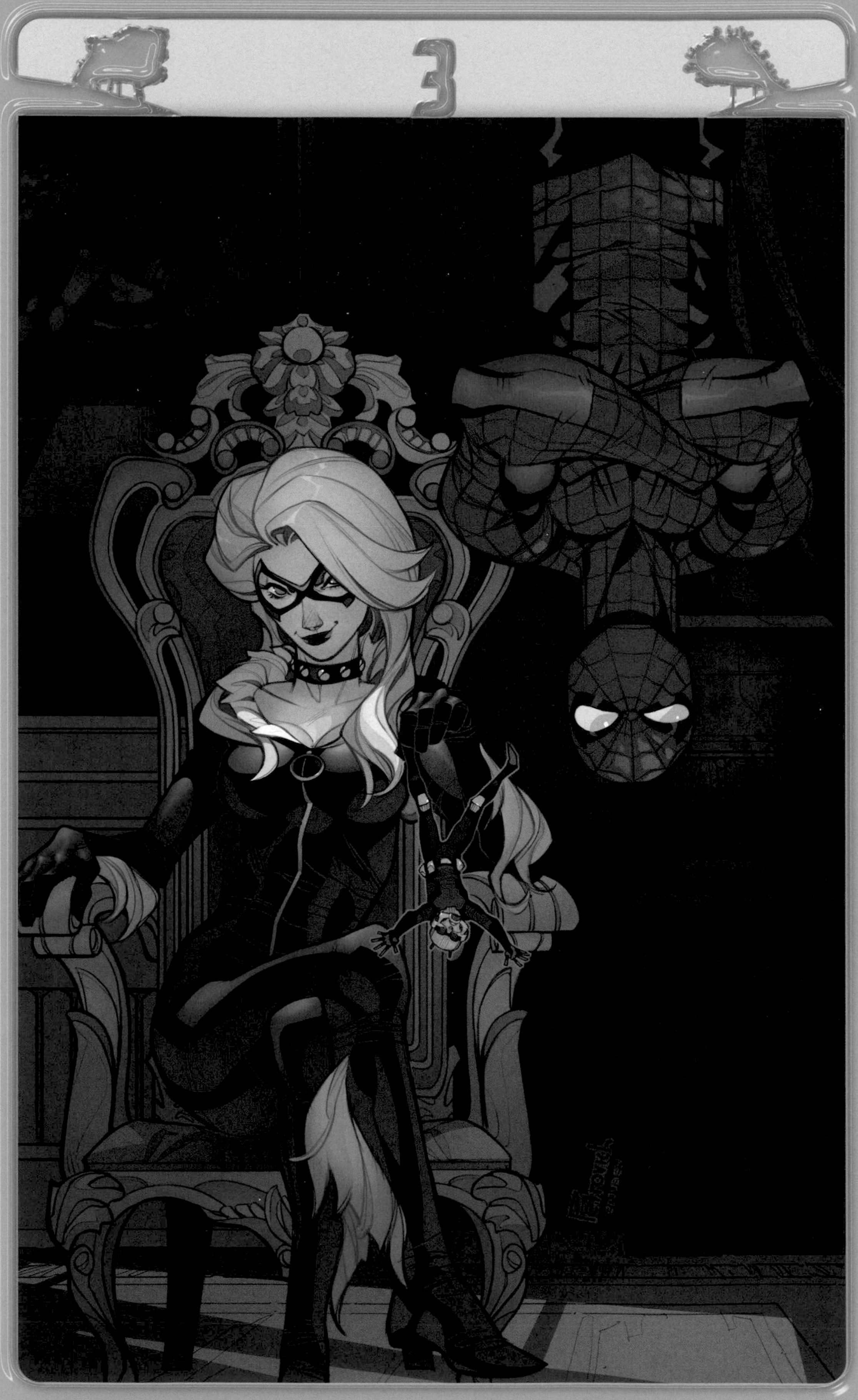
3

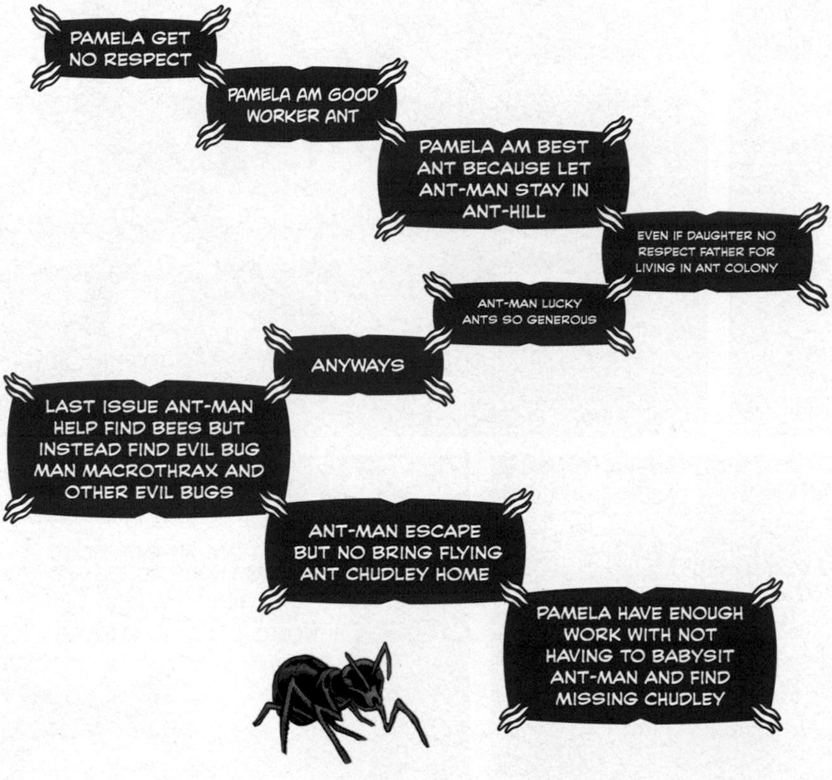
PAMELA GET NO RESPECT
PAMELA AM GOOD WORKER ANT
PAMELA AM BEST ANT BECAUSE LET ANT-MAN STAY IN ANT-HILL
EVEN IF DAUGHTER NO RESPECT FATHER FOR LIVING IN ANT COLONY
ANT-MAN LUCKY ANTS SO GENEROUS
ANYWAYS
LAST ISSUE ANT-MAN HELP FIND BEES BUT INSTEAD FIND EVIL BUG MAN MACROTHRAX AND OTHER EVIL BUGS
ANT-MAN ESCAPE BUT NO BRING FLYING ANT CHUDLEY HOME
PAMELA HAVE ENOUGH WORK WITH NOT HAVING TO BABYSIT ANT-MAN AND FIND MISSING CHUDLEY

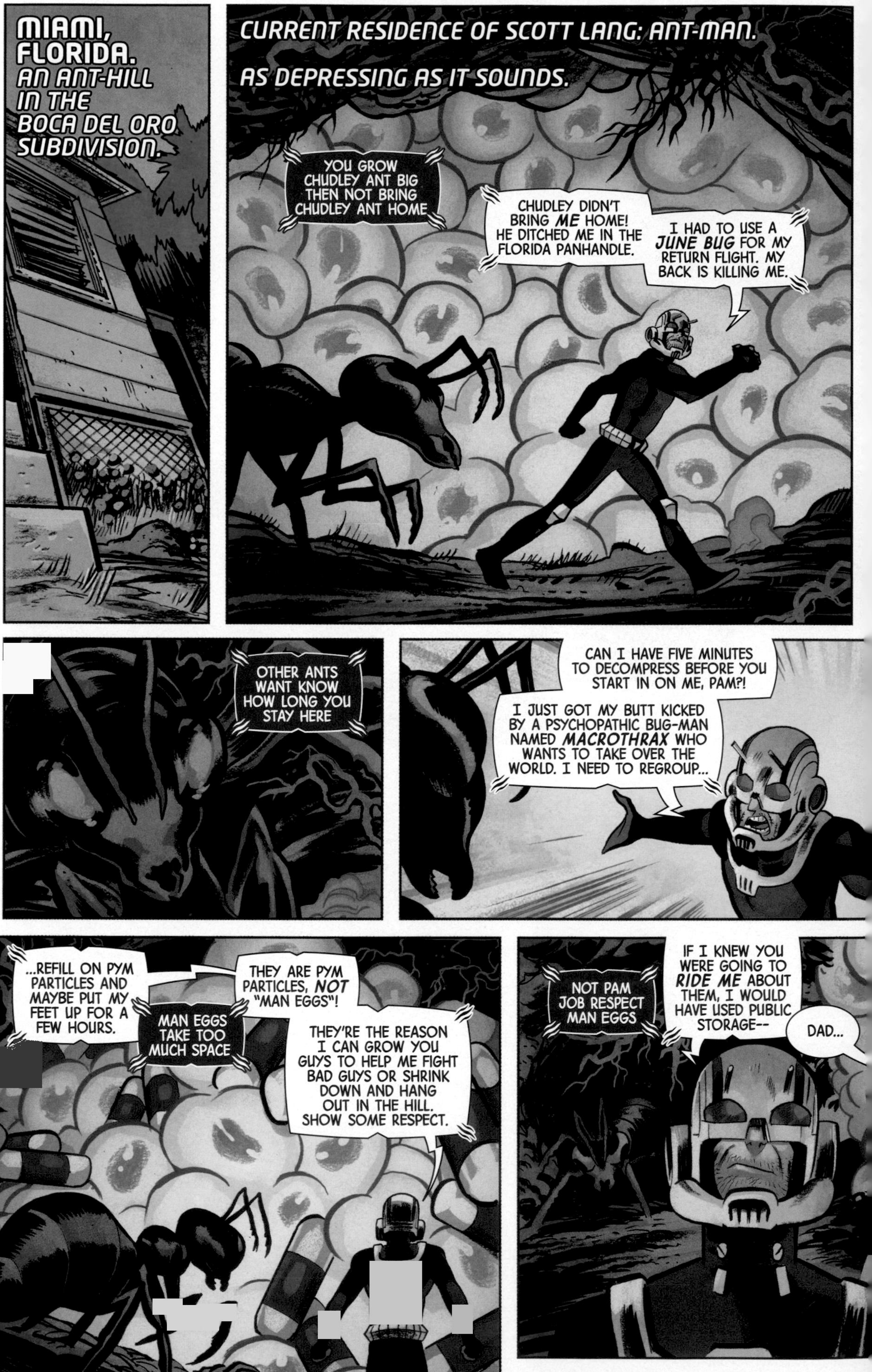
MIAMI, FLORIDA. AN ANT-HILL IN THE BOCA DEL ORO SUBDIVISION.
CURRENT RESIDENCE OF SCOTT LANG: ANT-MAN.
AS DEPRESSING AS IT SOUNDS.
YOU GROW CHUDLEY ANT BIG THEN NOT BRING CHUDLEY ANT HOME
CHUDLEY DIDN'T BRING ME HOME! HE DITCHED ME IN THE FLORIDA PANHANDLE.
I HAD TO USE A JUNE BUG FOR MY RETURN FLIGHT. MY BACK IS KILLING ME.
OTHER ANTS WANT KNOW HOW LONG YOU STAY HERE
CAN I HAVE FIVE MINUTES TO DECOMPRESS BEFORE YOU START IN ON ME, PAM?!
I JUST GOT MY BUTT KICKED BY A PSYCHOPATHIC BUG-MAN NAMED MACROTHRAX WHO WANTS TO TAKE OVER THE WORLD. I NEED TO REGROUP...
...REFILL ON PYM PARTICLES AND MAYBE PUT MY FEET UP FOR A FEW HOURS.
MAN EGGS TAKE TOO MUCH SPACE
THEY ARE PYM PARTICLES, NOT "MAN EGGS"!
THEY'RE THE REASON I CAN GROW YOU GUYS TO HELP ME FIGHT BAD GUYS OR SHRINK DOWN AND HANG OUT IN THE HILL. SHOW SOME RESPECT.
NOT PAM JOB RESPECT MAN EGGS
IF I KNEW YOU WERE GOING TO RIDE ME ABOUT THEM, I WOULD HAVE USED PUBLIC STORAGE--
DAD...

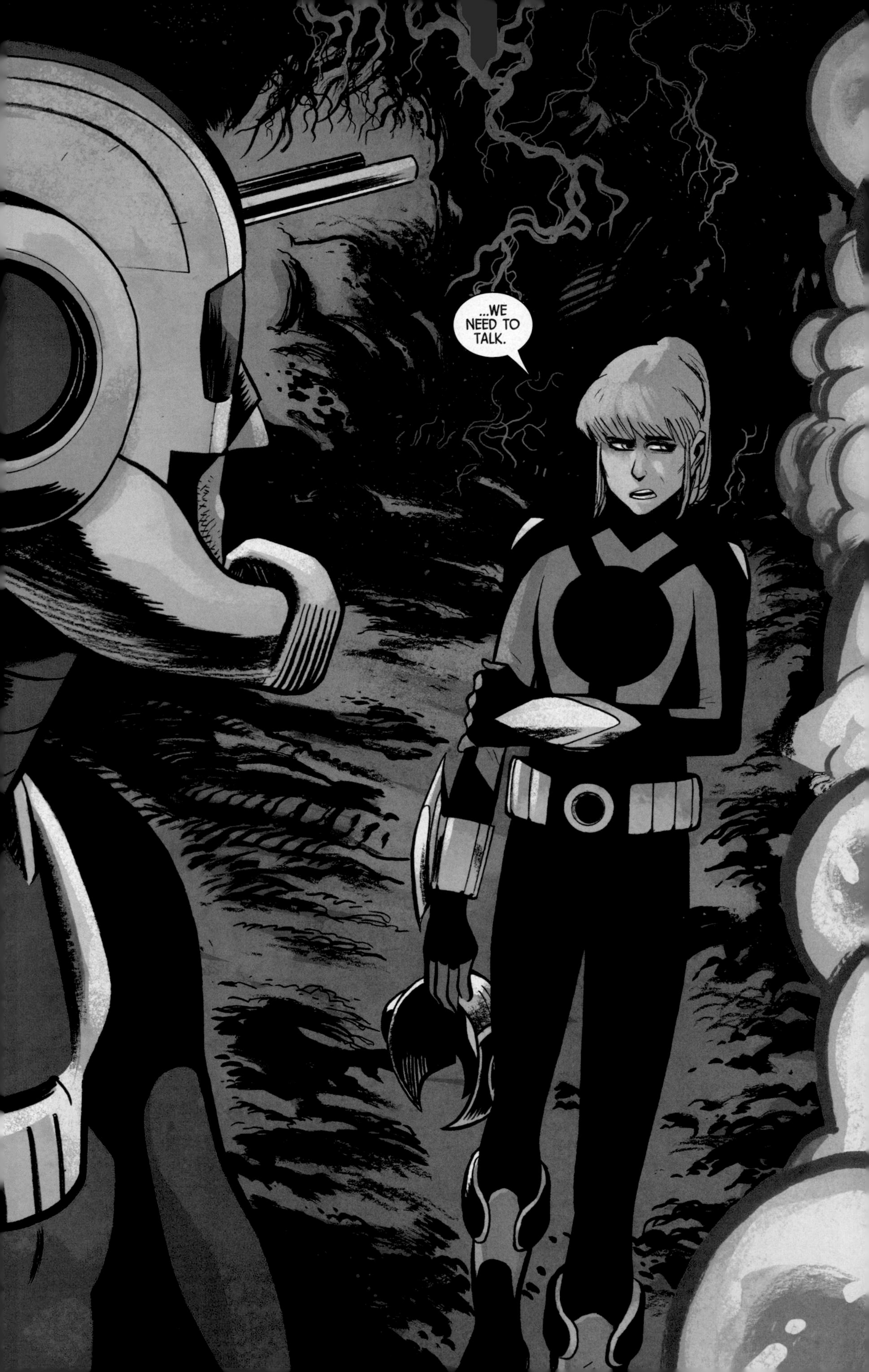
...WE NEED TO TALK.

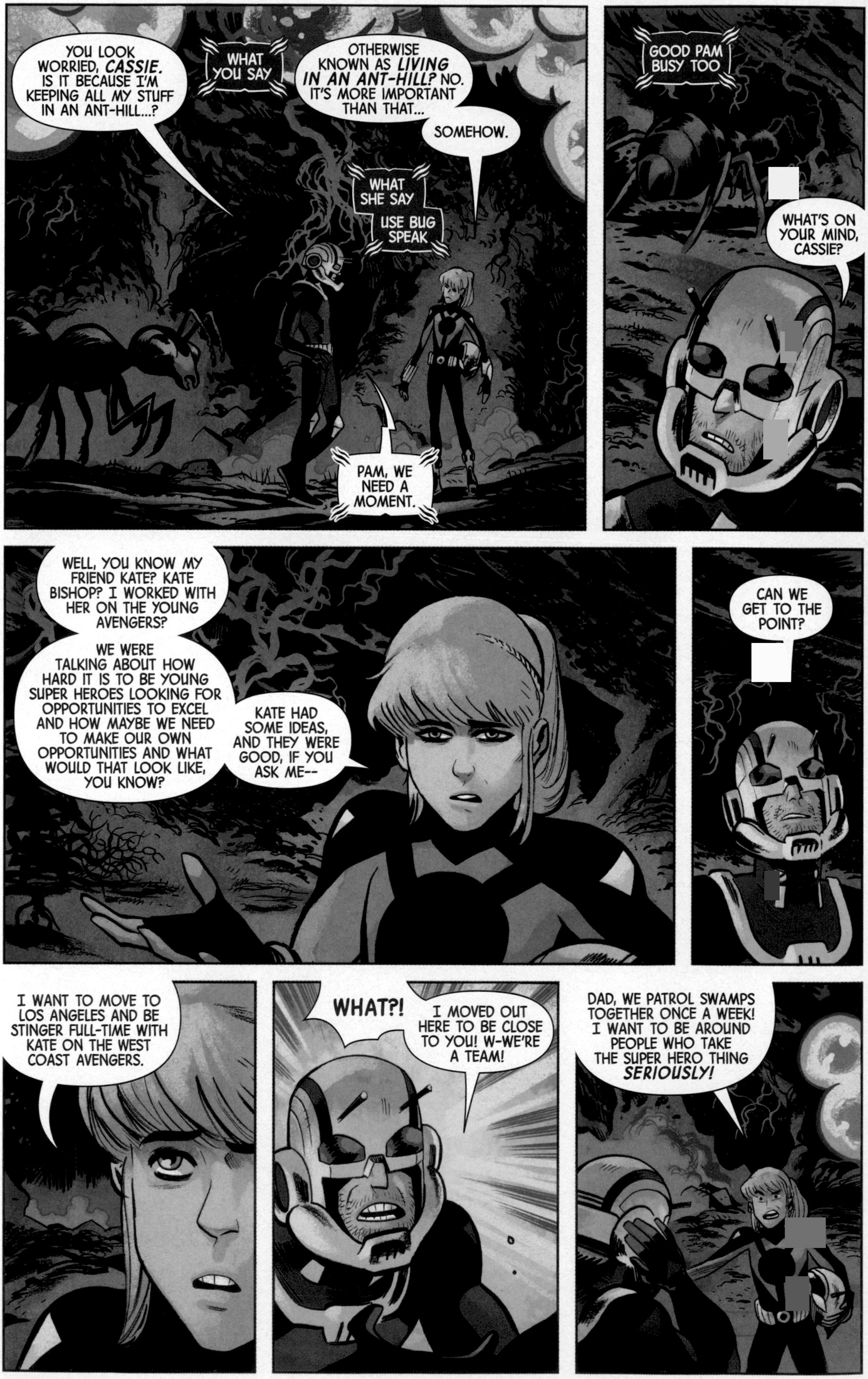
YOU LOOK WORRIED, CASSIE. IS IT BECAUSE I'M KEEPING ALL MY STUFF IN AN ANT-HILL...?
WHAT YOU SAY
OTHERWISE KNOWN AS LIVING IN AN ANT-HILL? NO. IT'S MORE IMPORTANT THAN THAT...
SOMEHOW.
WHAT SHE SAY
USE BUG SPEAK
PAM, WE NEED A MOMENT.
GOOD PAM BUSY TOO
WHAT'S ON YOUR MIND, CASSIE?
WELL, YOU KNOW MY FRIEND KATE? KATE BISHOP? I WORKED WITH HER ON THE YOUNG AVENGERS?
WE WERE TALKING ABOUT HOW HARD IT IS TO BE YOUNG SUPER HEROES LOOKING FOR OPPORTUNITIES TO EXCEL AND HOW MAYBE WE NEED TO MAKE OUR OWN OPPORTUNITIES AND WHAT WOULD THAT LOOK LIKE, YOU KNOW?
KATE HAD SOME IDEAS, AND THEY WERE GOOD, IF YOU ASK ME--
CAN WE GET TO THE POINT?
I WANT TO MOVE TO LOS ANGELES AND BE STINGER FULL-TIME WITH KATE ON THE WEST COAST AVENGERS.
WHAT?!
I MOVED OUT HERE TO BE CLOSE TO YOU! W-WE'RE A TEAM!
DAD, WE PATROL SWAMPS TOGETHER ONCE A WEEK! I WANT TO BE AROUND PEOPLE WHO TAKE THE SUPER HERO THING SERIOUSLY!

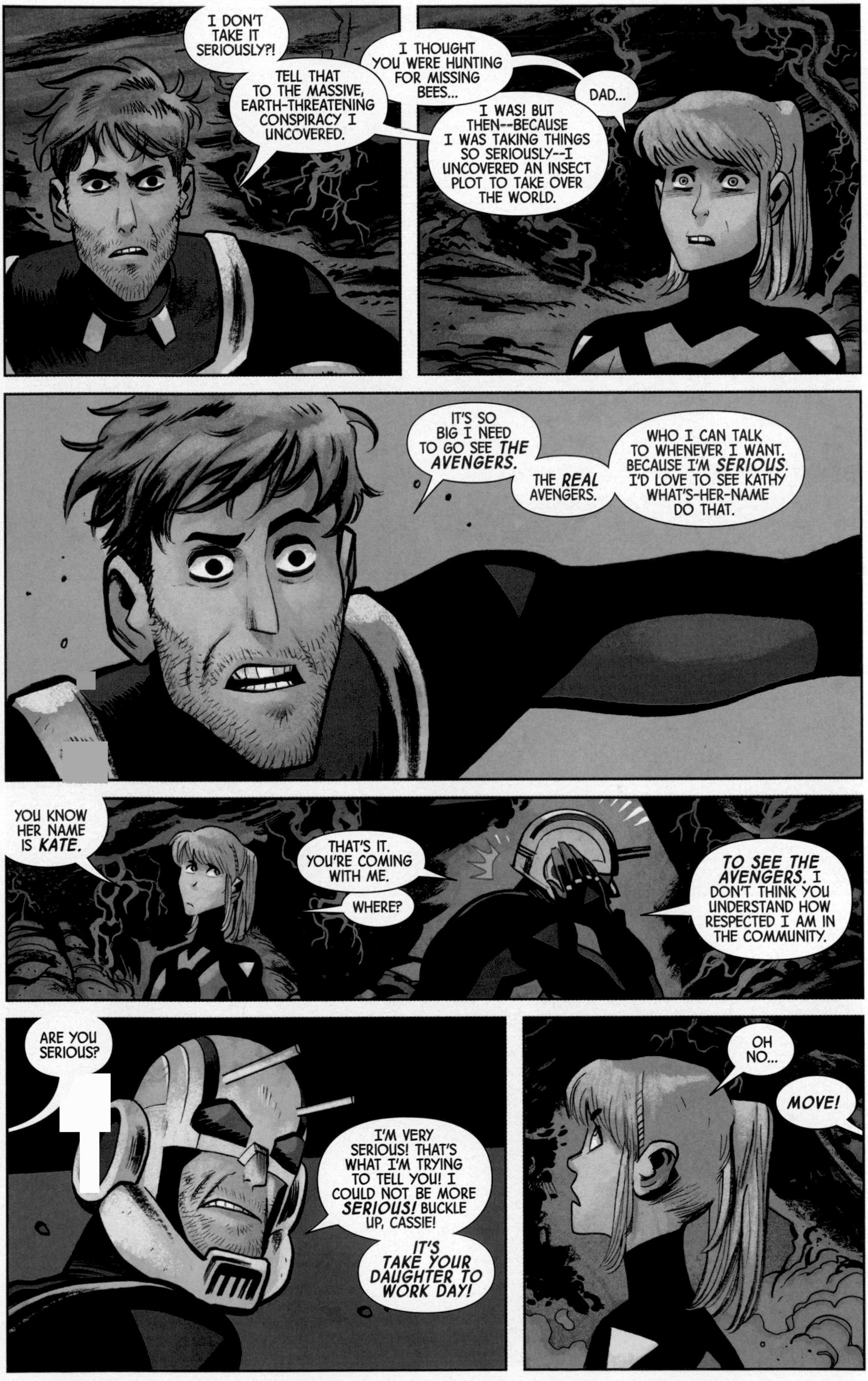

I DON'T TAKE IT SERIOUSLY?!
TELL THAT TO THE MASSIVE, EARTH-THREATENING CONSPIRACY I UNCOVERED.
I THOUGHT YOU WERE HUNTING FOR MISSING BEES...
DAD...
I WAS! BUT THEN--BECAUSE I WAS TAKING THINGS SO SERIOUSLY--I UNCOVERED AN INSECT PLOT TO TAKE OVER THE WORLD.
IT'S SO BIG I NEED TO GO SEE THE AVENGERS.
THE REAL AVENGERS.
WHO I CAN TALK TO WHENEVER I WANT. BECAUSE I'M SERIOUS. I'D LOVE TO SEE KATHY WHAT'S-HER-NAME DO THAT.
YOU KNOW HER NAME IS KATE.
THAT'S IT. YOU'RE COMING WITH ME.
WHERE?
TO SEE THE AVENGERS. I DON'T THINK YOU UNDERSTAND HOW RESPECTED I AM IN THE COMMUNITY.
ARE YOU SERIOUS?
I'M VERY SERIOUS! THAT'S WHAT I'M TRYING TO TELL YOU! I COULD NOT BE MORE SERIOUS! BUCKLE UP, CASSIE!
IT'S TAKE YOUR DAUGHTER TO WORK DAY!
OH NO...
MOVE!

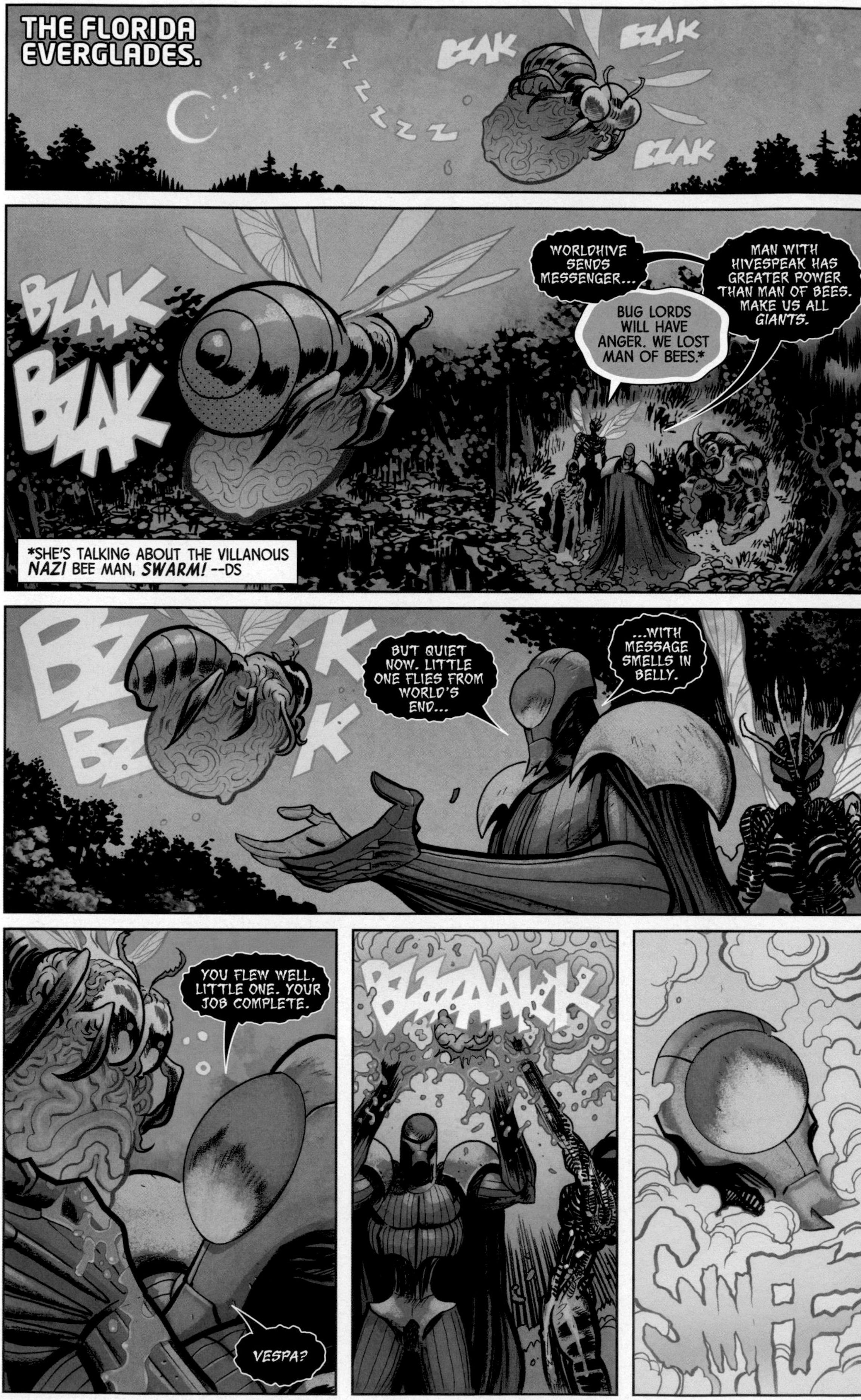
THE FLORIDA EVERGLADES.
BZAK
BZAK
BZAK
BZAK
BZAK
WORLDHIVE SENDS MESSENGER...
MAN WITH HIVESPEAK HAS GREATER POWER THAN MAN OF BEES. MAKE US ALL GIANTS.
BUG LORDS WILL HAVE ANGER. WE LOST MAN OF BEES.*
*SHE'S TALKING ABOUT THE VILLANOUS NAZI BEE MAN, SWARM! --DS
BUT QUIET NOW. LITTLE ONE FLIES FROM WORLD'S END...
...WITH MESSAGE SMELLS IN BELLY.
YOU FLEW WELL, LITTLE ONE. YOUR JOB COMPLETE.
VESPA?
BZZZAAKK

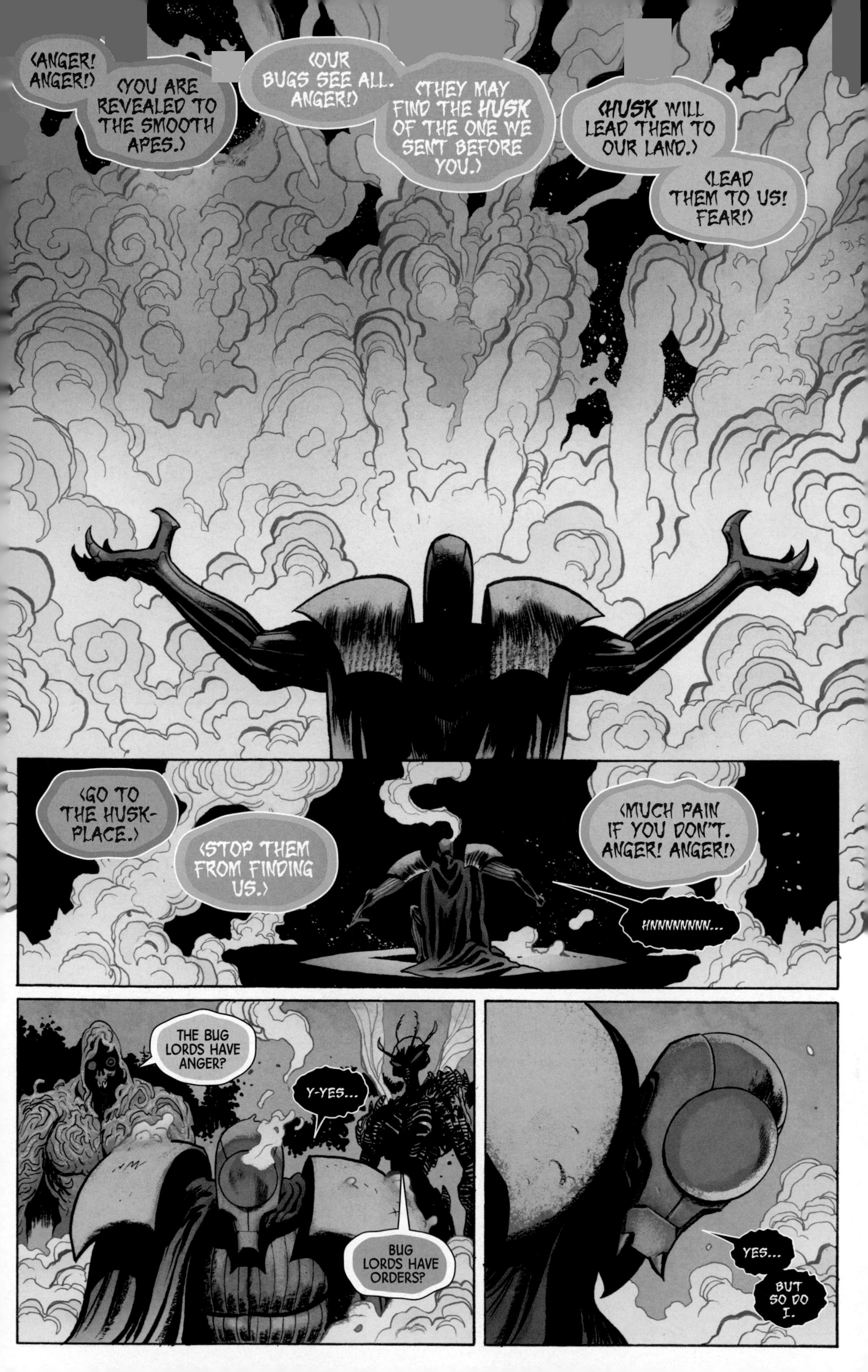
‹ANGER! ANGER!›
‹YOU ARE REVEALED TO THE SMOOTH APES.›
‹OUR BUGS SEE ALL. ANGER!›
‹THEY MAY FIND THE HUSK OF THE ONE WE SENT BEFORE YOU.›
‹HUSK WILL LEAD THEM TO OUR LAND.›
‹LEAD THEM TO US! FEAR!›
‹GO TO THE HUSK-PLACE.›
‹STOP THEM FROM FINDING US.›
‹MUCH PAIN IF YOU DON'T. ANGER! ANGER!›
HNNNNNNNN...
THE BUG LORDS HAVE ANGER?
Y-YES...
BUG LORDS HAVE ORDERS?
YES...
BUT SO DO I.

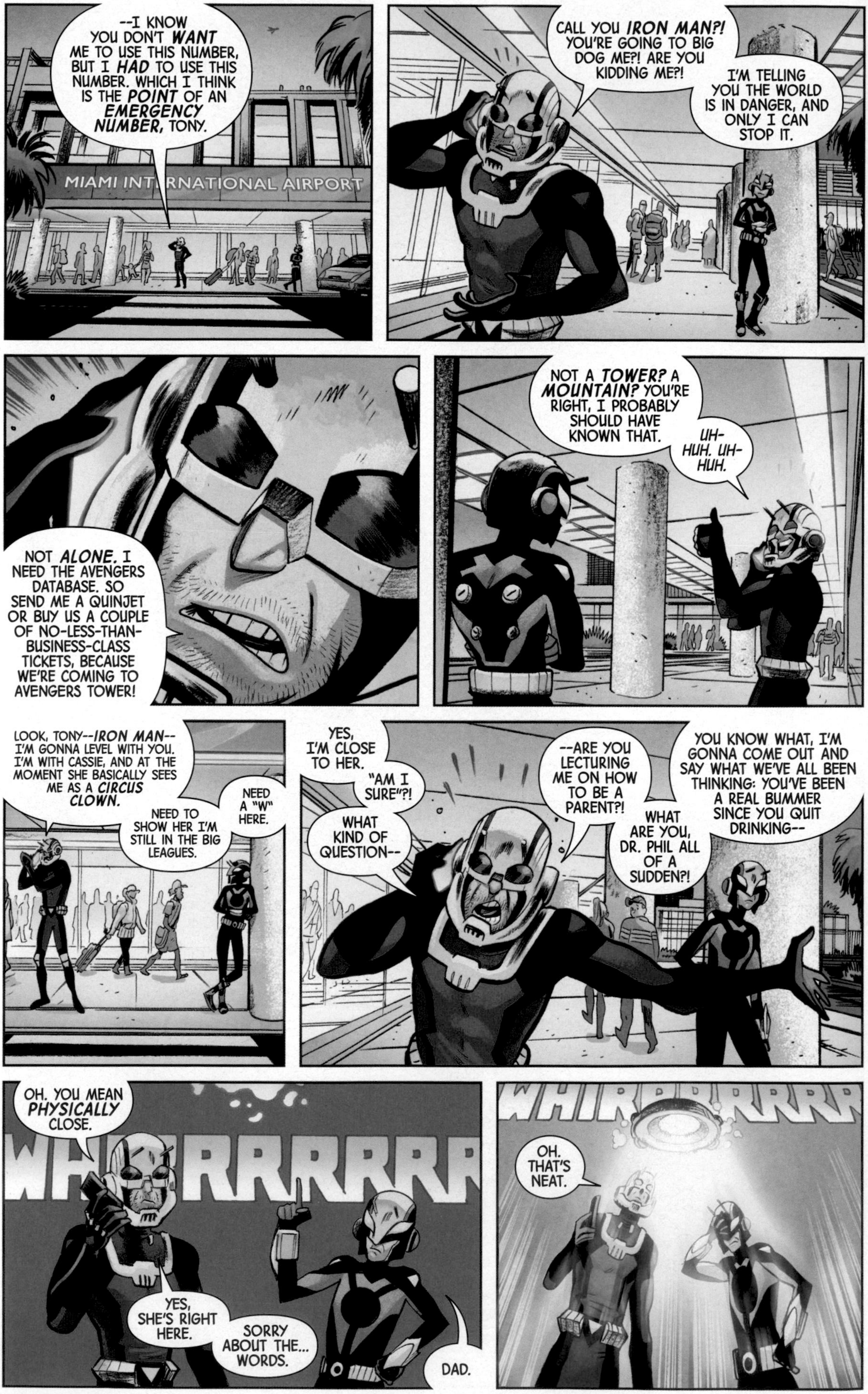
--I KNOW YOU DON'T WANT ME TO USE THIS NUMBER, BUT I HAD TO USE THIS NUMBER. WHICH I THINK IS THE POINT OF AN EMERGENCY NUMBER, TONY.
MIAMI INTERNATIONAL AIRPORT
CALL YOU IRON MAN?! YOU'RE GOING TO BIG DOG ME?! ARE YOU KIDDING ME?!
I'M TELLING YOU THE WORLD IS IN DANGER, AND ONLY I CAN STOP IT.
NOT ALONE. I NEED THE AVENGERS DATABASE. SO SEND ME A QUINJET OR BUY US A COUPLE OF NO-LESS-THAN-BUSINESS-CLASS TICKETS, BECAUSE WE'RE COMING TO AVENGERS TOWER!
NOT A TOWER? A MOUNTAIN? YOU'RE RIGHT, I PROBABLY SHOULD HAVE KNOWN THAT.
UH-HUH. UH-HUH.
LOOK, TONY--IRON MAN--I'M GONNA LEVEL WITH YOU. I'M WITH CASSIE, AND AT THE MOMENT SHE BASICALLY SEES ME AS A CIRCUS CLOWN.
NEED TO SHOW HER I'M STILL IN THE BIG LEAGUES.
NEED A "W" HERE.
YES, I'M CLOSE TO HER.
"AM I SURE"?!
WHAT KIND OF QUESTION--
--ARE YOU LECTURING ME ON HOW TO BE A PARENT?!
WHAT ARE YOU, DR. PHIL ALL OF A SUDDEN?!
YOU KNOW WHAT, I'M GONNA COME OUT AND SAY WHAT WE'VE ALL BEEN THINKING: YOU'VE BEEN A REAL BUMMER SINCE YOU QUIT DRINKING--
OH. YOU MEAN PHYSICALLY CLOSE.
WHIRRRRRRR
YES, SHE'S RIGHT HERE.
SORRY ABOUT THE... WORDS.
DAD.
WHIRRRRRRRR
OH. THAT'S NEAT.

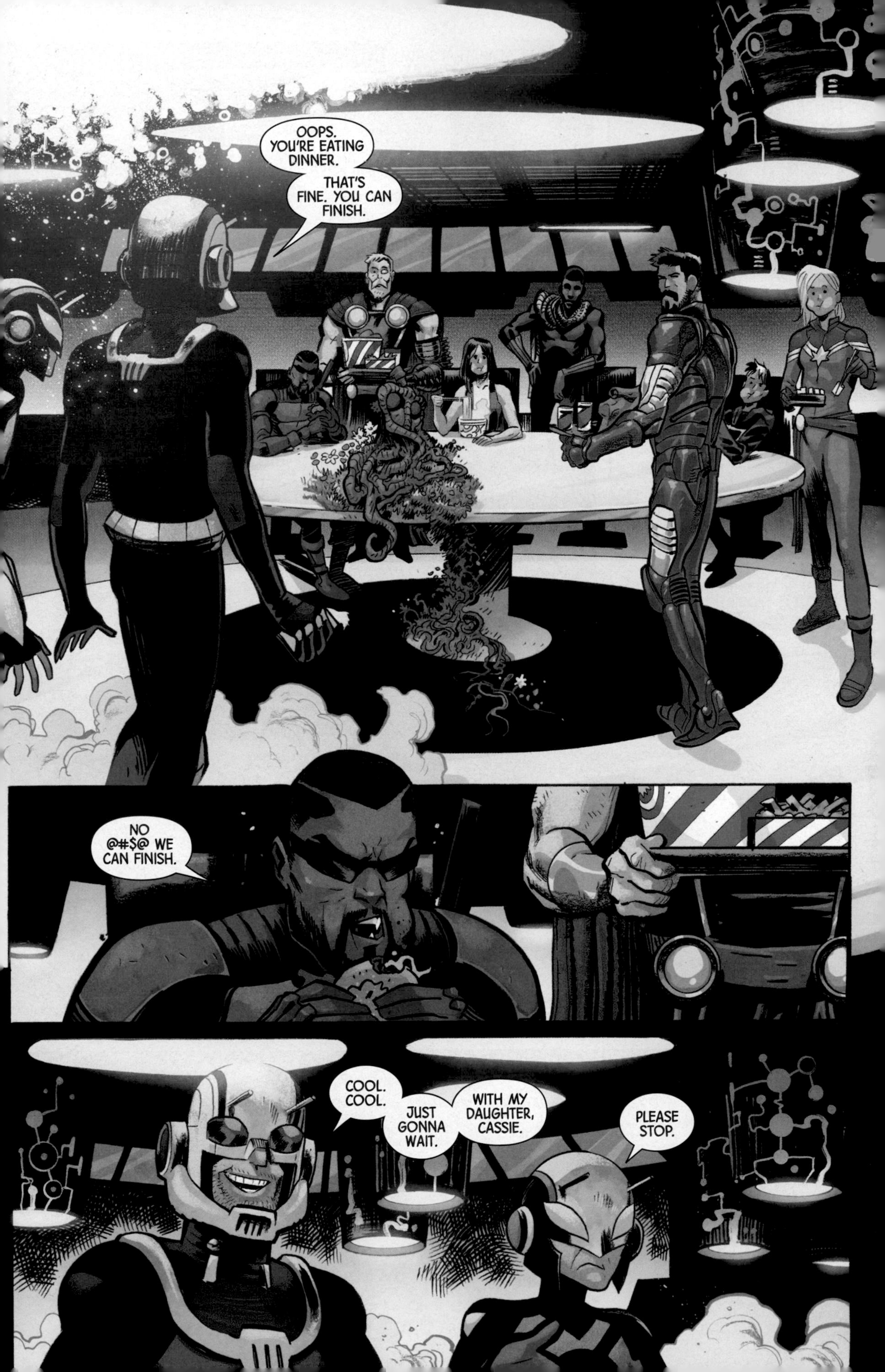
OOPS. YOU'RE EATING DINNER.
THAT'S FINE. YOU CAN FINISH.
NO @#$@ WE CAN FINISH.
COOL. COOL.
JUST GONNA WAIT.
WITH MY DAUGHTER, CASSIE.
PLEASE STOP.

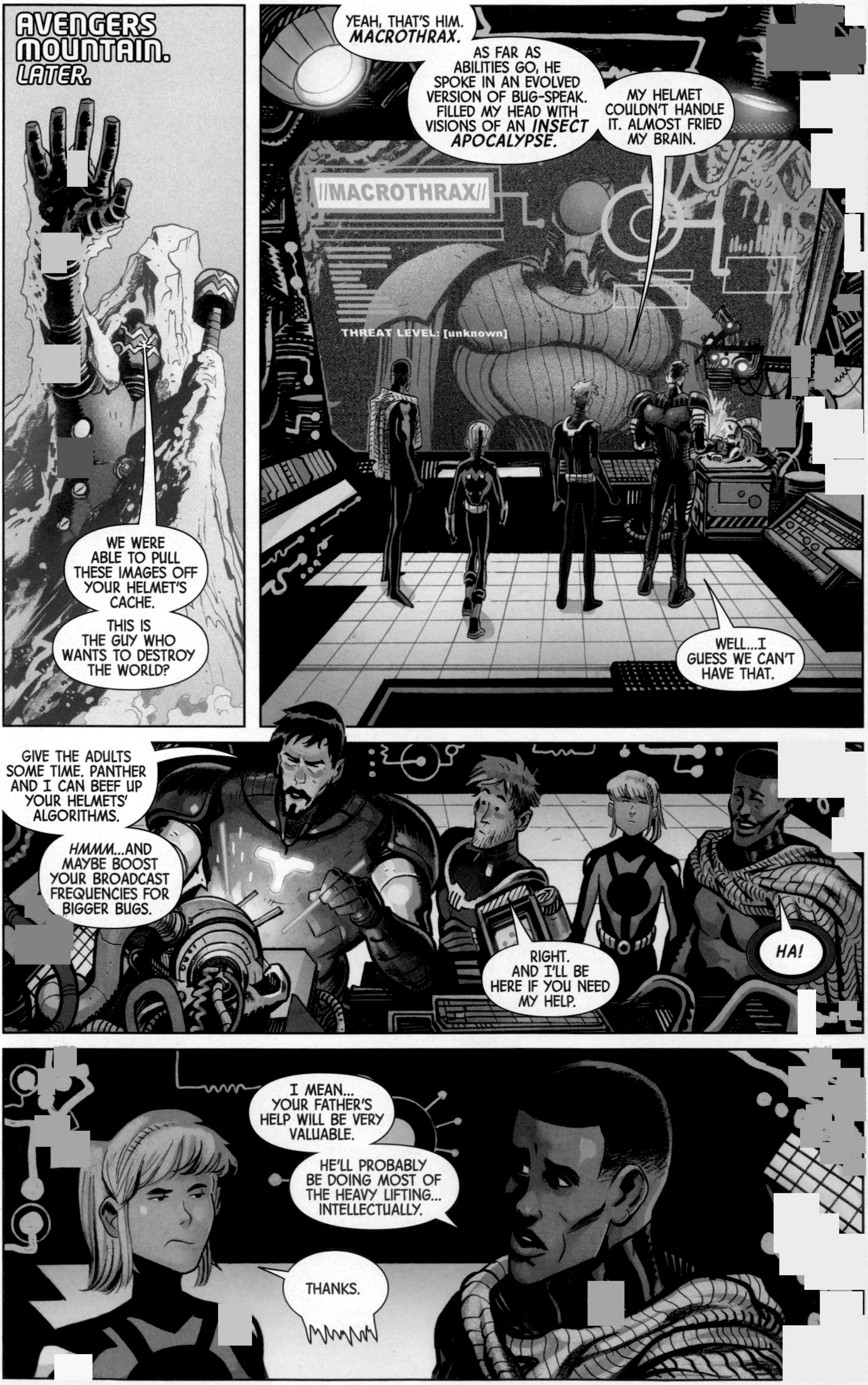
AVENGERS MOUNTAIN. LATER.
WE WERE ABLE TO PULL THESE IMAGES OFF YOUR HELMET'S CACHE.
THIS IS THE GUY WHO WANTS TO DESTROY THE WORLD?
YEAH, THAT'S HIM. MACROTHRAX.
AS FAR AS ABILITIES GO, HE SPOKE IN AN EVOLVED VERSION OF BUG-SPEAK. FILLED MY HEAD WITH VISIONS OF AN INSECT APOCALYPSE.
MY HELMET COULDN'T HANDLE IT. ALMOST FRIED MY BRAIN.
//MACROTHRAX//
THREAT LEVEL: [unknown]
WELL...I GUESS WE CAN'T HAVE THAT.
GIVE THE ADULTS SOME TIME. PANTHER AND I CAN BEEF UP YOUR HELMETS' ALGORITHMS.
HMMM...AND MAYBE BOOST YOUR BROADCAST FREQUENCIES FOR BIGGER BUGS.
RIGHT. AND I'LL BE HERE IF YOU NEED MY HELP.
HA!
I MEAN... YOUR FATHER'S HELP WILL BE VERY VALUABLE.
HE'LL PROBABLY BE DOING MOST OF THE HEAVY LIFTING... INTELLECTUALLY.
THANKS.

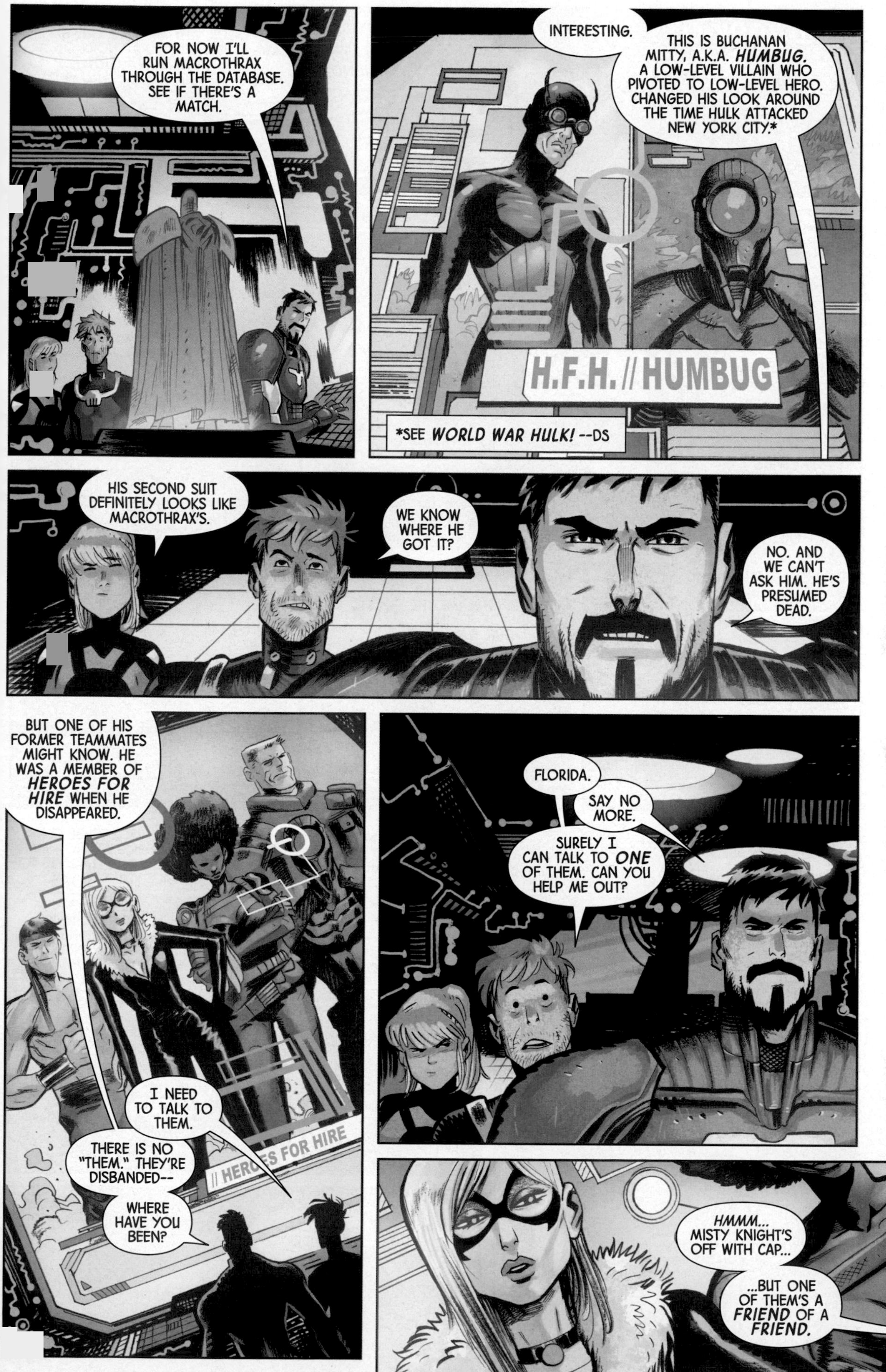

FOR NOW I'LL RUN MACROTHRAX THROUGH THE DATABASE. SEE IF THERE'S A MATCH.
INTERESTING.
THIS IS BUCHANAN MITTY, A.K.A. HUMBUG, A LOW-LEVEL VILLAIN WHO PIVOTED TO LOW-LEVEL HERO. CHANGED HIS LOOK AROUND THE TIME HULK ATTACKED NEW YORK CITY.*
H.F.H. // HUMBUG
*SEE WORLD WAR HULK! --DS
HIS SECOND SUIT DEFINITELY LOOKS LIKE MACROTHRAX'S.
WE KNOW WHERE HE GOT IT?
NO. AND WE CAN'T ASK HIM. HE'S PRESUMED DEAD.
BUT ONE OF HIS FORMER TEAMMATES MIGHT KNOW. HE WAS A MEMBER OF HEROES FOR HIRE WHEN HE DISAPPEARED.
// HEROES FOR HIRE
I NEED TO TALK TO THEM.
THERE IS NO "THEM." THEY'RE DISBANDED--
WHERE HAVE YOU BEEN?
FLORIDA.
SAY NO MORE.
SURELY I CAN TALK TO ONE OF THEM. CAN YOU HELP ME OUT?
HMMM... MISTY KNIGHT'S OFF WITH CAP...
...BUT ONE OF THEM'S A FRIEND OF A FRIEND.

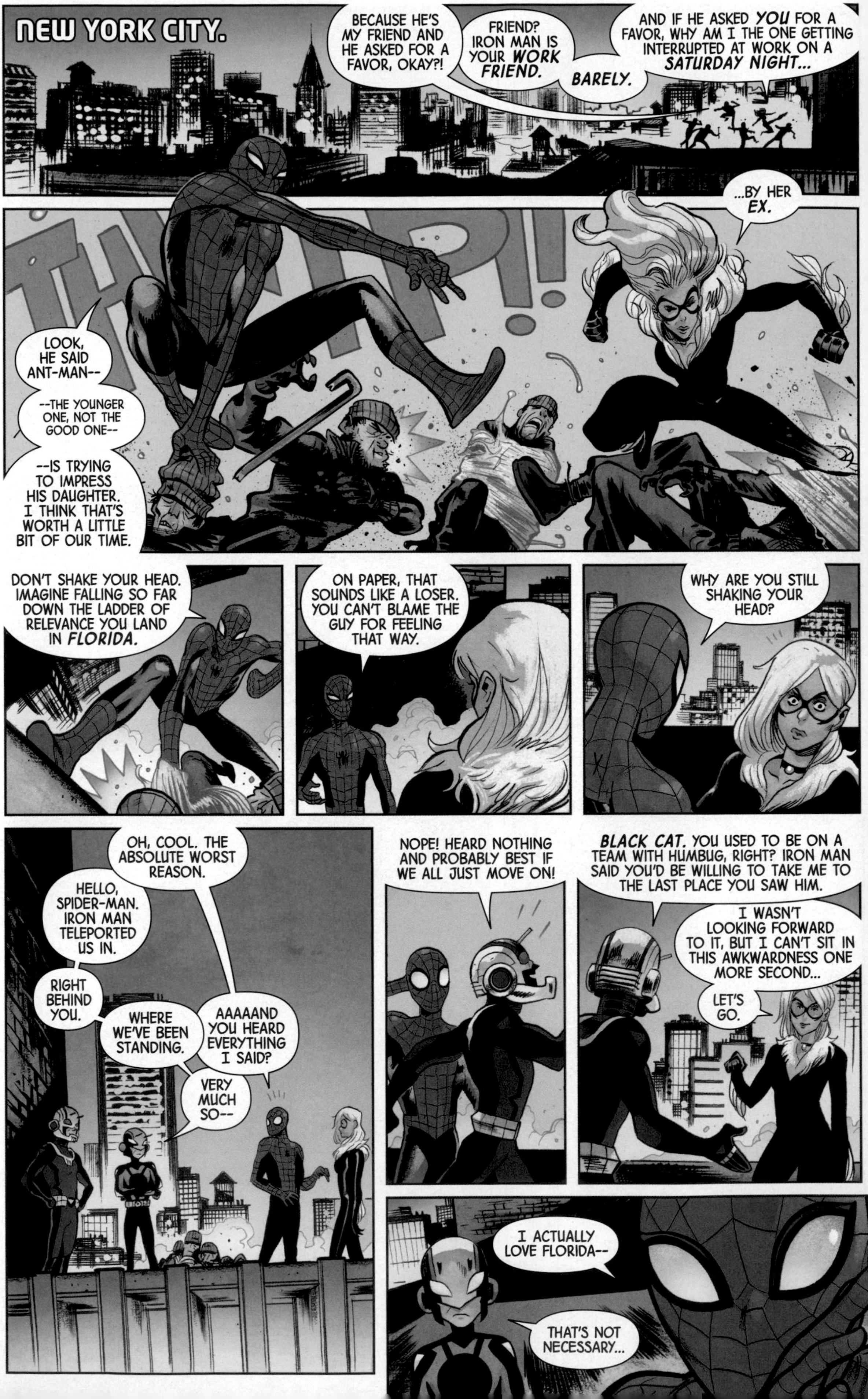
NEW YORK CITY.
BECAUSE HE'S MY FRIEND AND HE ASKED FOR A FAVOR, OKAY?!
FRIEND? IRON MAN IS YOUR WORK FRIEND.
BARELY.
AND IF HE ASKED YOU FOR A FAVOR, WHY AM I THE ONE GETTING INTERRUPTED AT WORK ON A SATURDAY NIGHT...
...BY HER EX.
LOOK, HE SAID ANT-MAN--
--THE YOUNGER ONE, NOT THE GOOD ONE--
--IS TRYING TO IMPRESS HIS DAUGHTER. I THINK THAT'S WORTH A LITTLE BIT OF OUR TIME.
DON'T SHAKE YOUR HEAD. IMAGINE FALLING SO FAR DOWN THE LADDER OF RELEVANCE YOU LAND IN FLORIDA.
ON PAPER, THAT SOUNDS LIKE A LOSER. YOU CAN'T BLAME THE GUY FOR FEELING THAT WAY.
WHY ARE YOU STILL SHAKING YOUR HEAD?
OH, COOL. THE ABSOLUTE WORST REASON.
HELLO, SPIDER-MAN. IRON MAN TELEPORTED US IN.
RIGHT BEHIND YOU.
WHERE WE'VE BEEN STANDING.
AAAAAND YOU HEARD EVERYTHING I SAID?
VERY MUCH SO--
NOPE! HEARD NOTHING AND PROBABLY BEST IF WE ALL JUST MOVE ON!
BLACK CAT. YOU USED TO BE ON A TEAM WITH HUMBUG, RIGHT? IRON MAN SAID YOU'D BE WILLING TO TAKE ME TO THE LAST PLACE YOU SAW HIM.
I WASN'T LOOKING FORWARD TO IT, BUT I CAN'T SIT IN THIS AWKWARDNESS ONE MORE SECOND...
LET'S GO.
I ACTUALLY LOVE FLORIDA--
THAT'S NOT NECESSARY...

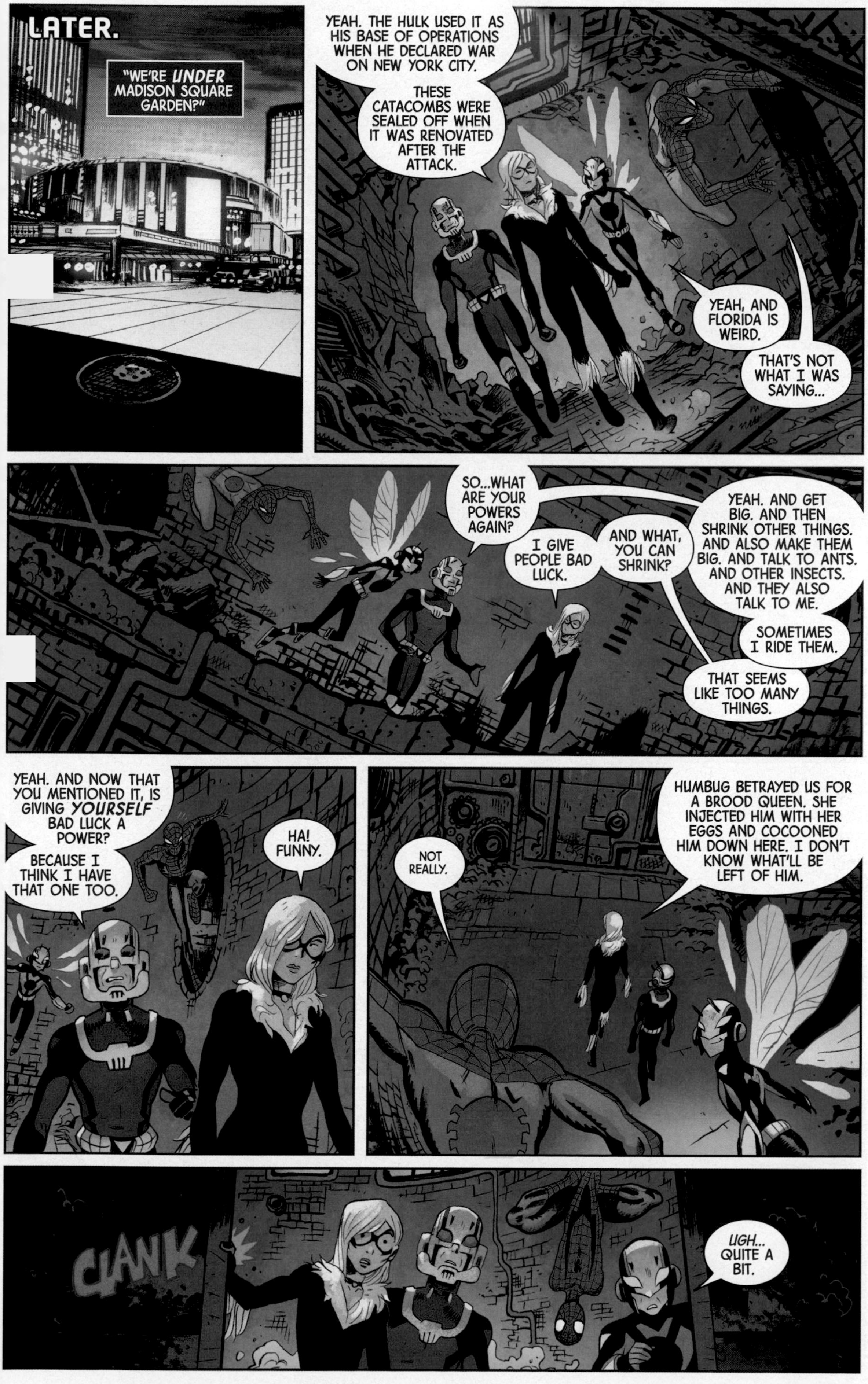
LATER.
"WE'RE UNDER MADISON SQUARE GARDEN?"
YEAH. THE HULK USED IT AS HIS BASE OF OPERATIONS WHEN HE DECLARED WAR ON NEW YORK CITY.
THESE CATACOMBS WERE SEALED OFF WHEN IT WAS RENOVATED AFTER THE ATTACK.
YEAH, AND FLORIDA IS WEIRD.
THAT'S NOT WHAT I WAS SAYING...
SO...WHAT ARE YOUR POWERS AGAIN?
I GIVE PEOPLE BAD LUCK.
AND WHAT, YOU CAN SHRINK?
YEAH. AND GET BIG. AND THEN SHRINK OTHER THINGS. AND ALSO MAKE THEM BIG. AND TALK TO ANTS. AND OTHER INSECTS. AND THEY ALSO TALK TO ME.
SOMETIMES I RIDE THEM.
THAT SEEMS LIKE TOO MANY THINGS.
YEAH. AND NOW THAT YOU MENTIONED IT, IS GIVING YOURSELF BAD LUCK A POWER?
BECAUSE I THINK I HAVE THAT ONE TOO.
HA! FUNNY.
NOT REALLY.
HUMBUG BETRAYED US FOR A BROOD QUEEN. SHE INJECTED HIM WITH HER EGGS AND COCOONED HIM DOWN HERE. I DON'T KNOW WHAT'LL BE LEFT OF HIM.
CLANK
UGH... QUITE A BIT.

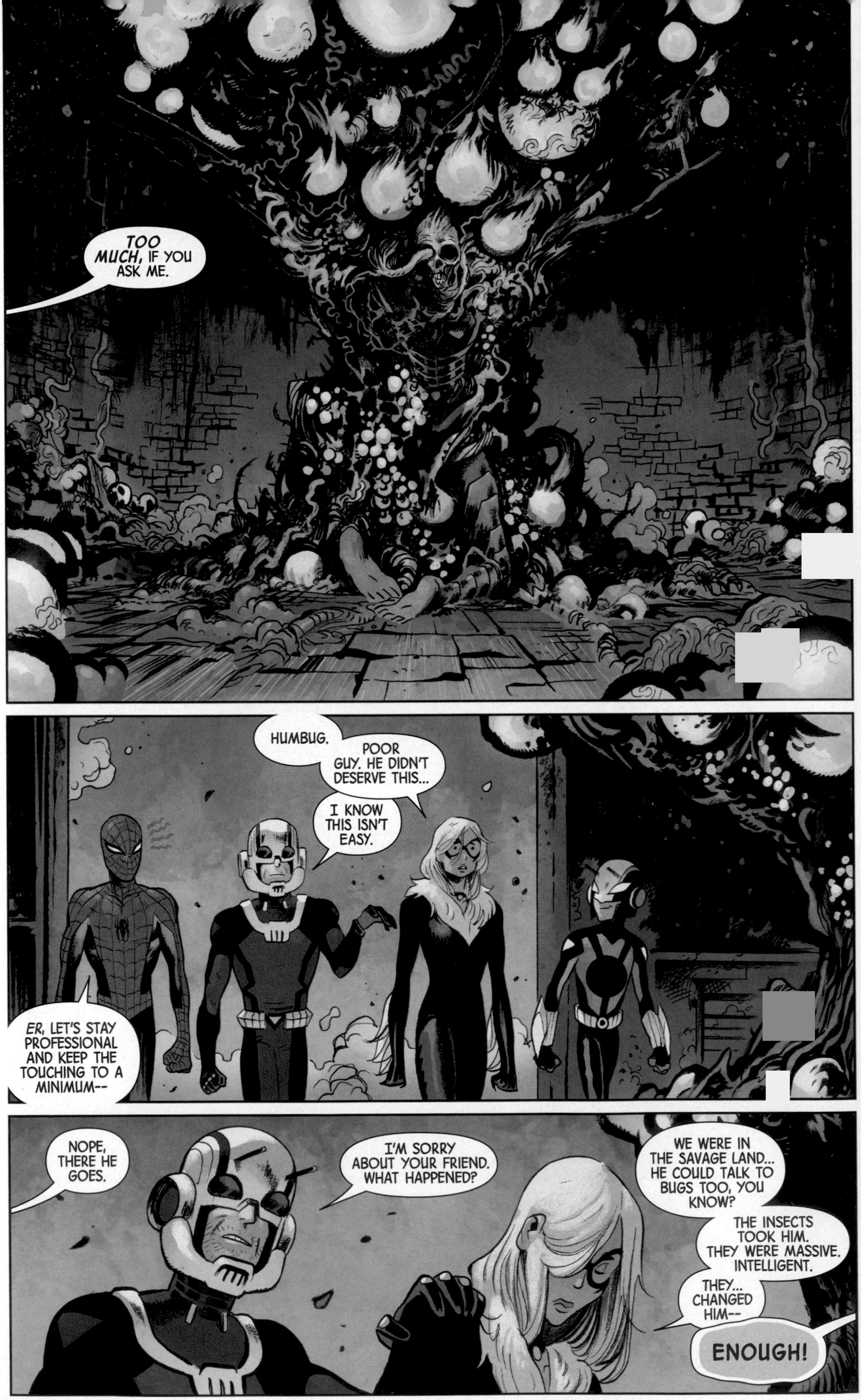
TOO MUCH, IF YOU ASK ME.
HUMBUG.
POOR GUY. HE DIDN'T DESERVE THIS...
I KNOW THIS ISN'T EASY.
ER, LET'S STAY PROFESSIONAL AND KEEP THE TOUCHING TO A MINIMUM--
NOPE, THERE HE GOES.
I'M SORRY ABOUT YOUR FRIEND. WHAT HAPPENED?
WE WERE IN THE SAVAGE LAND... HE COULD TALK TO BUGS TOO, YOU KNOW?
THE INSECTS TOOK HIM. THEY WERE MASSIVE. INTELLIGENT.
THEY... CHANGED HIM--
ENOUGH!

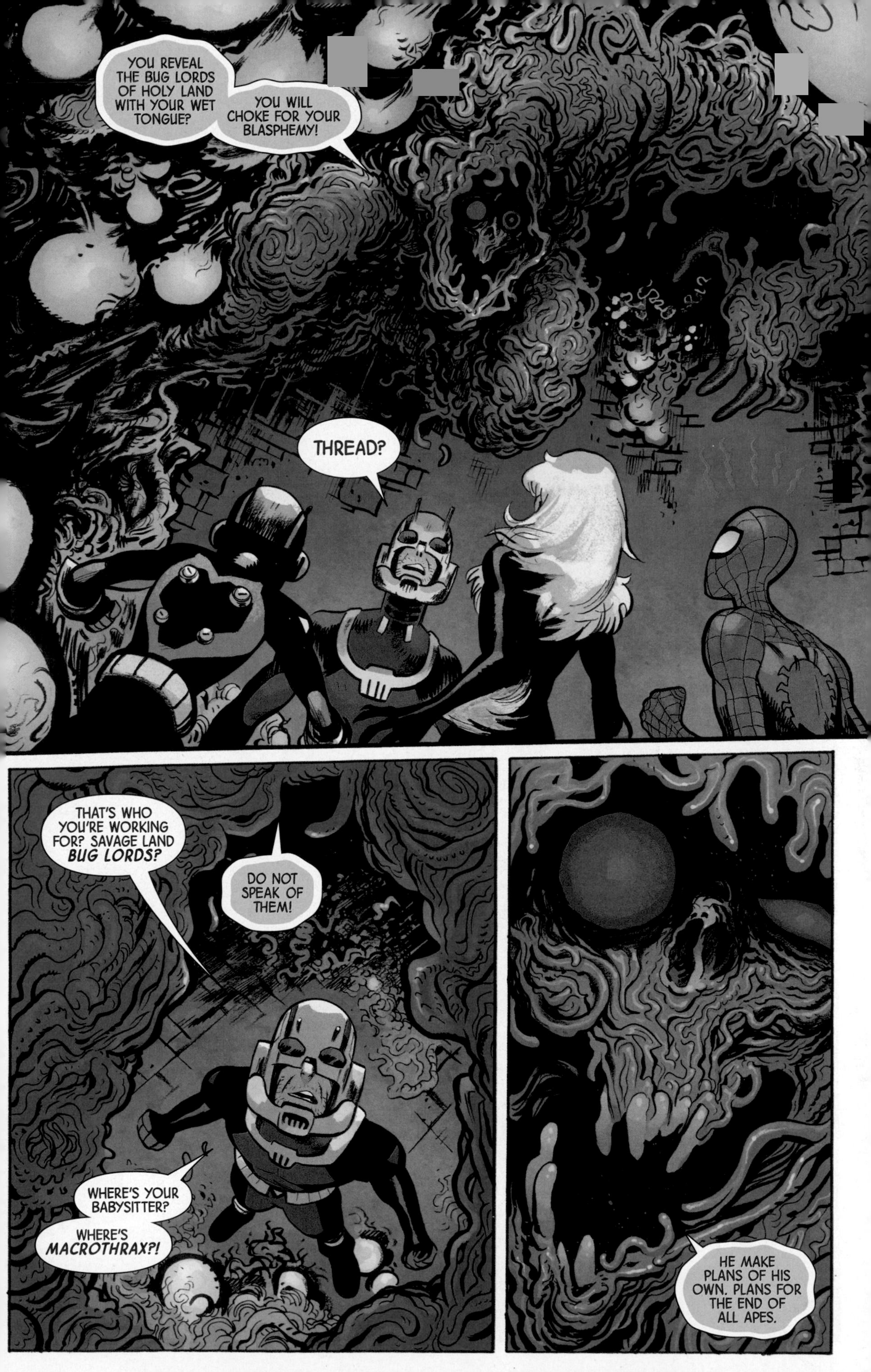

YOU REVEAL THE BUG LORDS OF HOLY LAND WITH YOUR WET TONGUE?
YOU WILL CHOKE FOR YOUR BLASPHEMY!
THREAD?
THAT'S WHO YOU'RE WORKING FOR? SAVAGE LAND *BUG LORDS?*
DO NOT SPEAK OF THEM!
WHERE'S YOUR BABYSITTER?
WHERE'S *MACROTHRAX?!*
HE MAKE PLANS OF HIS OWN. PLANS FOR THE END OF ALL APES.

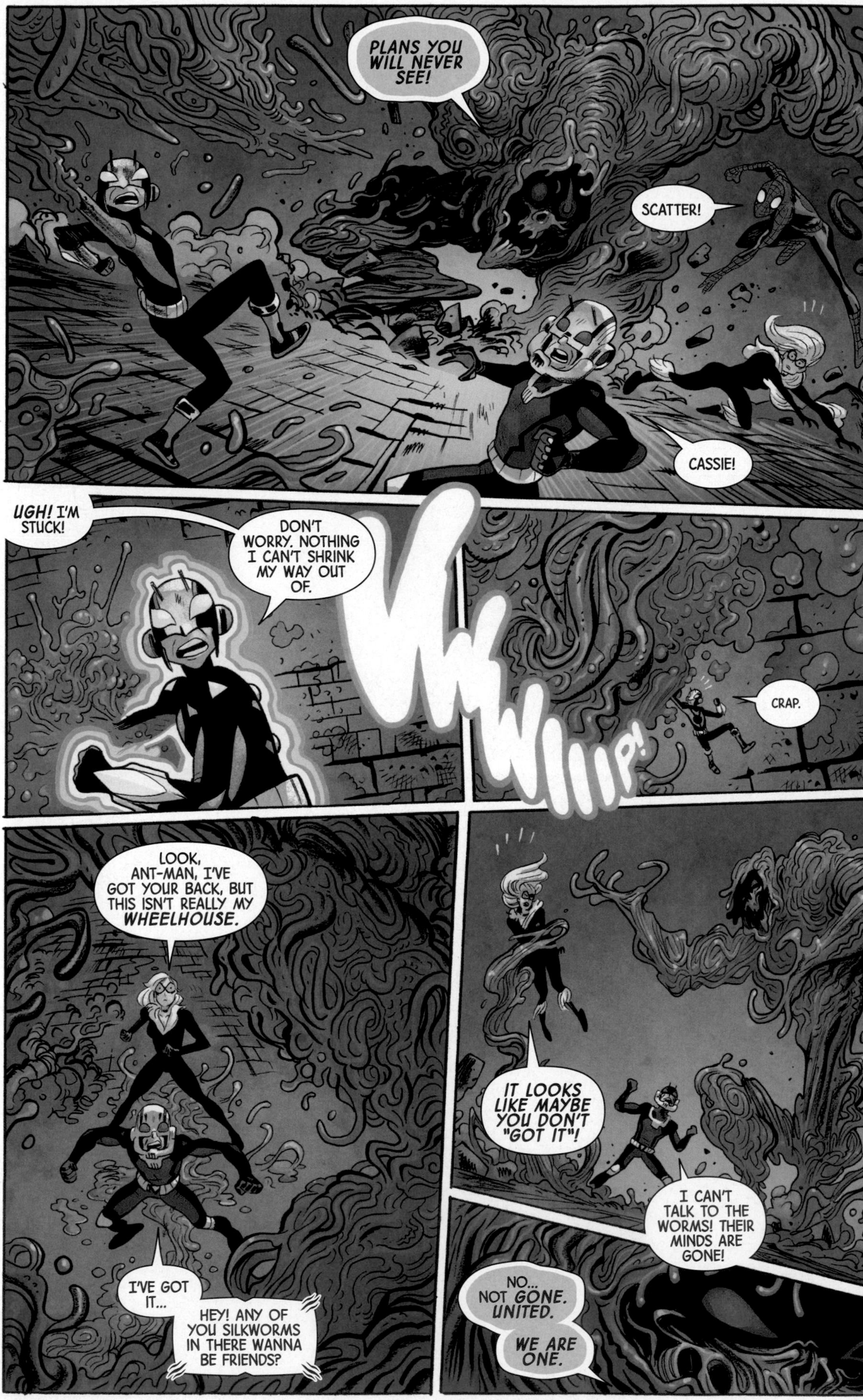
PLANS YOU WILL NEVER SEE!
SCATTER!
CASSIE!
UGH! I'M STUCK!
DON'T WORRY. NOTHING I CAN'T SHRINK MY WAY OUT OF.
VWWIIIIP!
CRAP.
LOOK, ANT-MAN, I'VE GOT YOUR BACK, BUT THIS ISN'T REALLY MY WHEELHOUSE.
I'VE GOT IT...
HEY! ANY OF YOU SILKWORMS IN THERE WANNA BE FRIENDS?
IT LOOKS LIKE MAYBE YOU DON'T "GOT IT"!
I CAN'T TALK TO THE WORMS! THEIR MINDS ARE GONE!
NO... NOT GONE. UNITED.
WE ARE ONE.

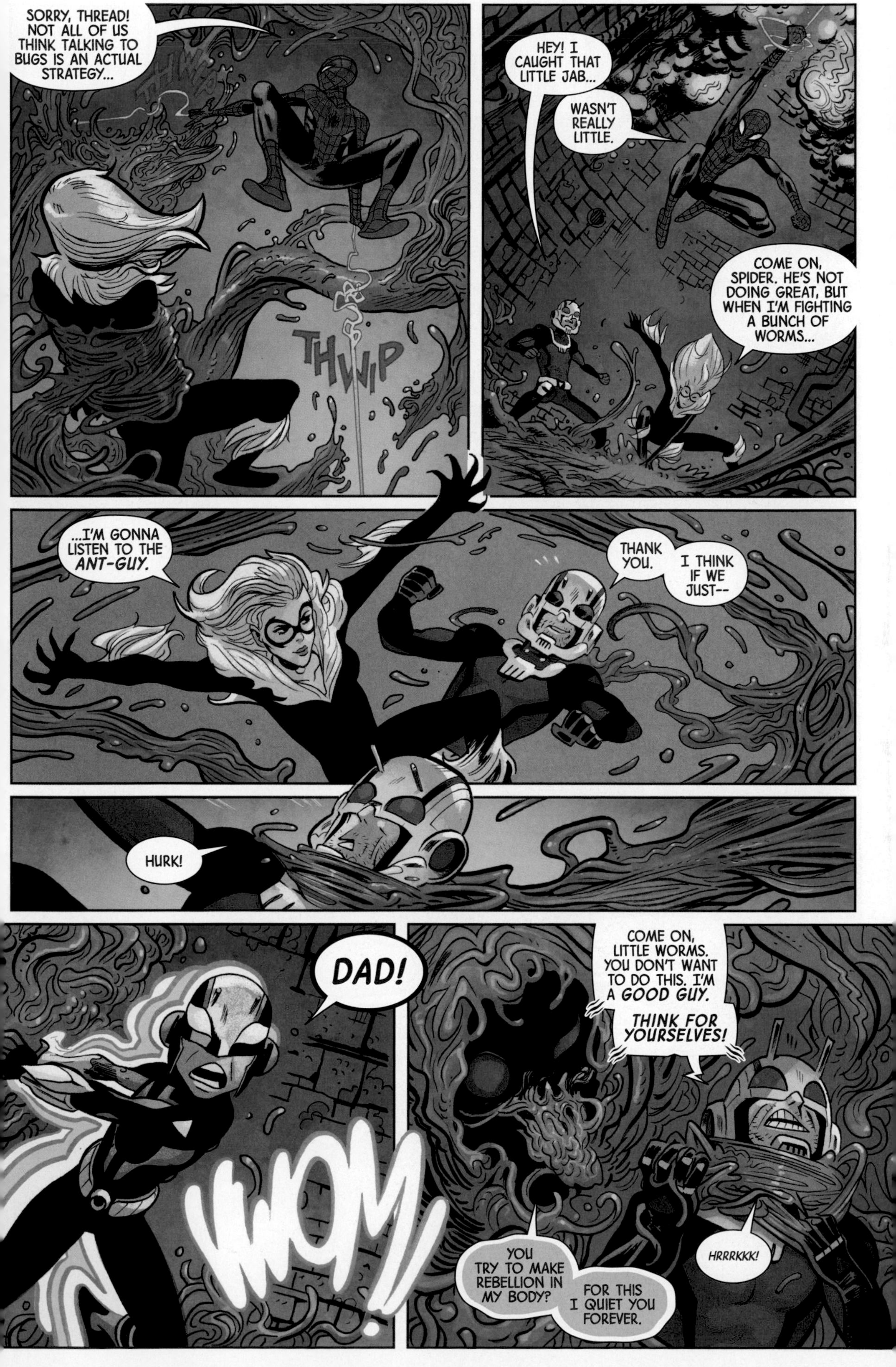
SORRY, THREAD! NOT ALL OF US THINK TALKING TO BUGS IS AN ACTUAL STRATEGY...
THWIP
THWIP
HEY! I CAUGHT THAT LITTLE JAB...
WASN'T REALLY LITTLE.
COME ON, SPIDER. HE'S NOT DOING GREAT, BUT WHEN I'M FIGHTING A BUNCH OF WORMS...
...I'M GONNA LISTEN TO THE ANT-GUY.
THANK YOU.
I THINK IF WE JUST--
HURK!
DAD!
COME ON, LITTLE WORMS. YOU DON'T WANT TO DO THIS. I'M A GOOD GUY.
THINK FOR YOURSELVES!
WOM!!
YOU TRY TO MAKE REBELLION IN MY BODY?
FOR THIS I QUIET YOU FOREVER.
HRRRKKK!

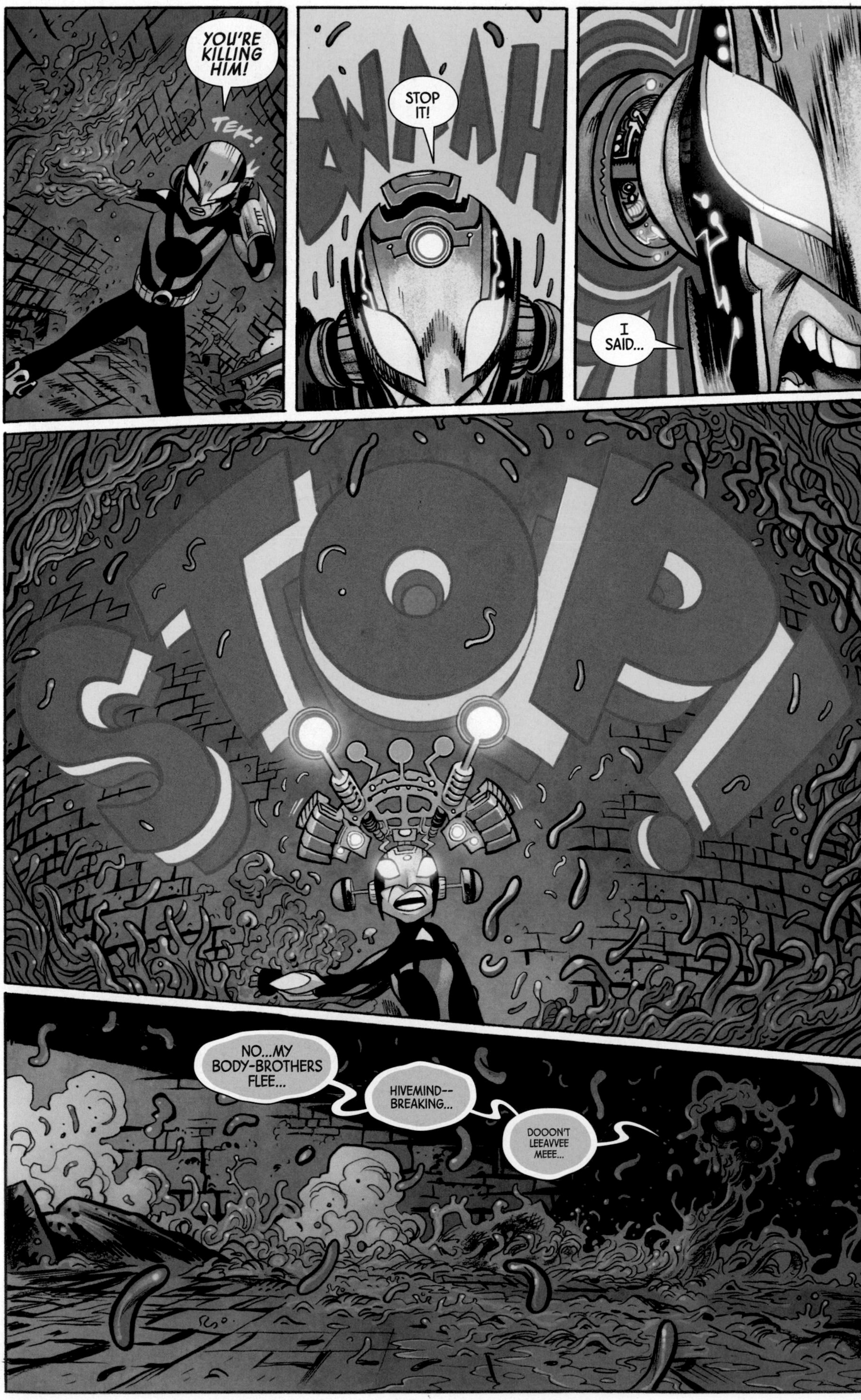
YOU'RE KILLING HIM!
TEK!
WAAAH
STOP IT!
I SAID...
STOP!
NO...MY BODY-BROTHERS FLEE...
HIVEMIND--BREAKING...
DOOON'T LEEAVVEE MEEE...

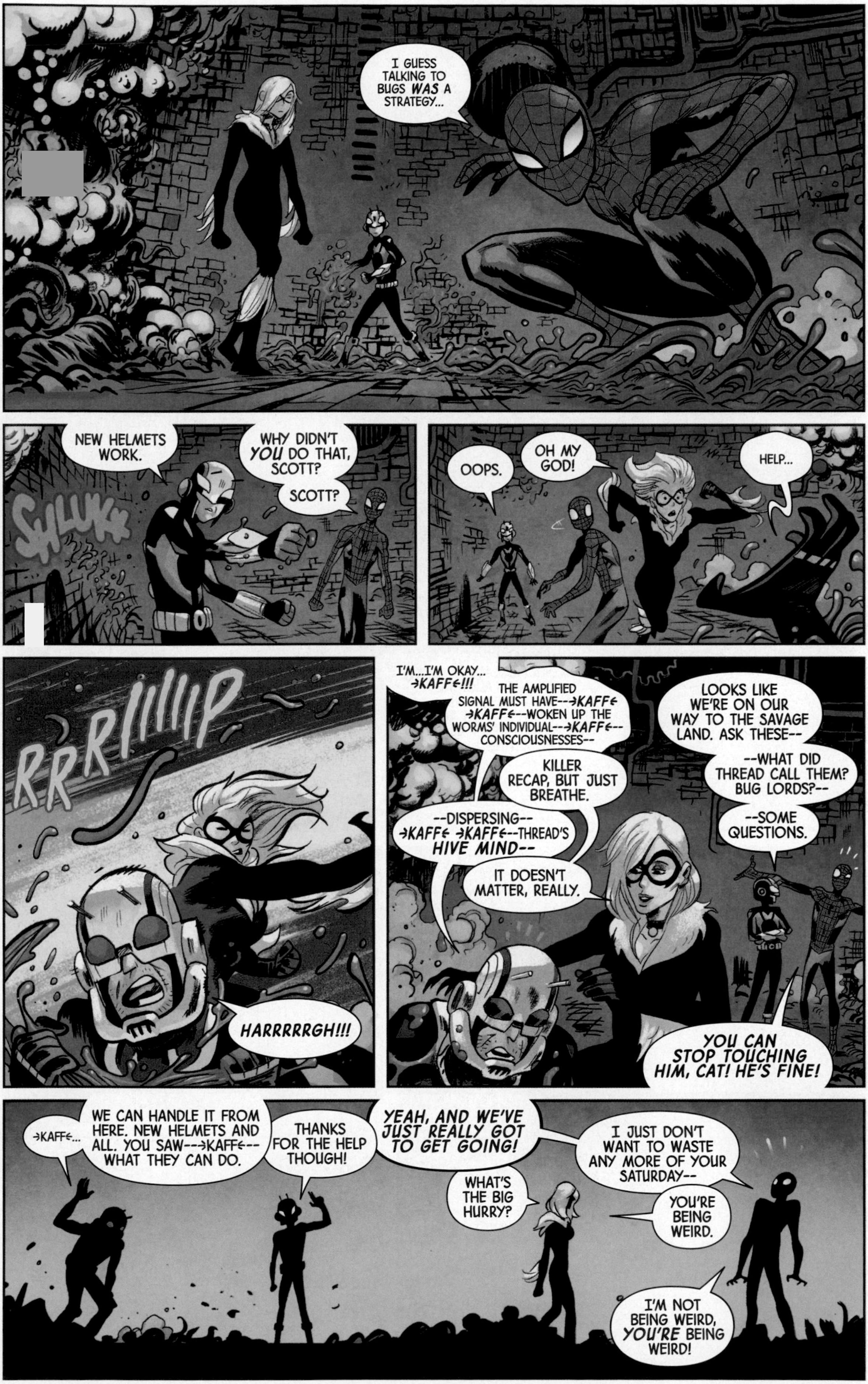

I GUESS TALKING TO BUGS *WAS* A STRATEGY...
NEW HELMETS WORK.
WHY DIDN'T *YOU* DO THAT, SCOTT?
SCOTT?
SHLUKK
OOPS.
OH MY GOD!
HELP...
RRRIIIIP
HARRRRRGH!!!
I'M...I'M OKAY... →KAFF←!!!
THE AMPLIFIED SIGNAL MUST HAVE--→KAFF← →KAFF←--WOKEN UP THE WORMS' INDIVIDUAL--→KAFF←--CONSCIOUSNESSES--
KILLER RECAP, BUT JUST BREATHE.
--DISPERSING-- →KAFF← →KAFF←--THREAD'S *HIVE MIND--*
IT DOESN'T MATTER, REALLY.
LOOKS LIKE WE'RE ON OUR WAY TO THE SAVAGE LAND. ASK THESE--
--WHAT DID THREAD CALL THEM? BUG LORDS?--
--SOME QUESTIONS.
YOU CAN STOP TOUCHING HIM, CAT! HE'S FINE!
→KAFF←...
WE CAN HANDLE IT FROM HERE. NEW HELMETS AND ALL. YOU SAW--→KAFF←--WHAT THEY CAN DO.
THANKS FOR THE HELP THOUGH!
YEAH, AND WE'VE JUST REALLY GOT TO GET GOING!
I JUST DON'T WANT TO WASTE ANY MORE OF YOUR SATURDAY--
WHAT'S THE BIG HURRY?
YOU'RE BEING WEIRD.
I'M NOT BEING WEIRD, *YOU'RE* BEING WEIRD!

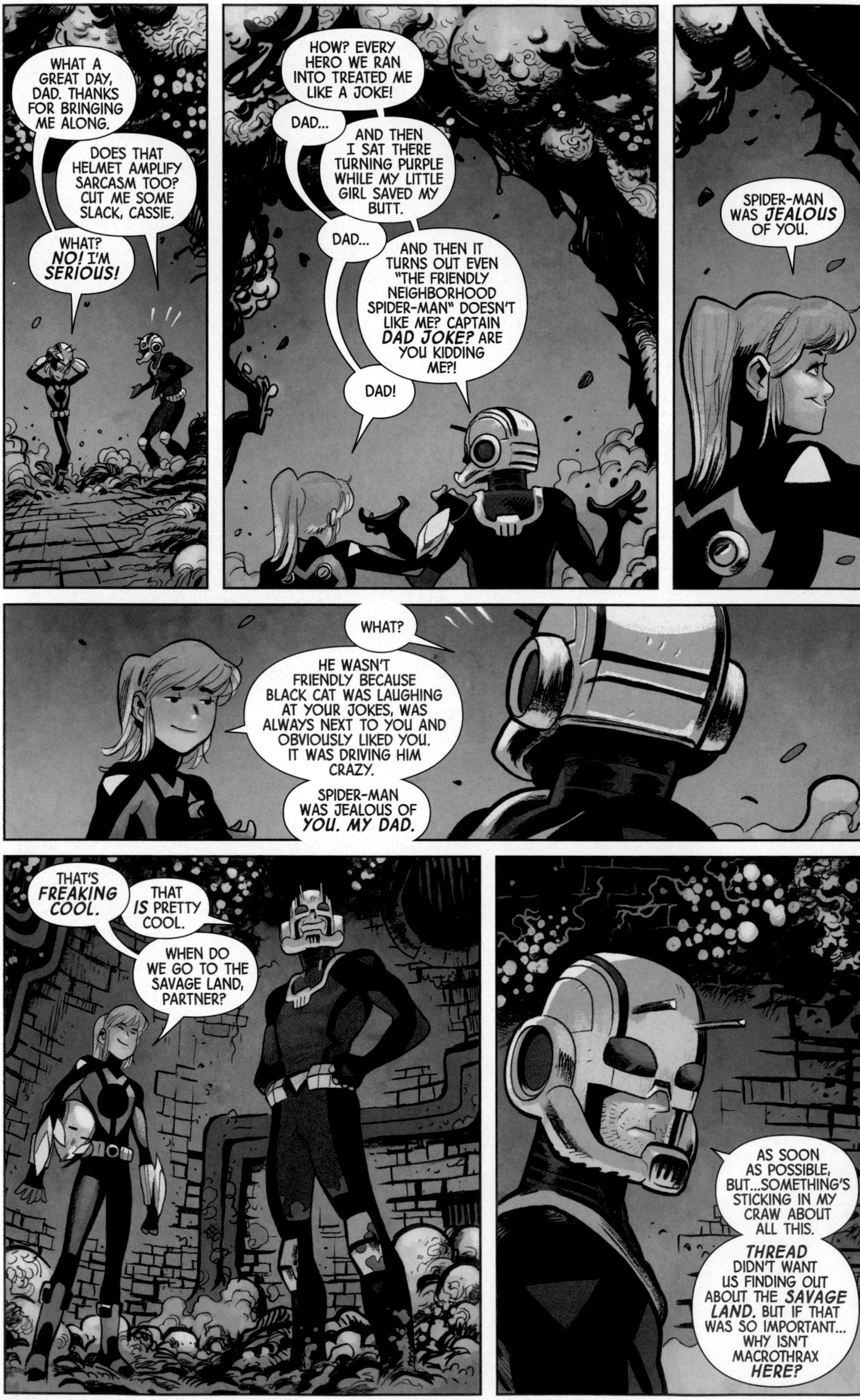

WHAT A GREAT DAY, DAD. THANKS FOR BRINGING ME ALONG.
DOES THAT HELMET AMPLIFY SARCASM TOO? CUT ME SOME SLACK, CASSIE.
WHAT? NO! I'M SERIOUS!
HOW? EVERY HERO WE RAN INTO TREATED ME LIKE A JOKE!
DAD...
AND THEN I SAT THERE TURNING PURPLE WHILE MY LITTLE GIRL SAVED MY BUTT.
DAD...
AND THEN IT TURNS OUT EVEN "THE FRIENDLY NEIGHBORHOOD SPIDER-MAN" DOESN'T LIKE ME? CAPTAIN DAD JOKE? ARE YOU KIDDING ME?!
DAD!
SPIDER-MAN WAS JEALOUS OF YOU.
WHAT?
HE WASN'T FRIENDLY BECAUSE BLACK CAT WAS LAUGHING AT YOUR JOKES, WAS ALWAYS NEXT TO YOU AND OBVIOUSLY LIKED YOU. IT WAS DRIVING HIM CRAZY.
SPIDER-MAN WAS JEALOUS OF YOU. MY DAD.
THAT'S FREAKING COOL.
THAT IS PRETTY COOL.
WHEN DO WE GO TO THE SAVAGE LAND, PARTNER?
AS SOON AS POSSIBLE, BUT...SOMETHING'S STICKING IN MY CRAW ABOUT ALL THIS.
THREAD DIDN'T WANT US FINDING OUT ABOUT THE SAVAGE LAND. BUT IF THAT WAS SO IMPORTANT... WHY ISN'T MACROTHRAX HERE?

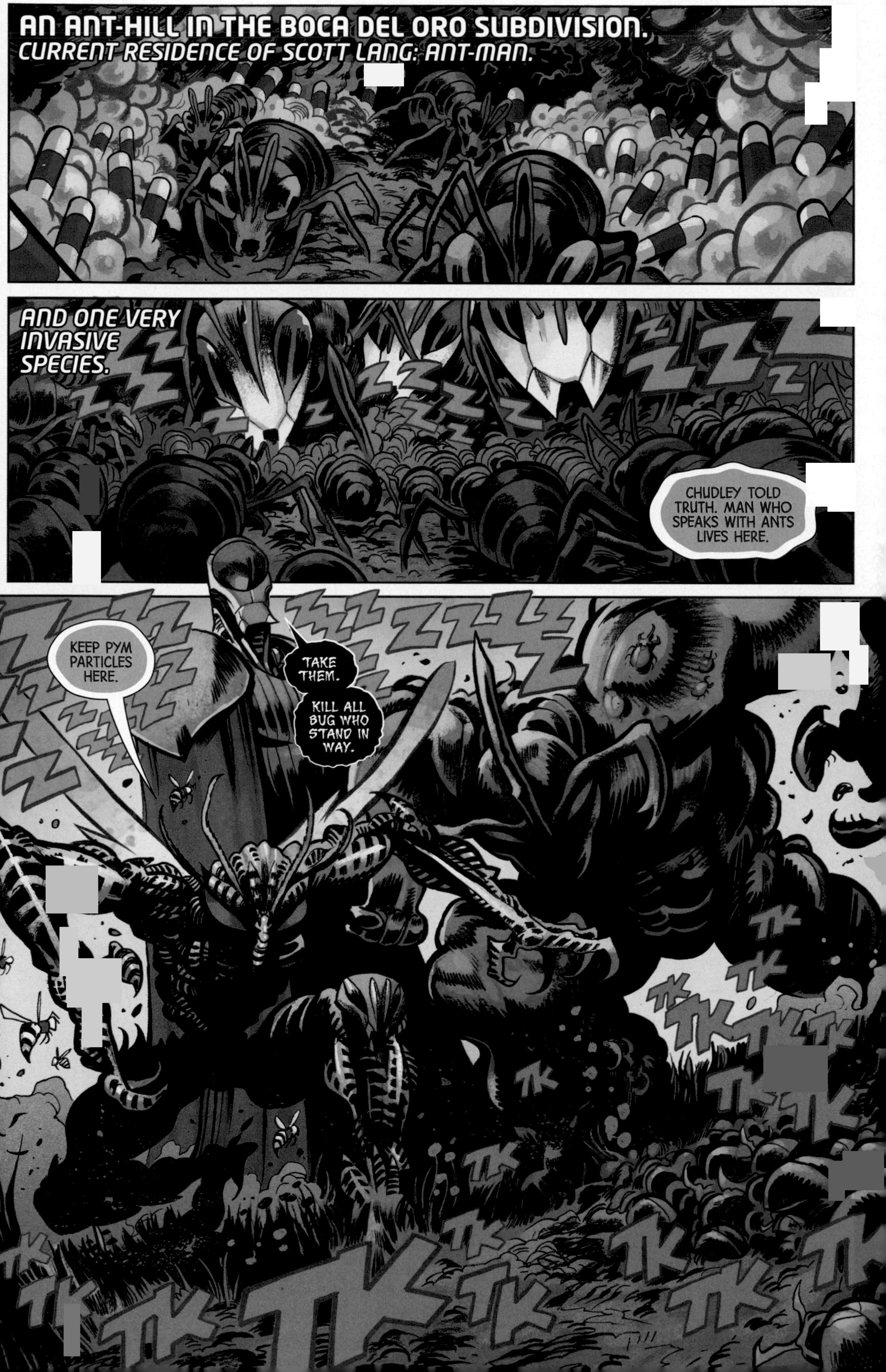
AN ANT-HILL IN THE BOCA DEL ORO SUBDIVISION.
CURRENT RESIDENCE OF SCOTT LANG: ANT-MAN.
AND ONE VERY INVASIVE SPECIES.
CHUDLEY TOLD TRUTH. MAN WHO SPEAKS WITH ANTS LIVES HERE.
KEEP PYM PARTICLES HERE.
TAKE THEM.
KILL ALL BUG WHO STAND IN WAY.
TK

4

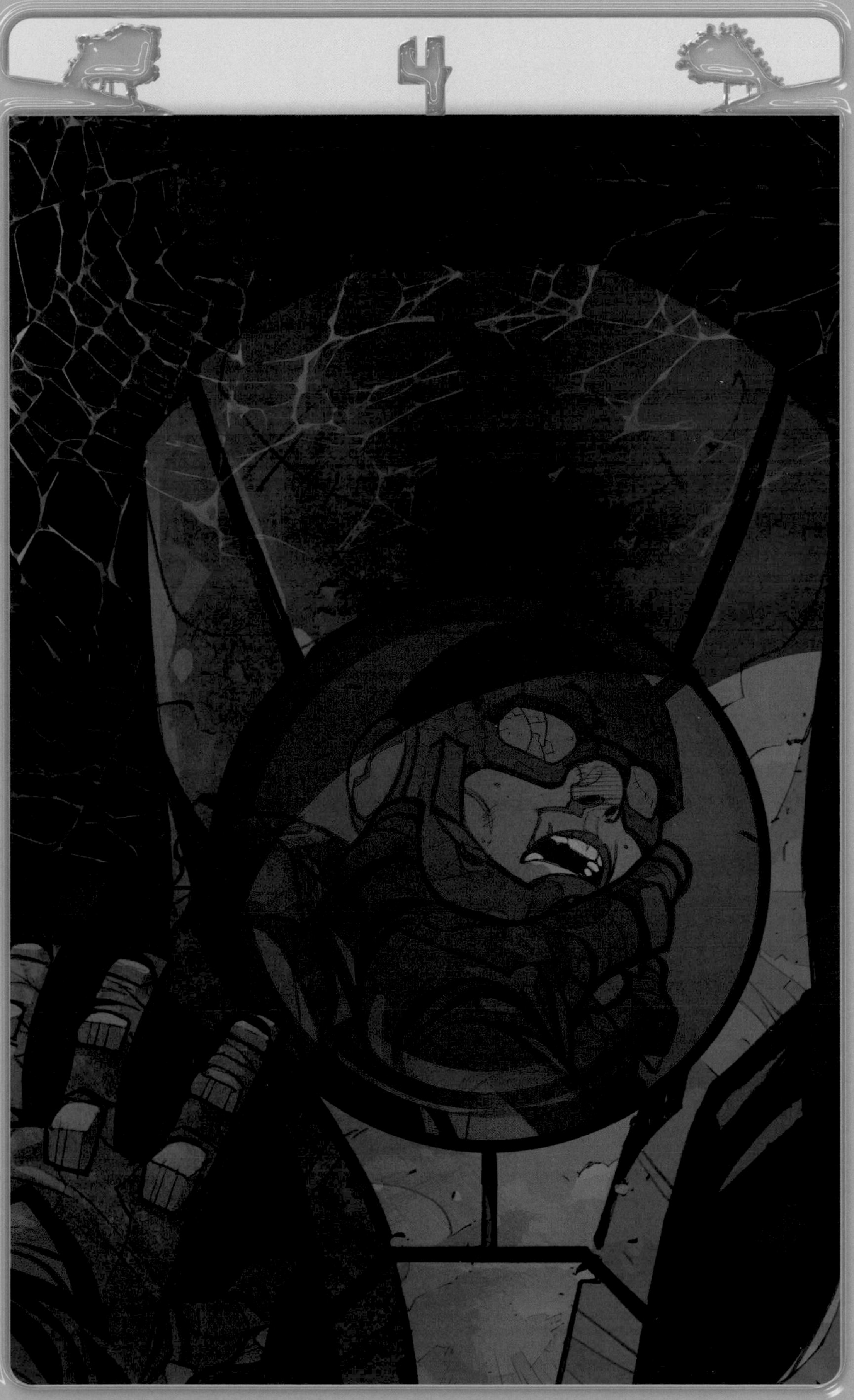

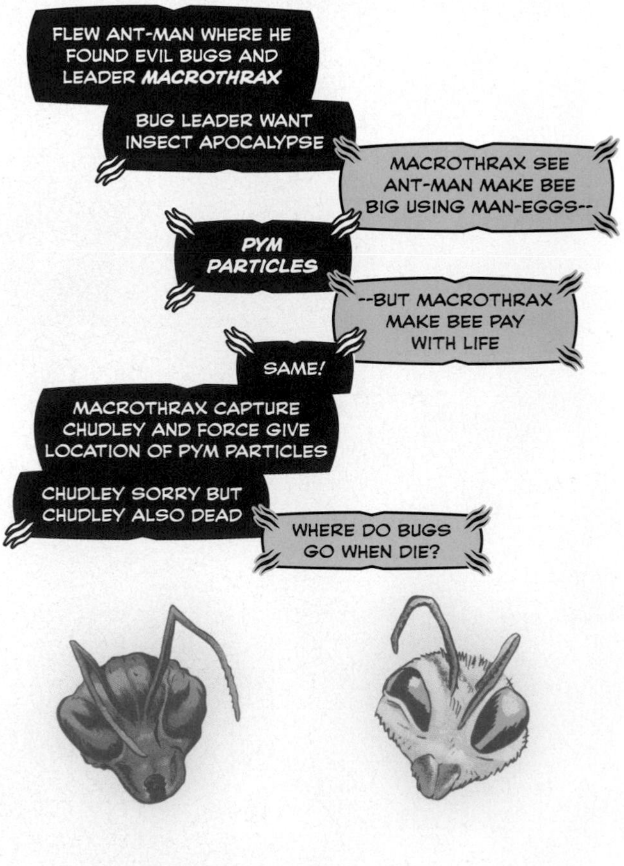
FLEW ANT-MAN WHERE HE FOUND EVIL BUGS AND LEADER ***MACROTHRAX***
BUG LEADER WANT INSECT APOCALYPSE
MACROTHRAX SEE ANT-MAN MAKE BEE BIG USING MAN-EGGS--
PYM PARTICLES
--BUT MACROTHRAX MAKE BEE PAY WITH LIFE
SAME!
MACROTHRAX CAPTURE CHUDLEY AND FORCE GIVE LOCATION OF PYM PARTICLES
CHUDLEY SORRY BUT CHUDLEY ALSO DEAD
WHERE DO BUGS GO WHEN DIE?

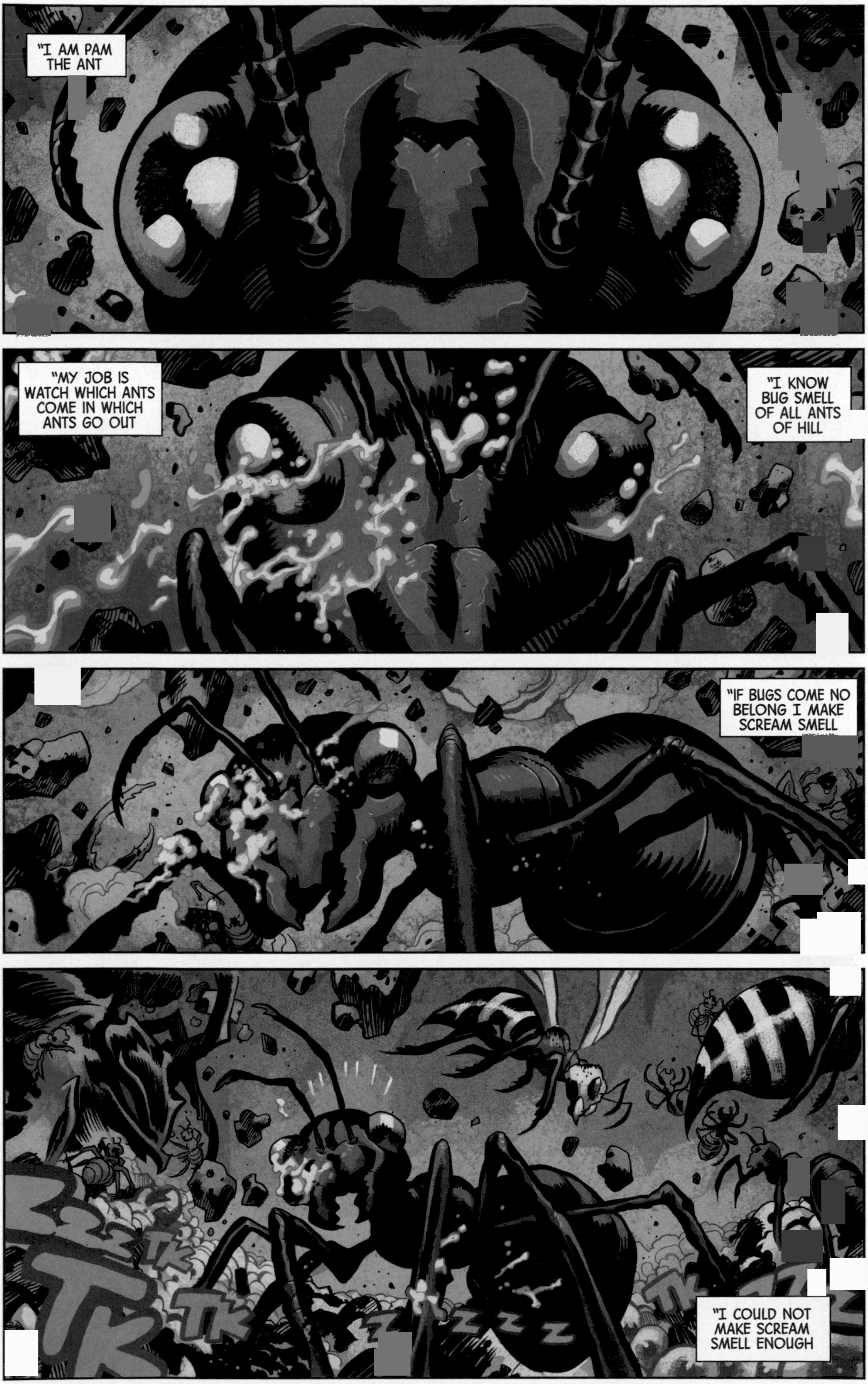
"I AM PAM THE ANT
"MY JOB IS WATCH WHICH ANTS COME IN WHICH ANTS GO OUT
"I KNOW BUG SMELL OF ALL ANTS OF HILL
"IF BUGS COME NO BELONG I MAKE SCREAM SMELL
TK
TK
"I COULD NOT MAKE SCREAM SMELL ENOUGH

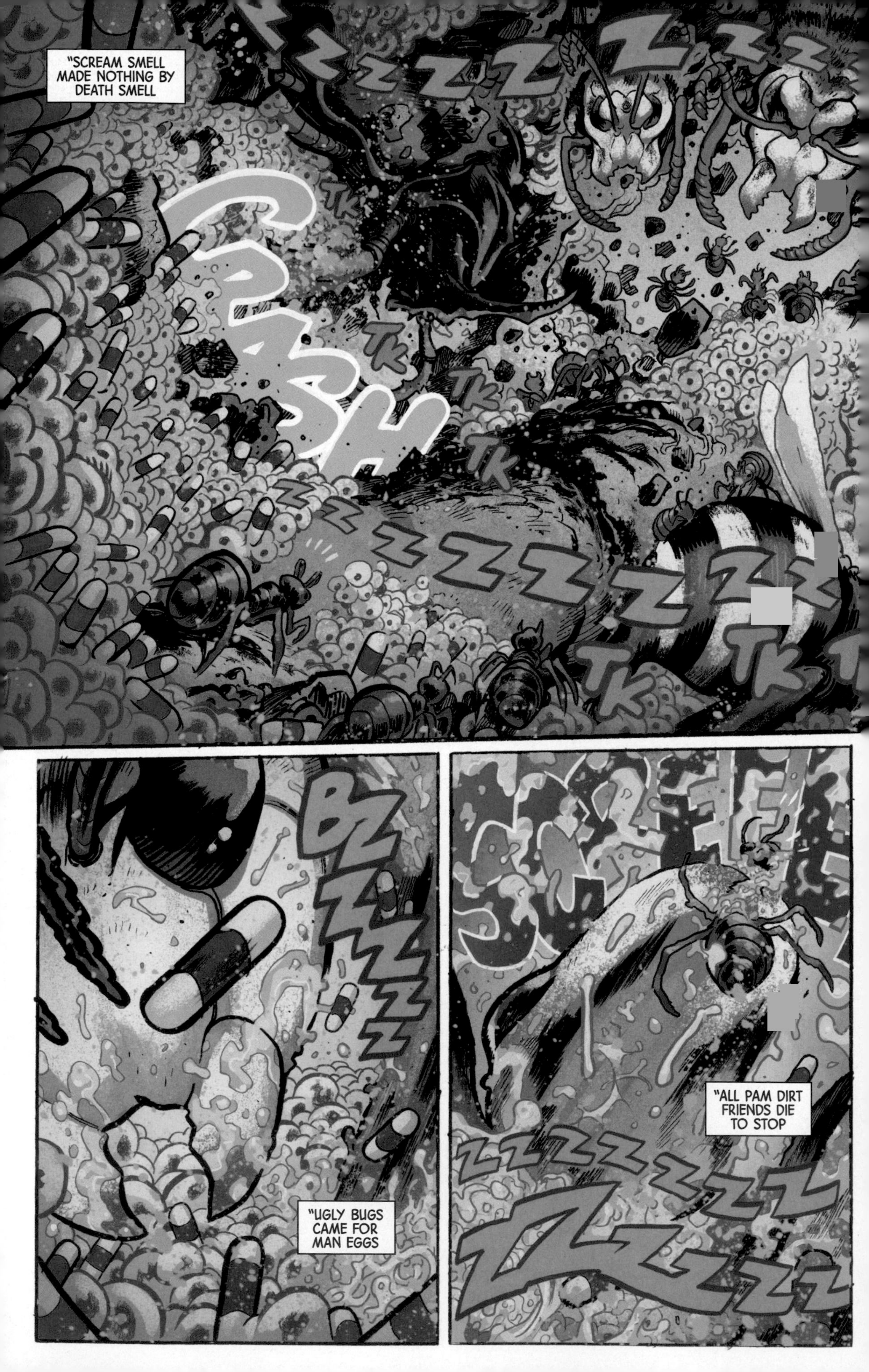
"SCREAM SMELL MADE NOTHING BY DEATH SMELL
ZZZZZZ
CRASH
TK TK TK
ZZZZZZZZ
TK TK
BZZZZZZZZ
"UGLY BUGS CAME FOR MAN EGGS
"ALL PAM DIRT FRIENDS DIE TO STOP
ZZZZZZZZZ
ZZZZZ

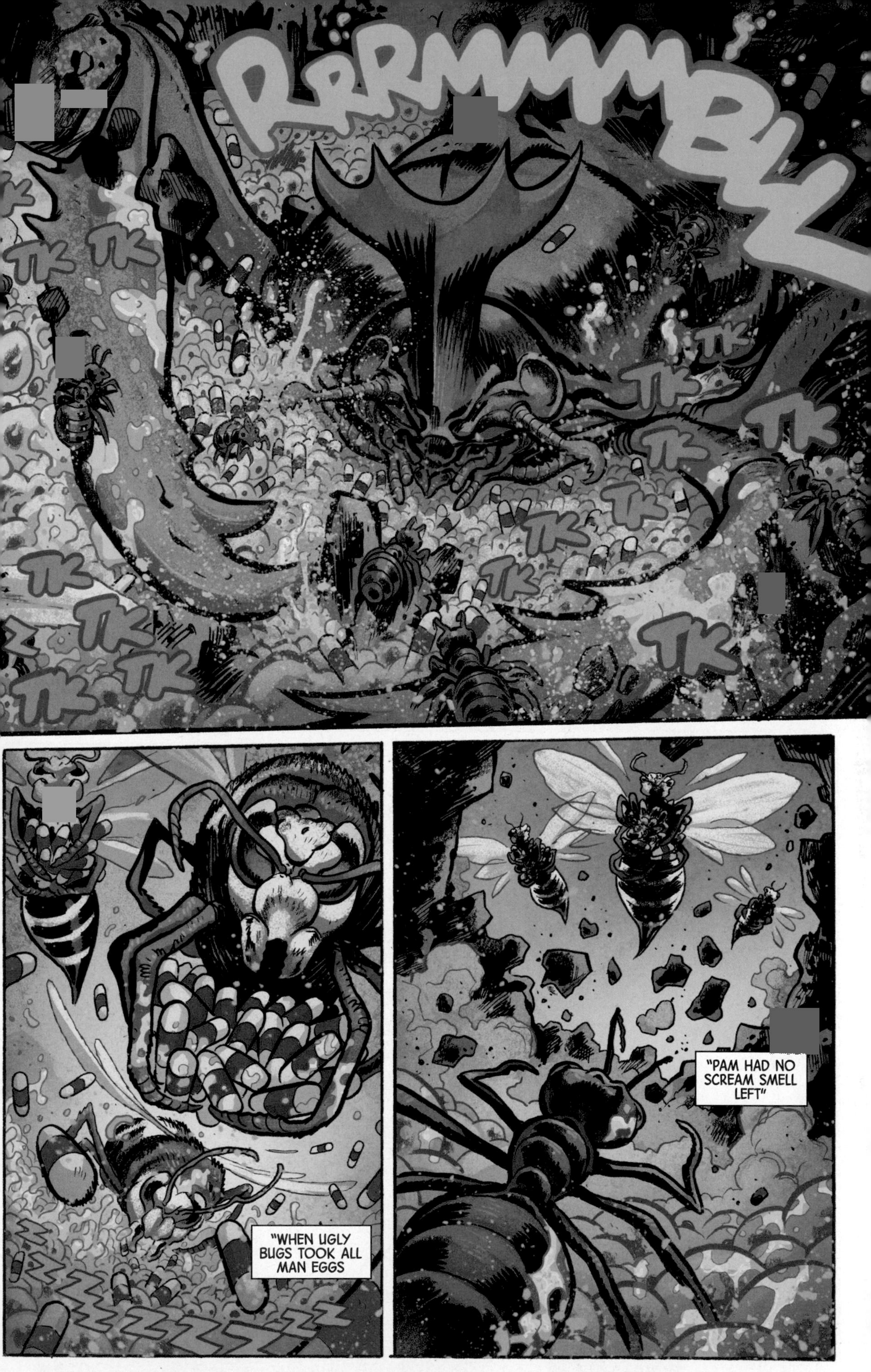
TK TK
TK
TK
TK
TK
"WHEN UGLY BUGS TOOK ALL MAN EGGS
"PAM HAD NO SCREAM SMELL LEFT"

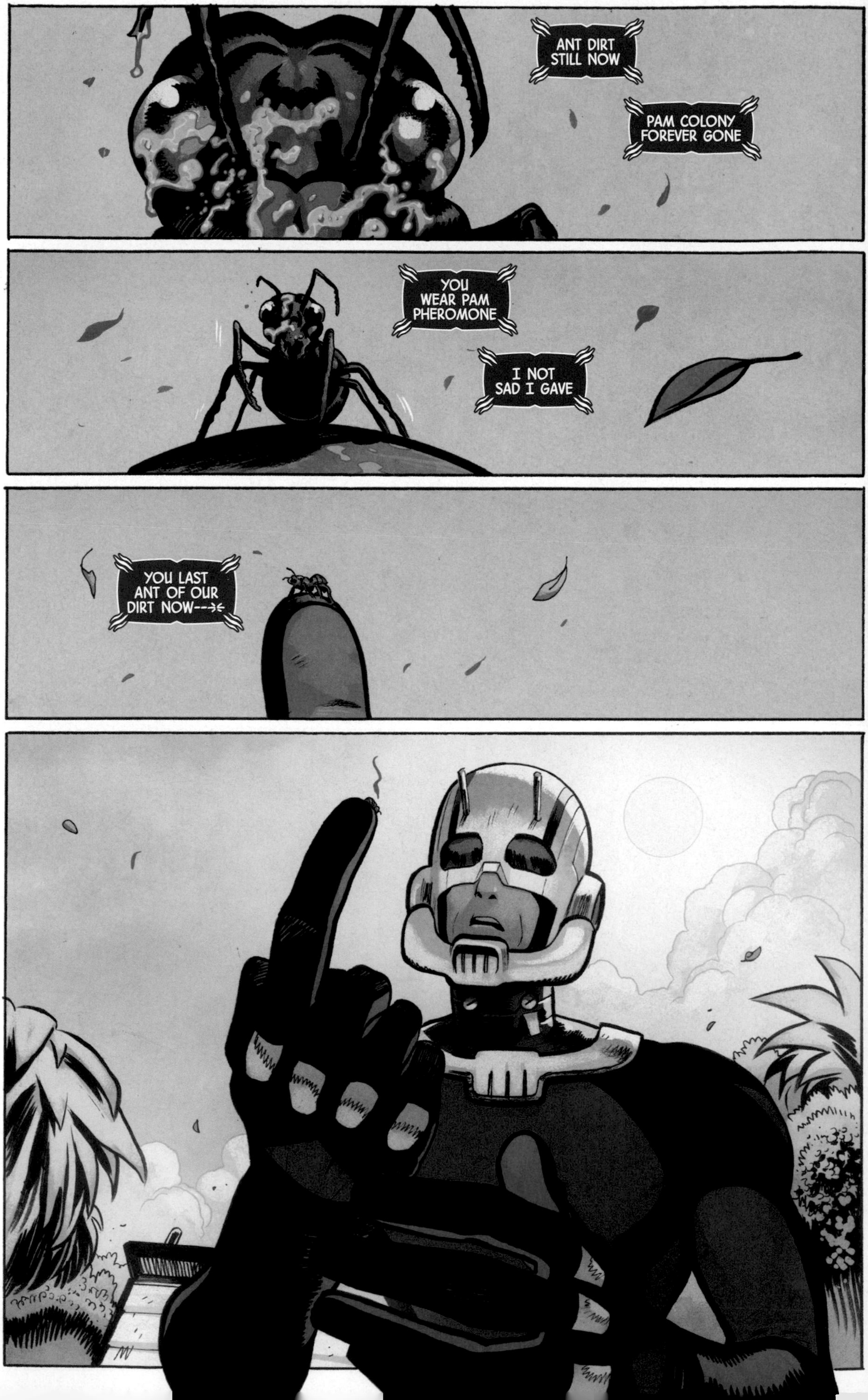
ANT DIRT STILL NOW
PAM COLONY FOREVER GONE
YOU WEAR PAM PHEROMONE
I NOT SAD I GAVE
YOU LAST ANT OF OUR DIRT NOW--

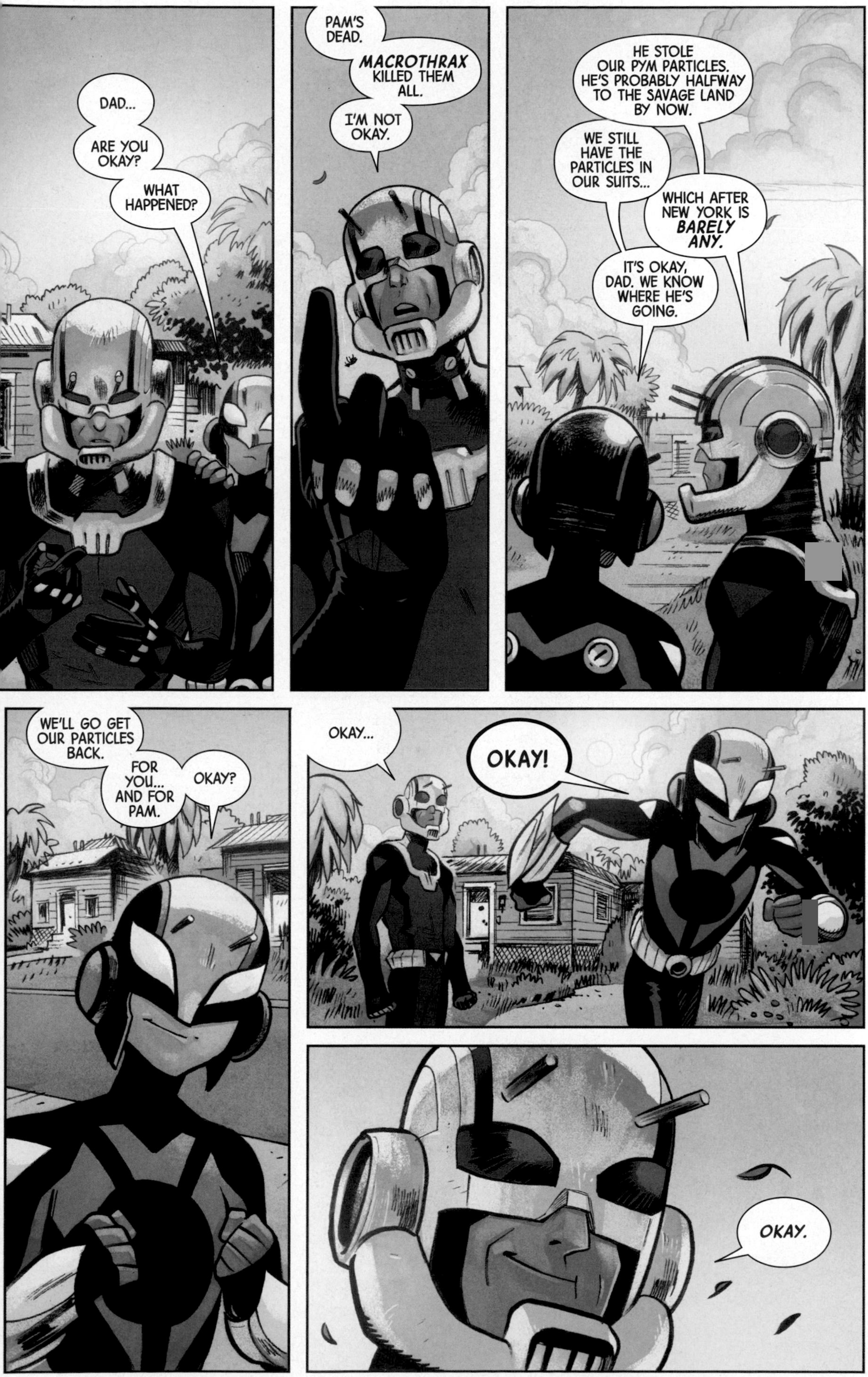
DAD...
ARE YOU OKAY?
WHAT HAPPENED?
PAM'S DEAD.
MACROTHRAX KILLED THEM ALL.
I'M NOT OKAY.
HE STOLE OUR PYM PARTICLES. HE'S PROBABLY HALFWAY TO THE SAVAGE LAND BY NOW.
WE STILL HAVE THE PARTICLES IN OUR SUITS...
WHICH AFTER NEW YORK IS BARELY ANY.
IT'S OKAY, DAD. WE KNOW WHERE HE'S GOING.
WE'LL GO GET OUR PARTICLES BACK.
FOR YOU... AND FOR PAM.
OKAY?
OKAY...
OKAY!
OKAY.

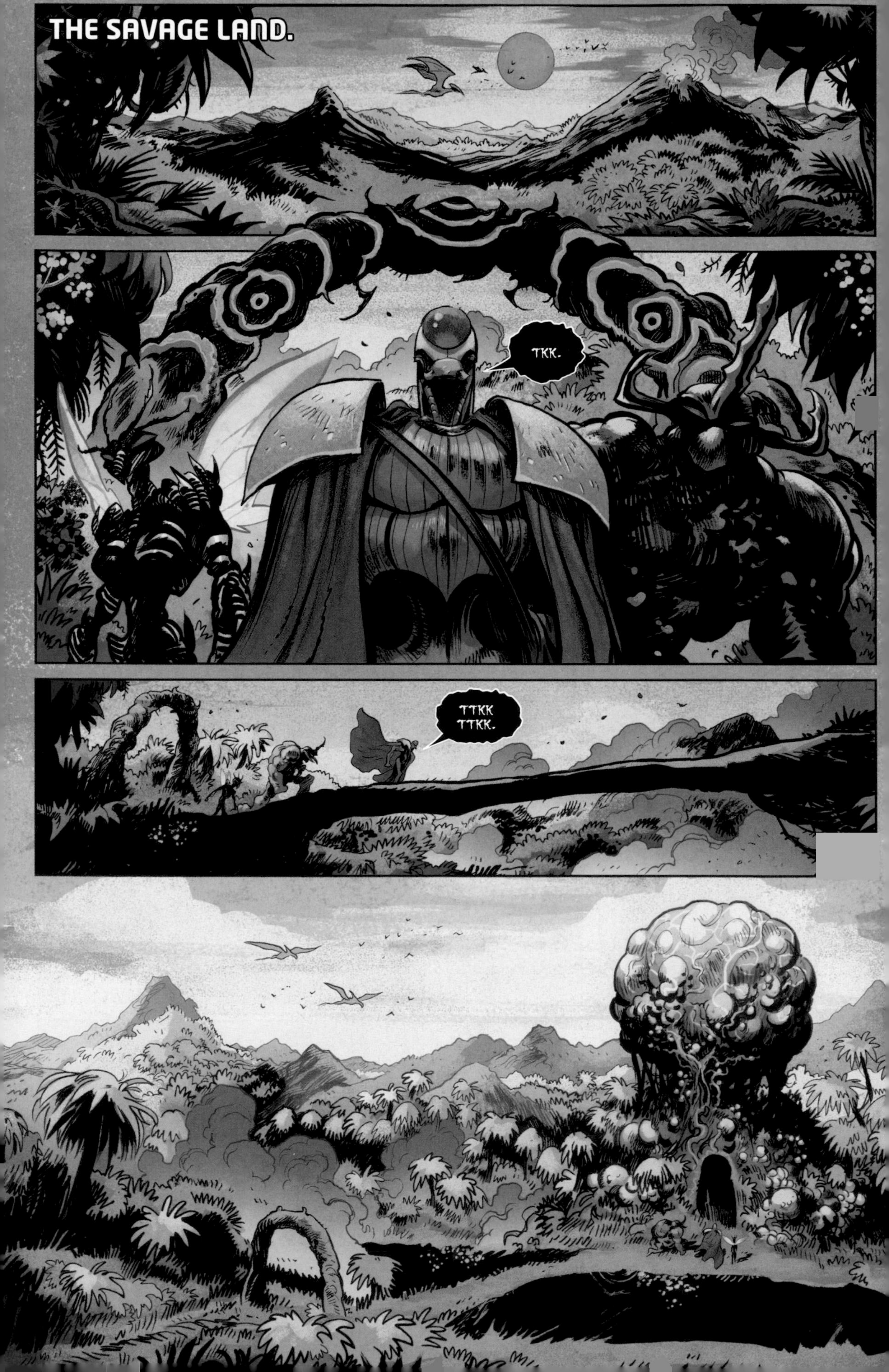
THE SAVAGE LAND.
TKK.
TTKK
TTKK.

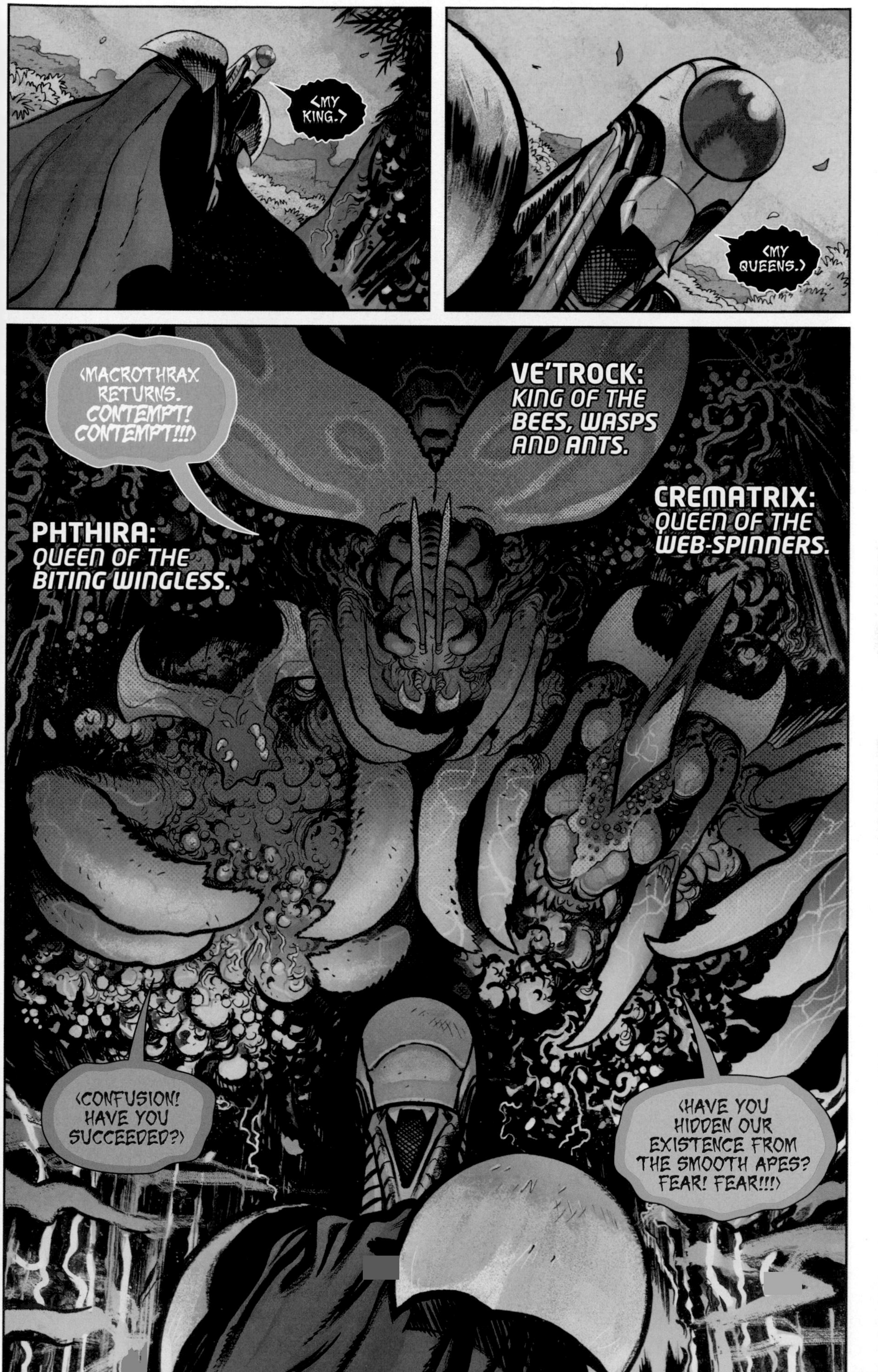
<MY KING.>
<MY QUEENS.>
<MACROTHRAX RETURNS. CONTEMPT! CONTEMPT!!!>
VE'TROCK: KING OF THE BEES, WASPS AND ANTS.
PHTHIRA: QUEEN OF THE BITING WINGLESS.
CREMATRIX: QUEEN OF THE WEB-SPINNERS.
<CONFUSION! HAVE YOU SUCCEEDED?>
<HAVE YOU HIDDEN OUR EXISTENCE FROM THE SMOOTH APES? FEAR! FEAR!!!>

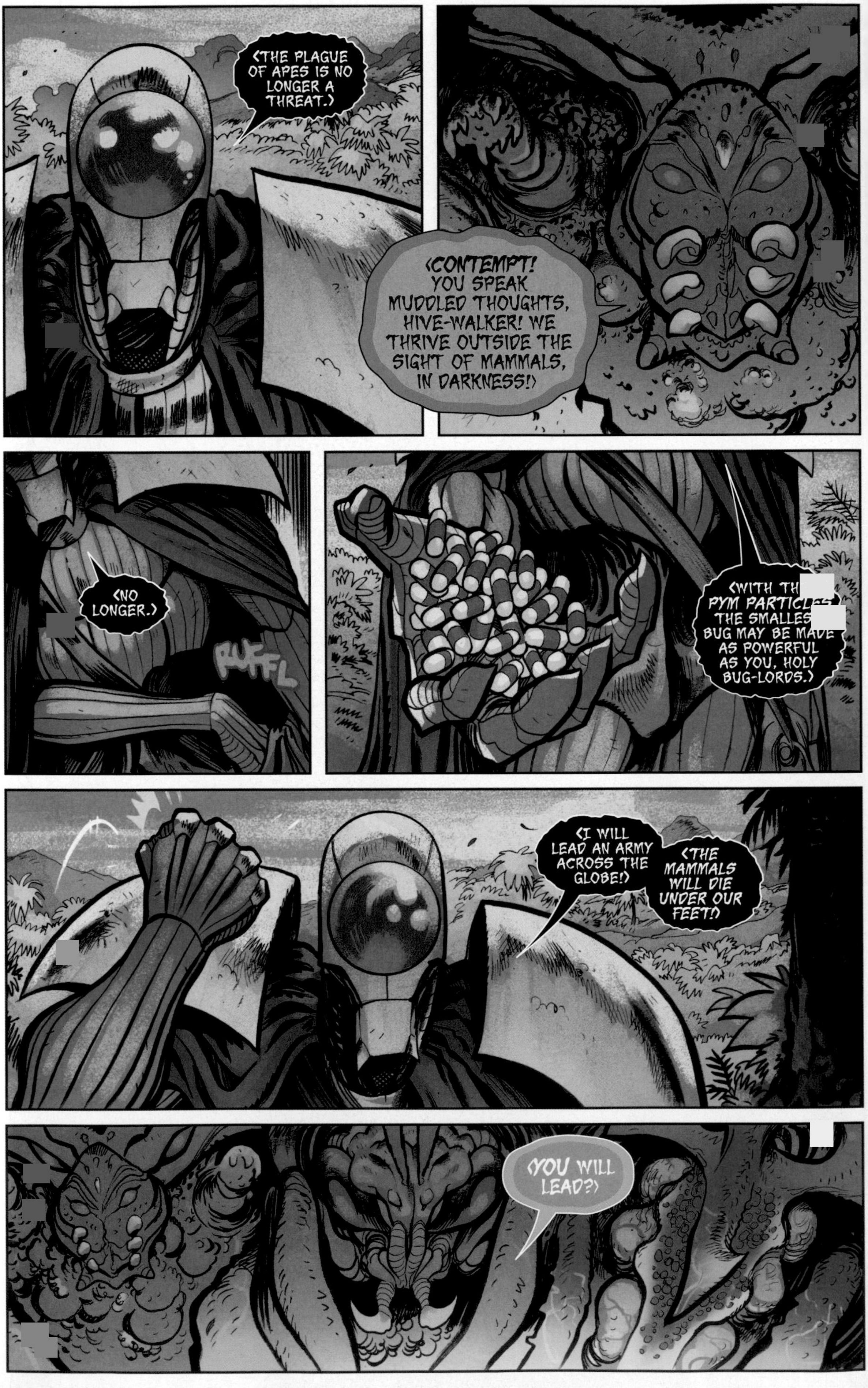
‹THE PLAGUE OF APES IS NO LONGER A THREAT.›
‹CONTEMPT! YOU SPEAK MUDDLED THOUGHTS, HIVE-WALKER! WE THRIVE OUTSIDE THE SIGHT OF MAMMALS, IN DARKNESS!›
‹NO LONGER.›
RUFFL
‹WITH TH PYM PARTICL THE SMALLES BUG MAY BE MADE AS POWERFUL AS YOU, HOLY BUG-LORDS.›
‹I WILL LEAD AN ARMY ACROSS THE GLOBE!›
‹THE MAMMALS WILL DIE UNDER OUR FEET!›
‹YOU WILL LEAD?›

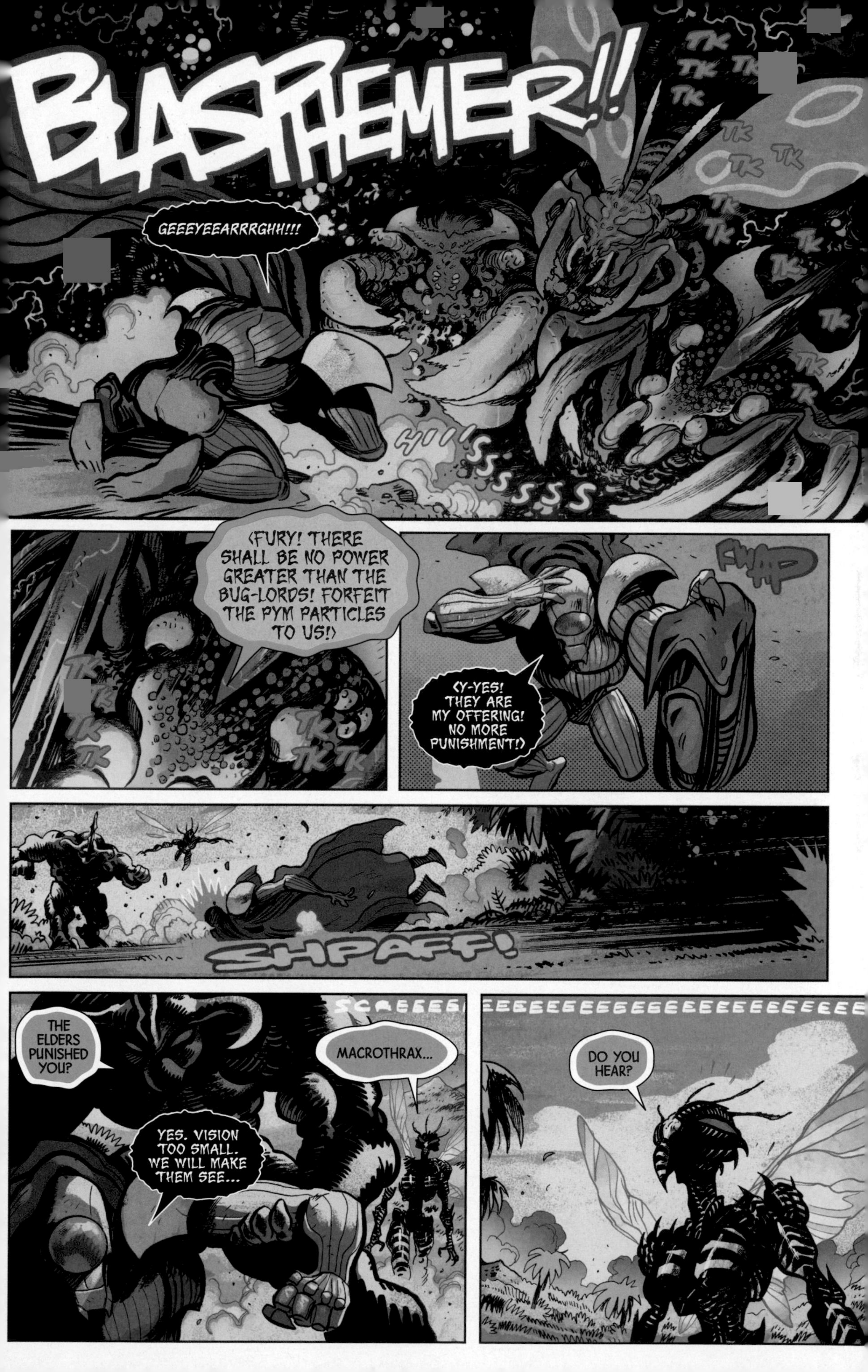
BLASPHEMER!!
TK TK TK TK TK TK TK TK TK TK TK TK
GEEEYEEARRRGHH!!!
HIIISSSSSSS
‹FURY! THERE SHALL BE NO POWER GREATER THAN THE BUG-LORDS! FORFEIT THE PYM PARTICLES TO US!›
TK TK TK TK TK TK
FWAP
‹Y-YES! THEY ARE MY OFFERING! NO MORE PUNISHMENT!›
SHPAFF!
THE ELDERS PUNISHED YOU?
SCREEEEEEEEEEEEEEEEEEEEEEEEEEEEE
MACROTHRAX...
YES. VISION TOO SMALL. WE WILL MAKE THEM SEE...
DO YOU HEAR?

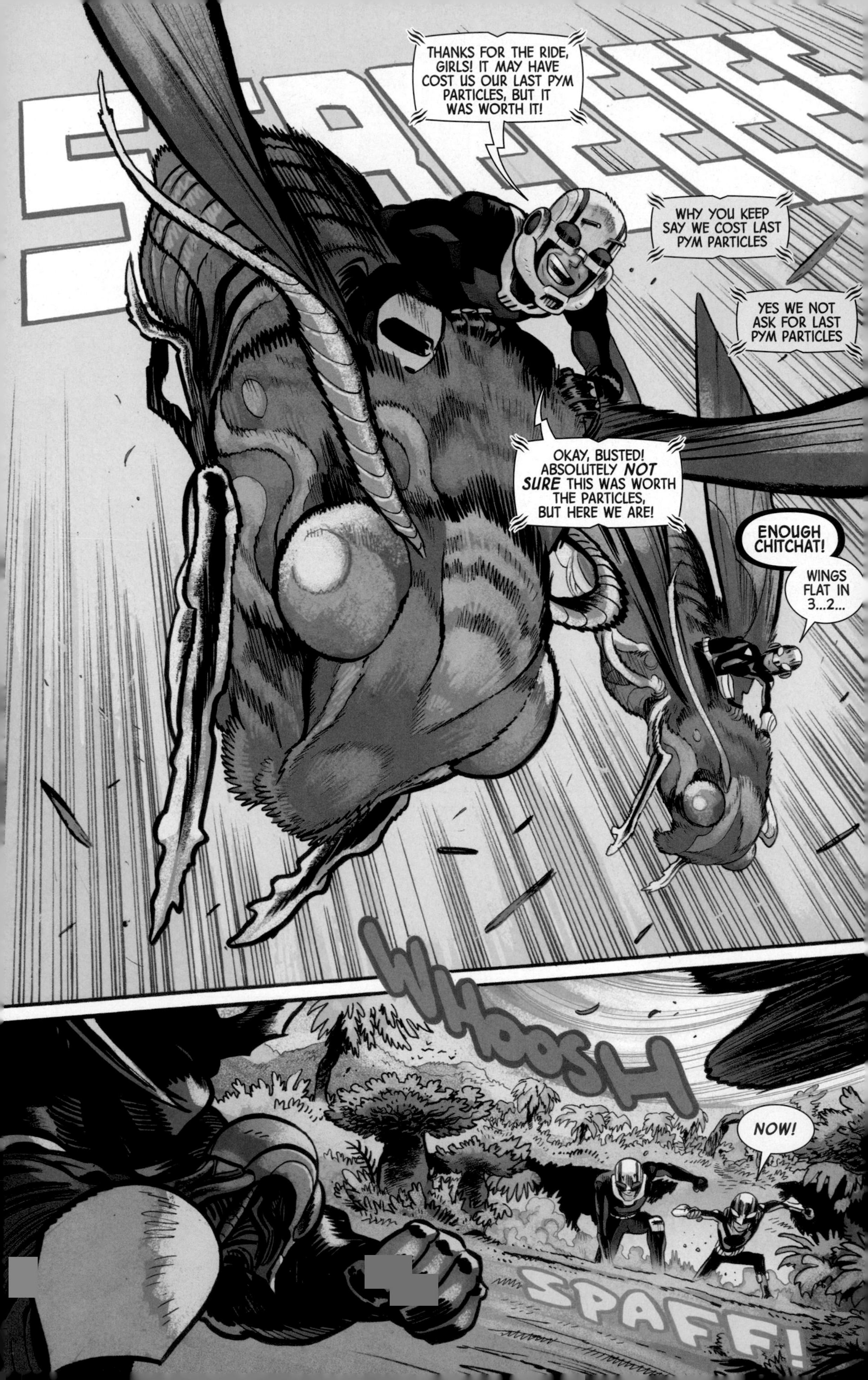
THANKS FOR THE RIDE, GIRLS! IT MAY HAVE COST US OUR LAST PYM PARTICLES, BUT IT WAS WORTH IT!
WHY YOU KEEP SAY WE COST LAST PYM PARTICLES
YES WE NOT ASK FOR LAST PYM PARTICLES
OKAY, BUSTED! ABSOLUTELY ***NOT SURE*** THIS WAS WORTH THE PARTICLES, BUT HERE WE ARE!
ENOUGH CHITCHAT!
WINGS FLAT IN 3...2...
WHOOSH
NOW!
SPAFF!

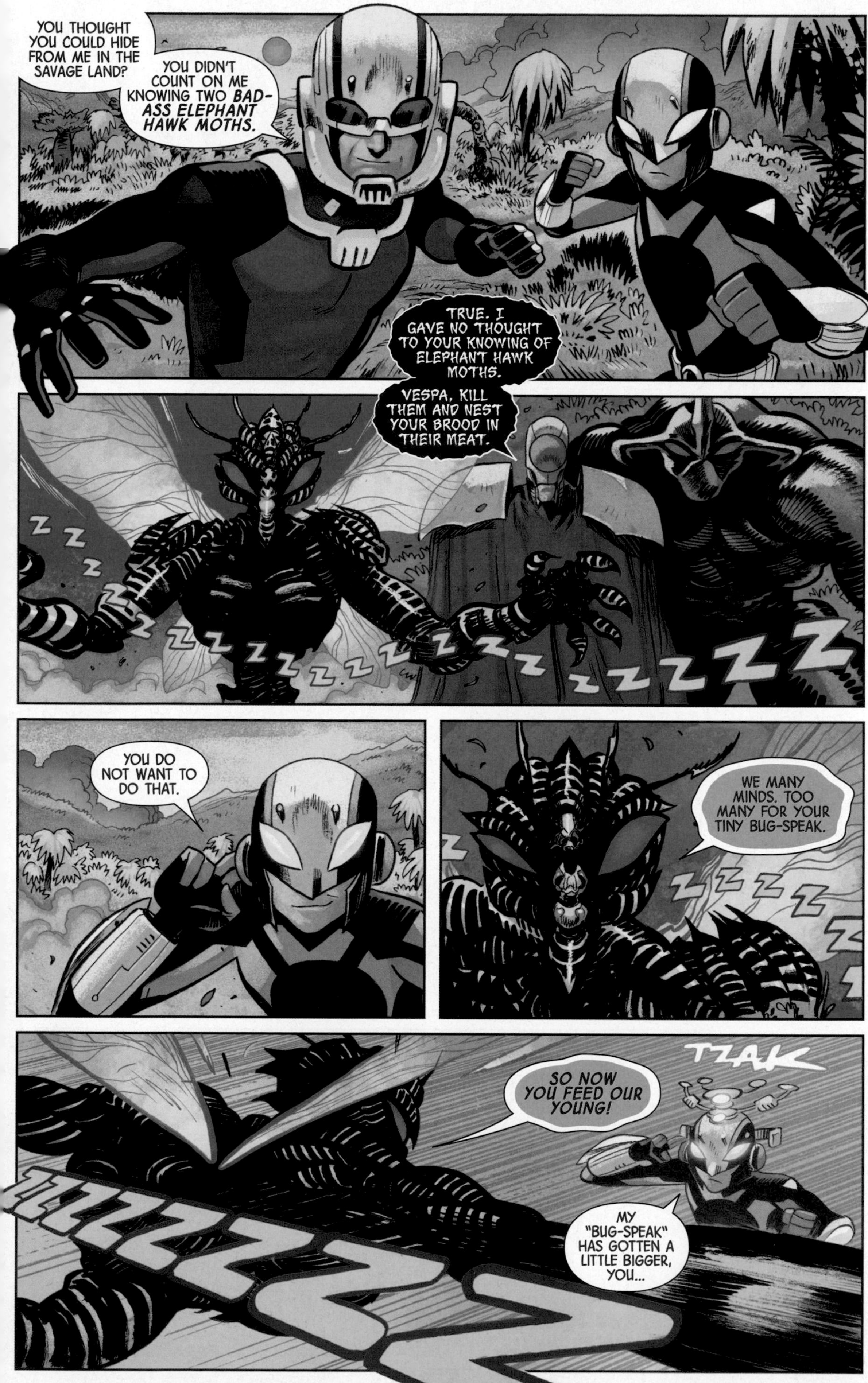
YOU THOUGHT YOU COULD HIDE FROM ME IN THE SAVAGE LAND?
YOU DIDN'T COUNT ON ME KNOWING TWO BAD-ASS ELEPHANT HAWK MOTHS.
TRUE. I GAVE NO THOUGHT TO YOUR KNOWING OF ELEPHANT HAWK MOTHS.
VESPA, KILL THEM AND NEST YOUR BROOD IN THEIR MEAT.
YOU DO NOT WANT TO DO THAT.
WE MANY MINDS. TOO MANY FOR YOUR TINY BUG-SPEAK.
TZAK
SO NOW YOU FEED OUR YOUNG!
MY "BUG-SPEAK" HAS GOTTEN A LITTLE BIGGER, YOU...

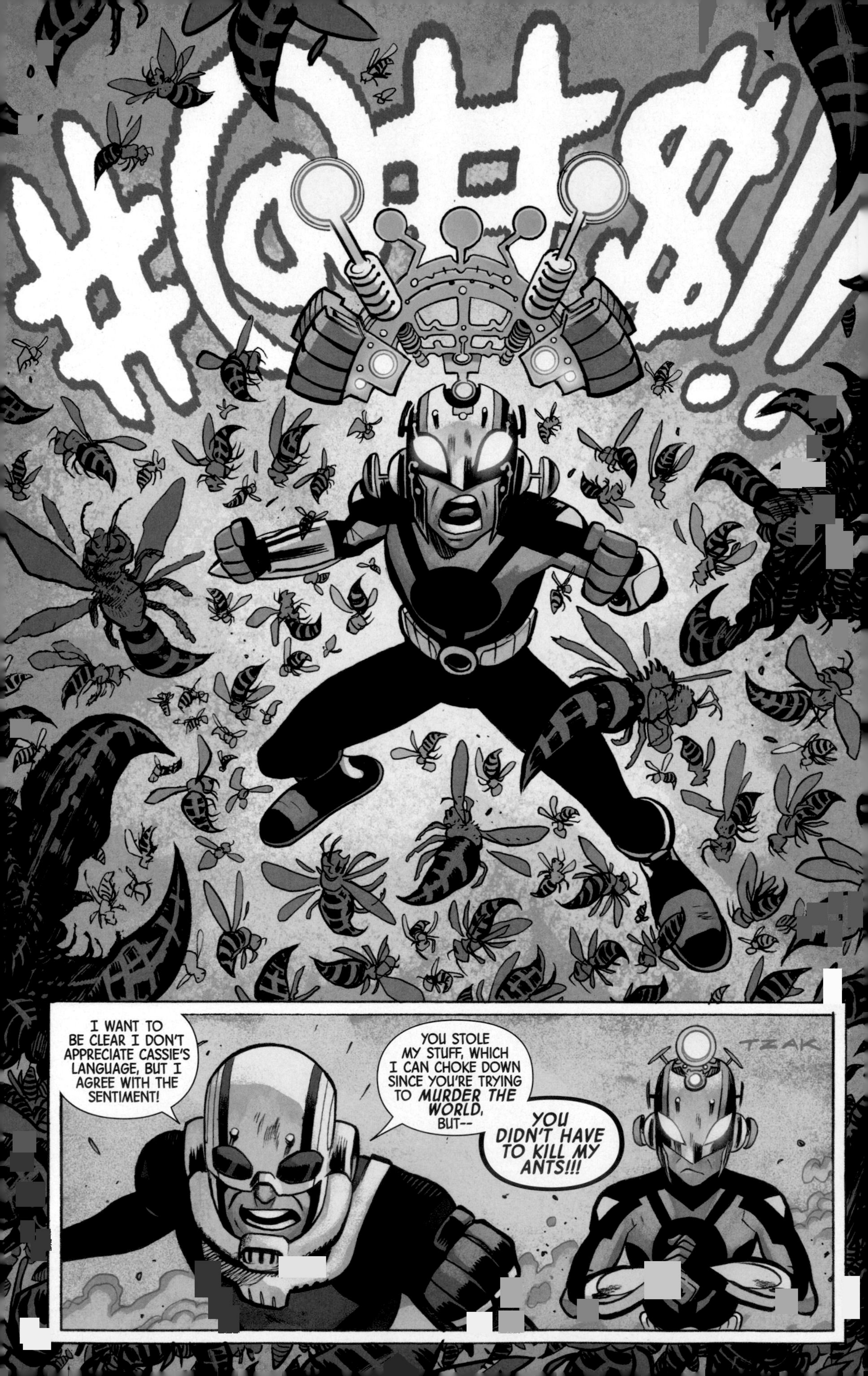
I WANT TO BE CLEAR I DON'T APPRECIATE CASSIE'S LANGUAGE, BUT I AGREE WITH THE SENTIMENT!
YOU STOLE MY STUFF, WHICH I CAN CHOKE DOWN SINCE YOU'RE TRYING TO *MURDER THE WORLD,* BUT--
YOU DIDN'T HAVE TO KILL MY ANTS!!!
TZAK

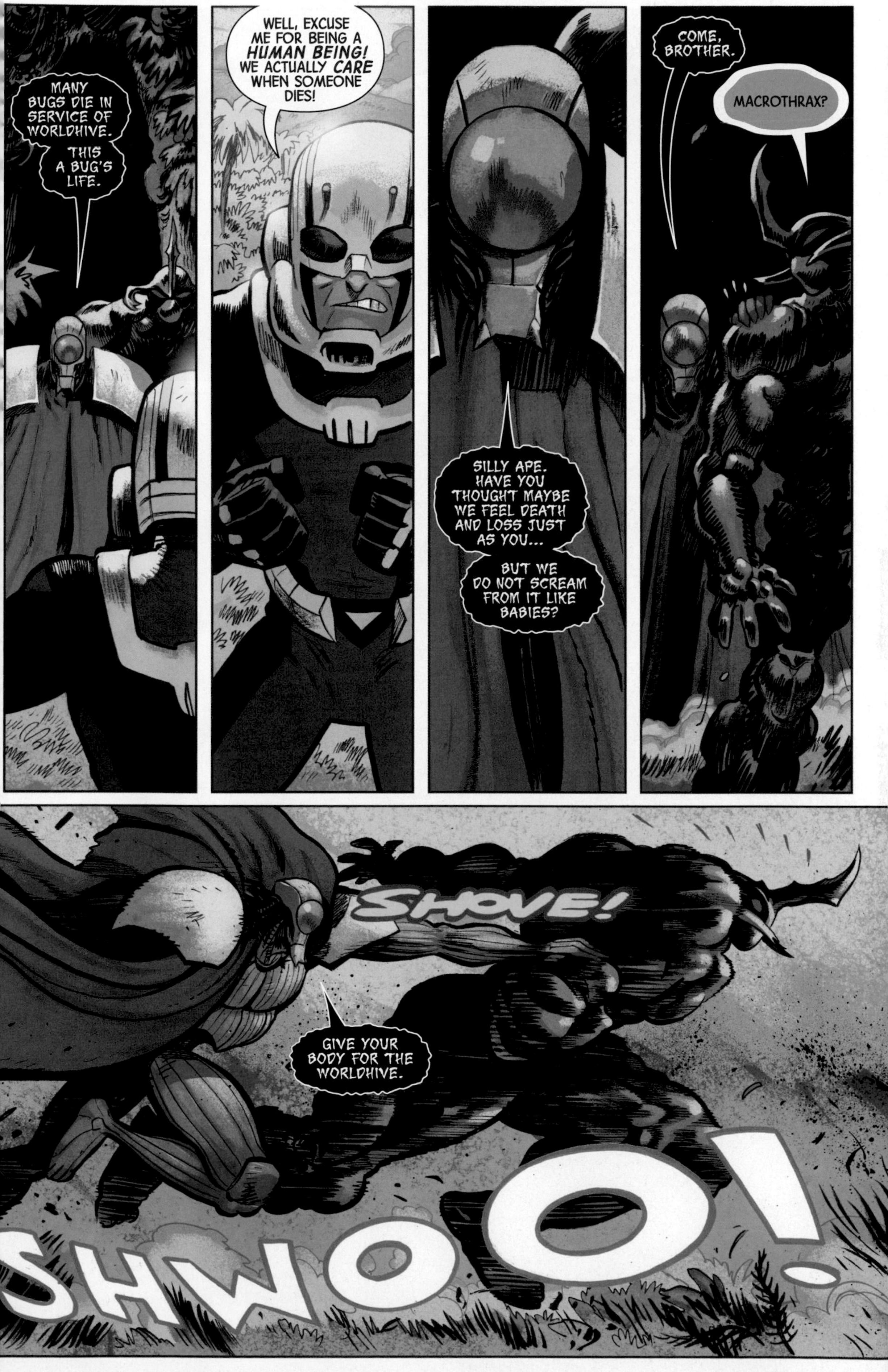
MANY BUGS DIE IN SERVICE OF WORLDHIVE.
THIS A BUG'S LIFE.
WELL, EXCUSE ME FOR BEING A *HUMAN BEING!* WE ACTUALLY *CARE* WHEN SOMEONE DIES!
SILLY APE. HAVE YOU THOUGHT MAYBE WE FEEL DEATH AND LOSS JUST AS YOU...
BUT WE DO NOT SCREAM FROM IT LIKE BABIES?
COME, BROTHER.
MACROTHRAX?
SHOVE!
GIVE YOUR BODY FOR THE WORLDHIVE.
SHWOO!

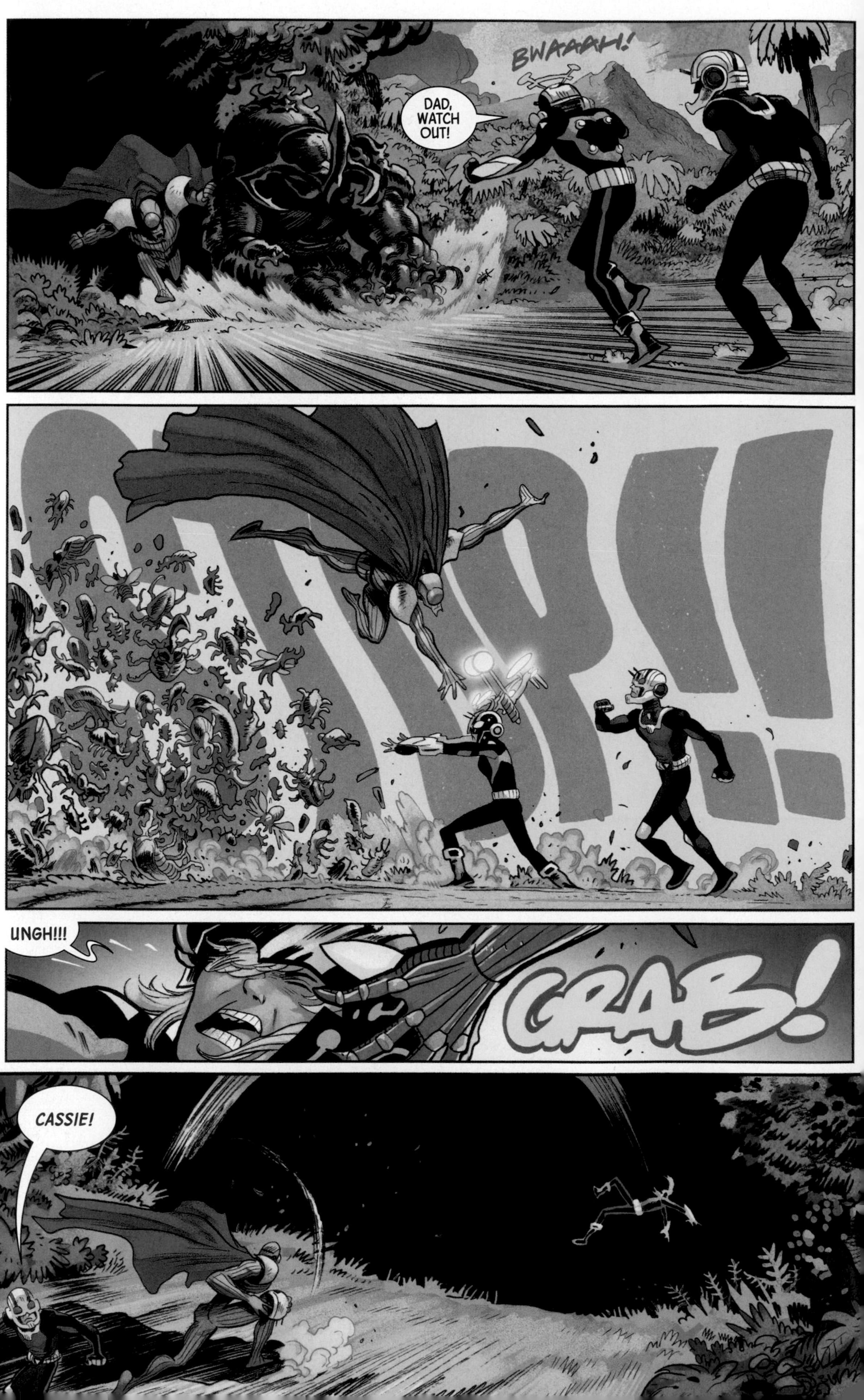
BWAAAH!
DAD, WATCH OUT!
UNGH!!!
GRAB!
CASSIE!

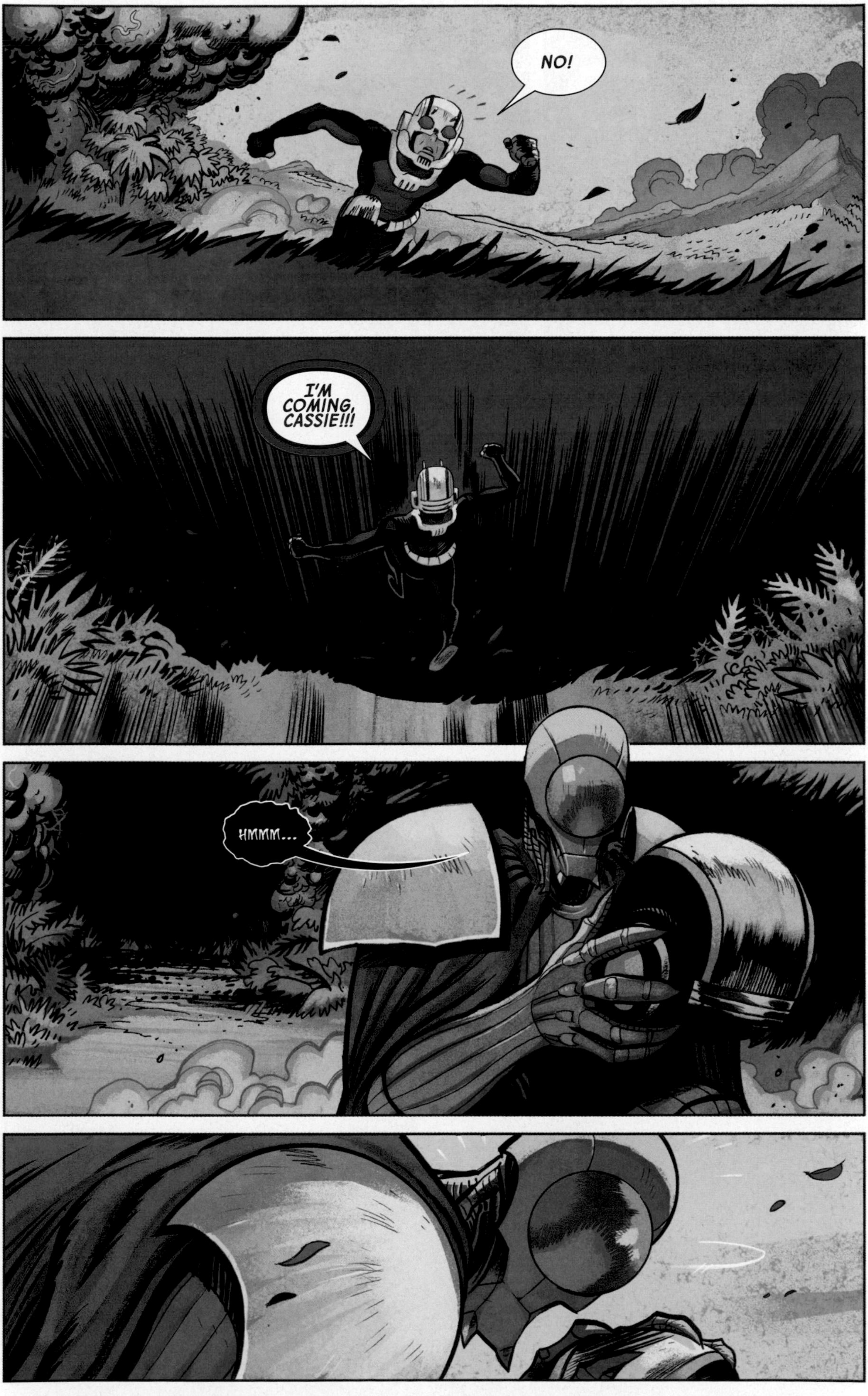
NO!
I'M COMING, CASSIE!!!
HMMM...

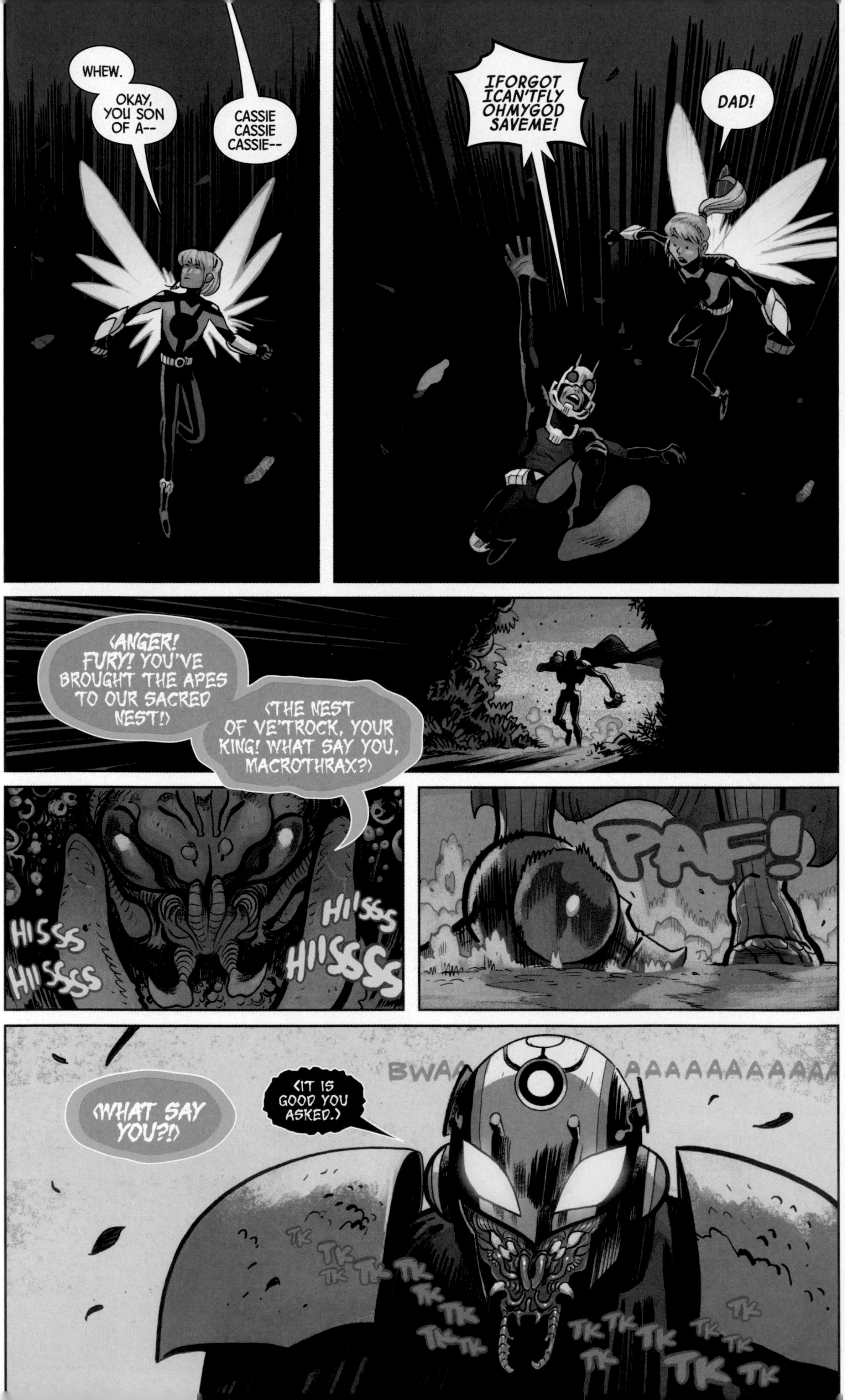
WHEW.
OKAY, YOU SON OF A--
CASSIE CASSIE CASSIE--
IFORGOT ICAN'TFLY OHMYGOD SAVEME!
DAD!
‹ANGER! FURY! YOU'VE BROUGHT THE APES TO OUR SACRED NEST!›
‹THE NEST OF VE'TROCK, YOUR KING! WHAT SAY YOU, MACROTHRAX?›
HISSS HIISSSS
HIISSS HIISSSS
PAF!
BWAAAAAAAAAAAA
‹WHAT SAY YOU?!›
‹IT IS GOOD YOU ASKED.›
TK TK TK TK TK TK TK TK TK TK TK TK TK TK TK TK TK

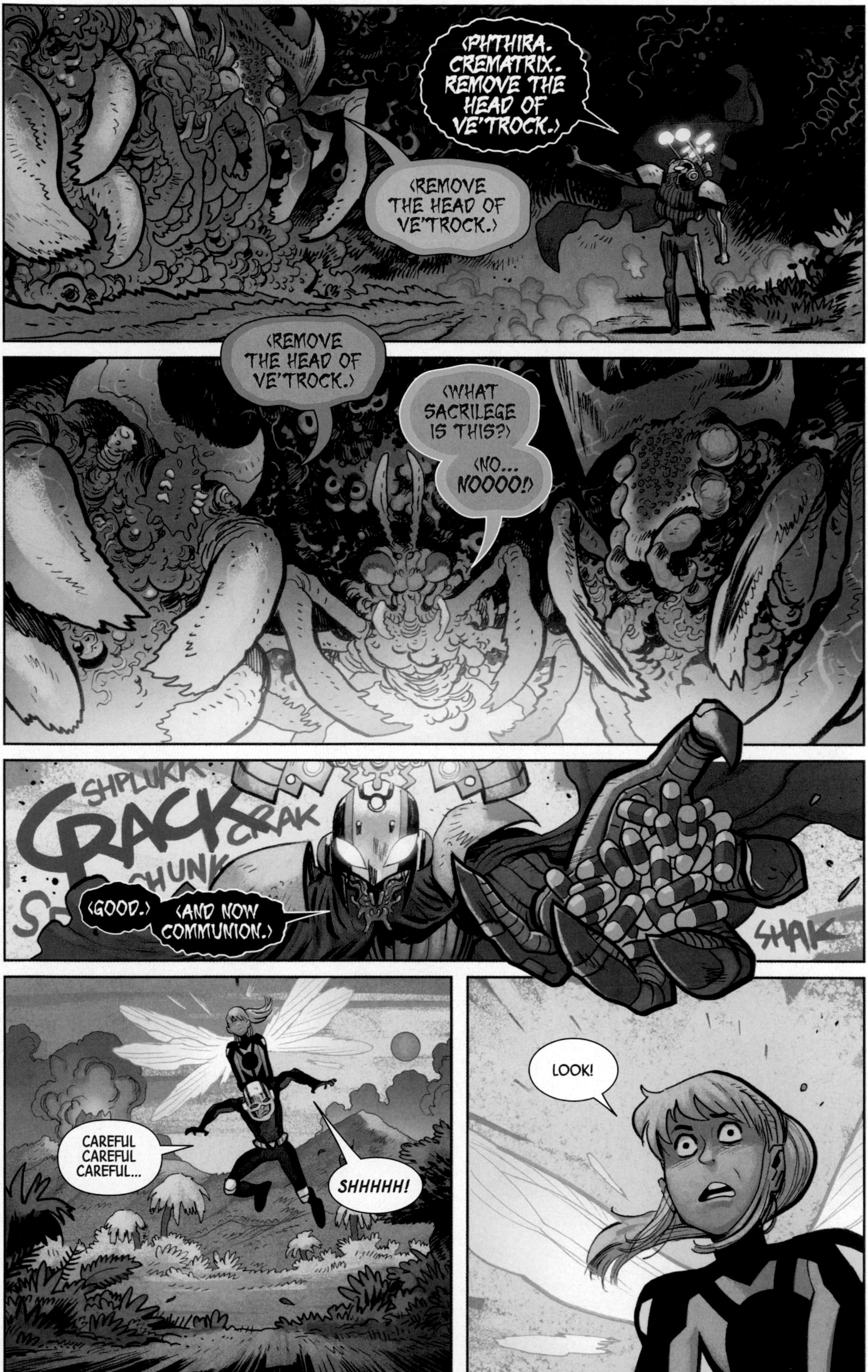
‹PHTHIRA. CREMATRIX. REMOVE THE HEAD OF VE'TROCK.›
‹REMOVE THE HEAD OF VE'TROCK.›
‹REMOVE THE HEAD OF VE'TROCK.›
‹WHAT SACRILEGE IS THIS?›
‹NO... NOOOO!›
SHPLUKK
CRACK
CRAK
CHUNK
SHAK
‹GOOD.›
‹AND NOW COMMUNION.›
CAREFUL CAREFUL CAREFUL...
SHHHHH!
LOOK!

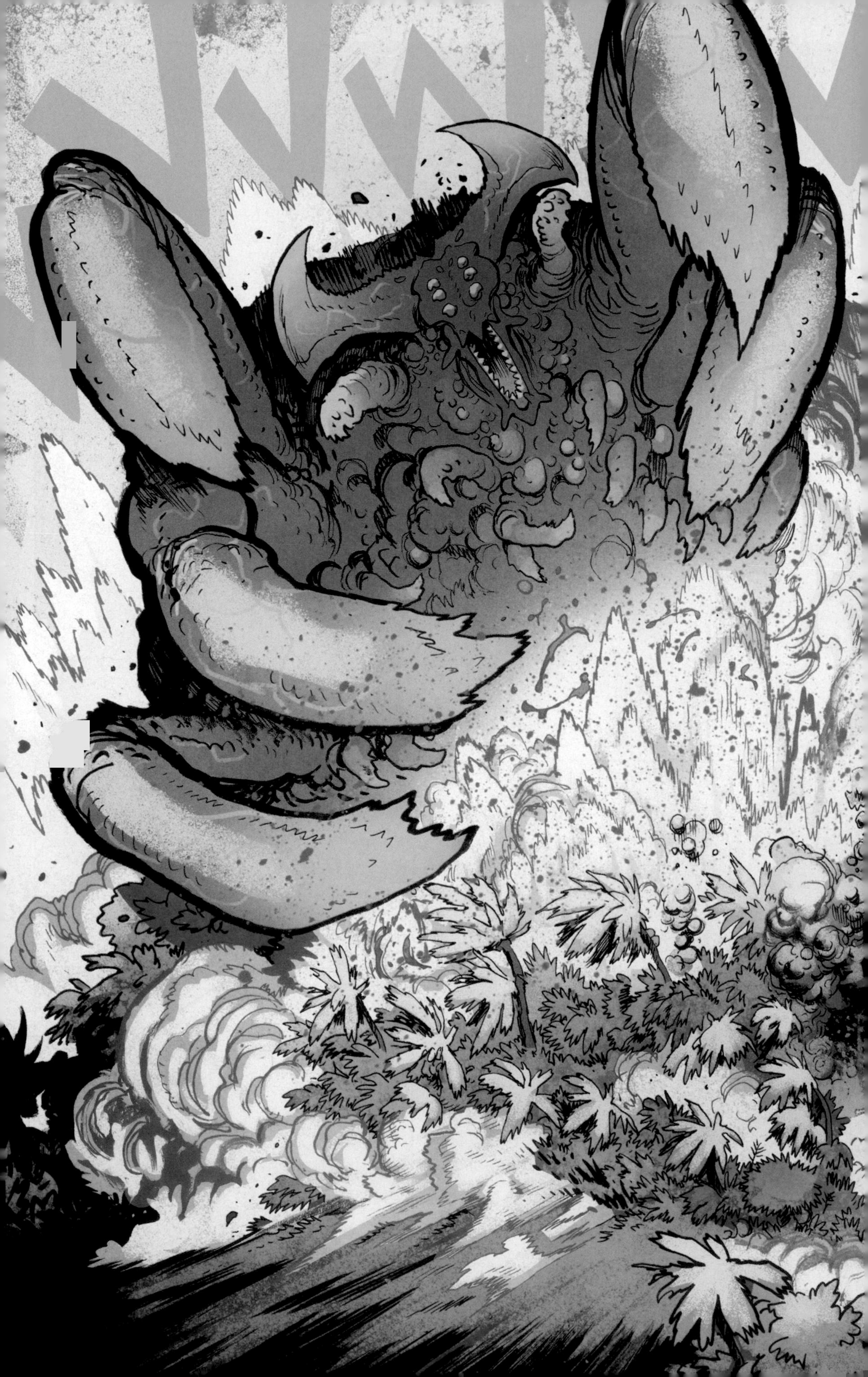

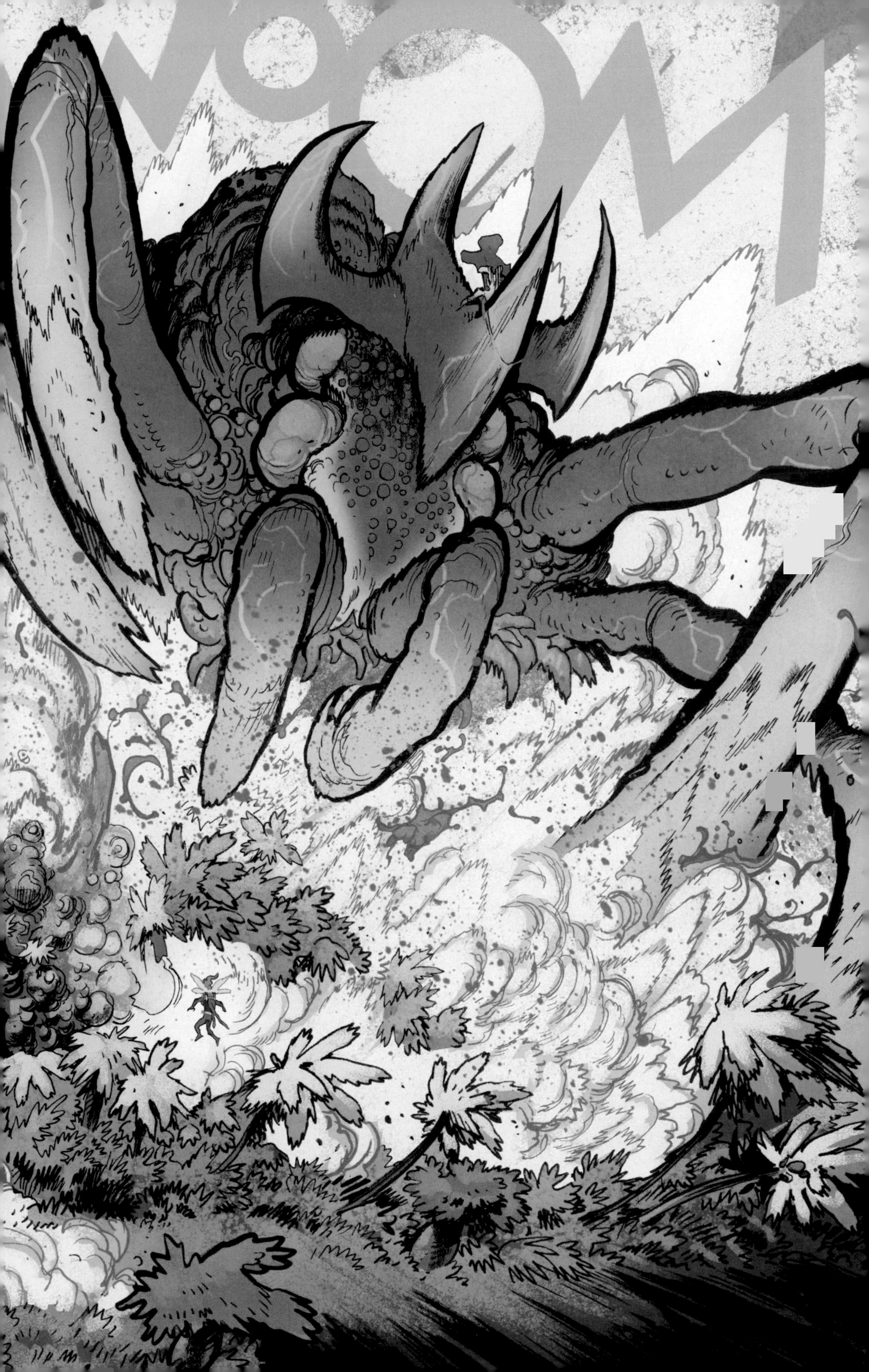
WOOM

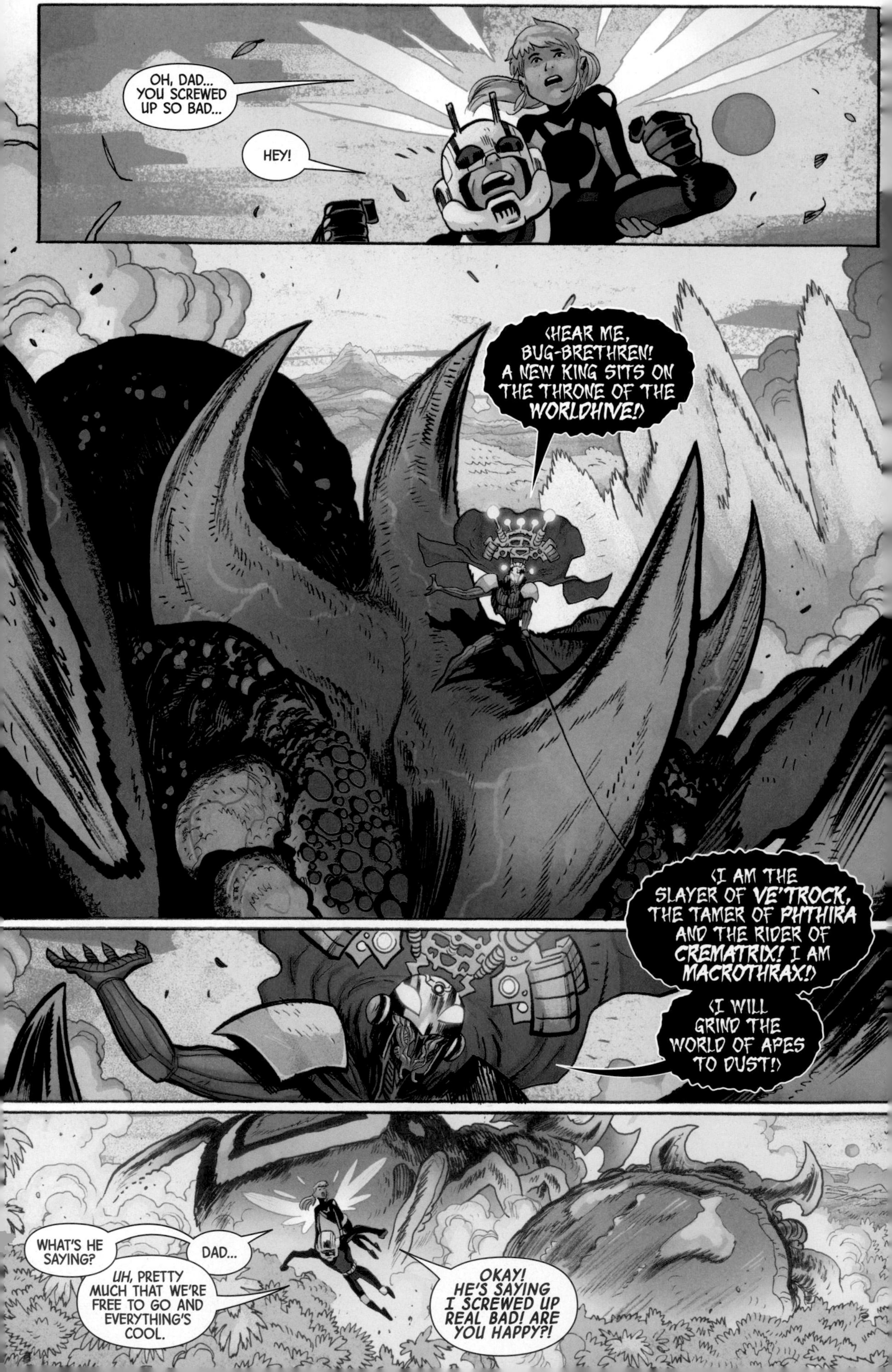

OH, DAD... YOU SCREWED UP SO BAD...
HEY!
‹HEAR ME, BUG-BRETHREN! A NEW KING SITS ON THE THRONE OF THE WORLDHIVE!›
‹I AM THE SLAYER OF VE'TROCK, THE TAMER OF PHTHIRA AND THE RIDER OF CREMATRIX! I AM MACROTHRAX!›
‹I WILL GRIND THE WORLD OF APES TO DUST!›
WHAT'S HE SAYING?
DAD...
UH, PRETTY MUCH THAT WE'RE FREE TO GO AND EVERYTHING'S COOL.
OKAY! HE'S SAYING I SCREWED UP REAL BAD! ARE YOU HAPPY?!

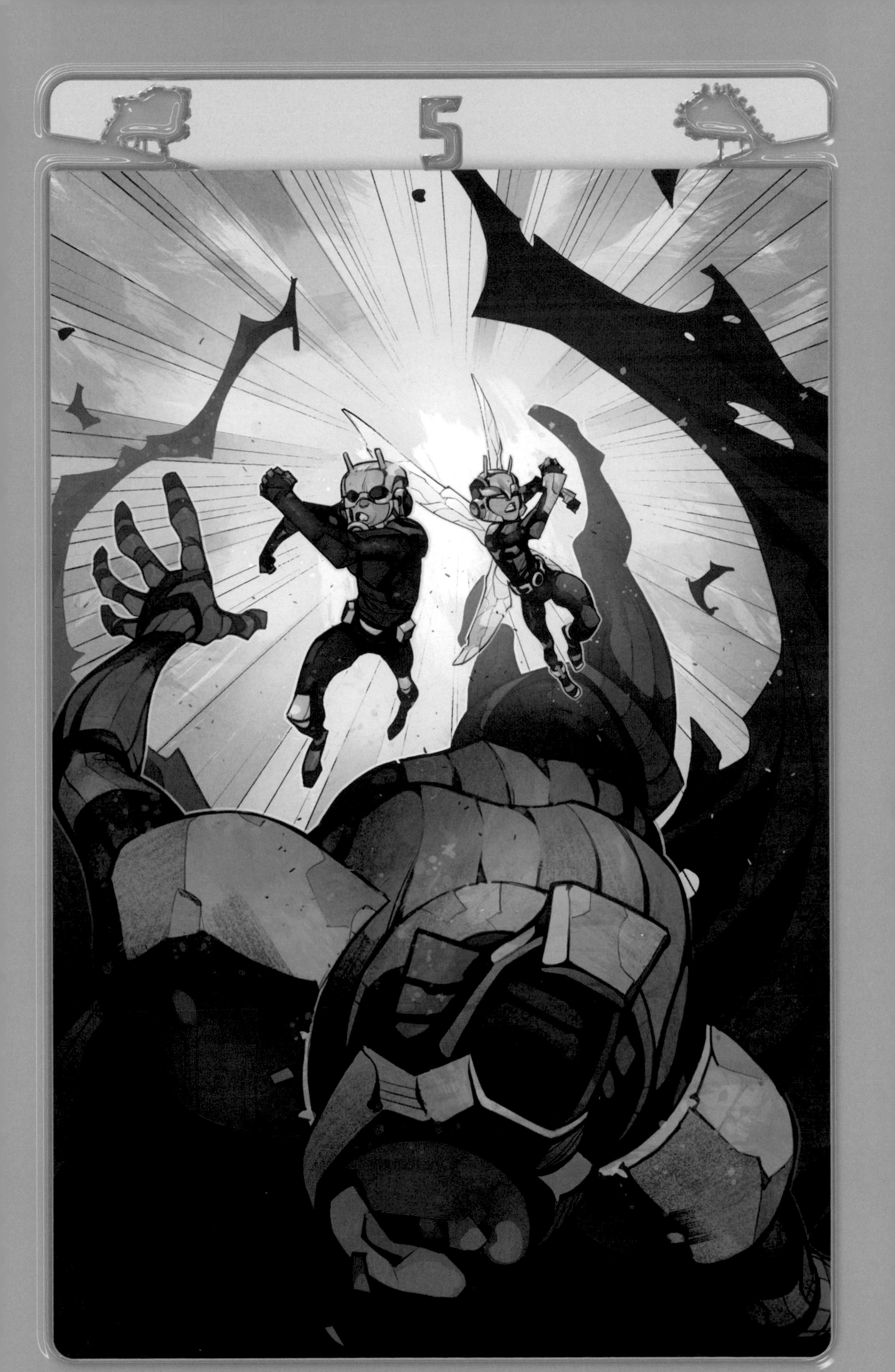

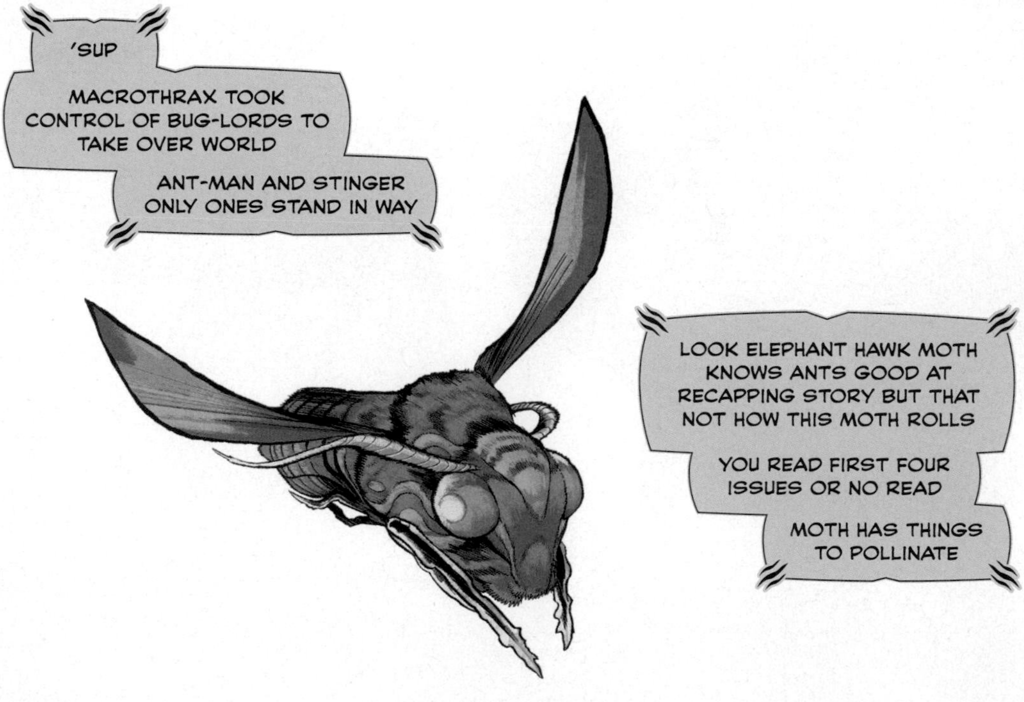
'SUP
MACROTHRAX TOOK CONTROL OF BUG-LORDS TO TAKE OVER WORLD
ANT-MAN AND STINGER ONLY ONES STAND IN WAY
LOOK ELEPHANT HAWK MOTH KNOWS ANTS GOOD AT RECAPPING STORY BUT THAT NOT HOW THIS MOTH ROLLS
YOU READ FIRST FOUR ISSUES OR NO READ
MOTH HAS THINGS TO POLLINATE

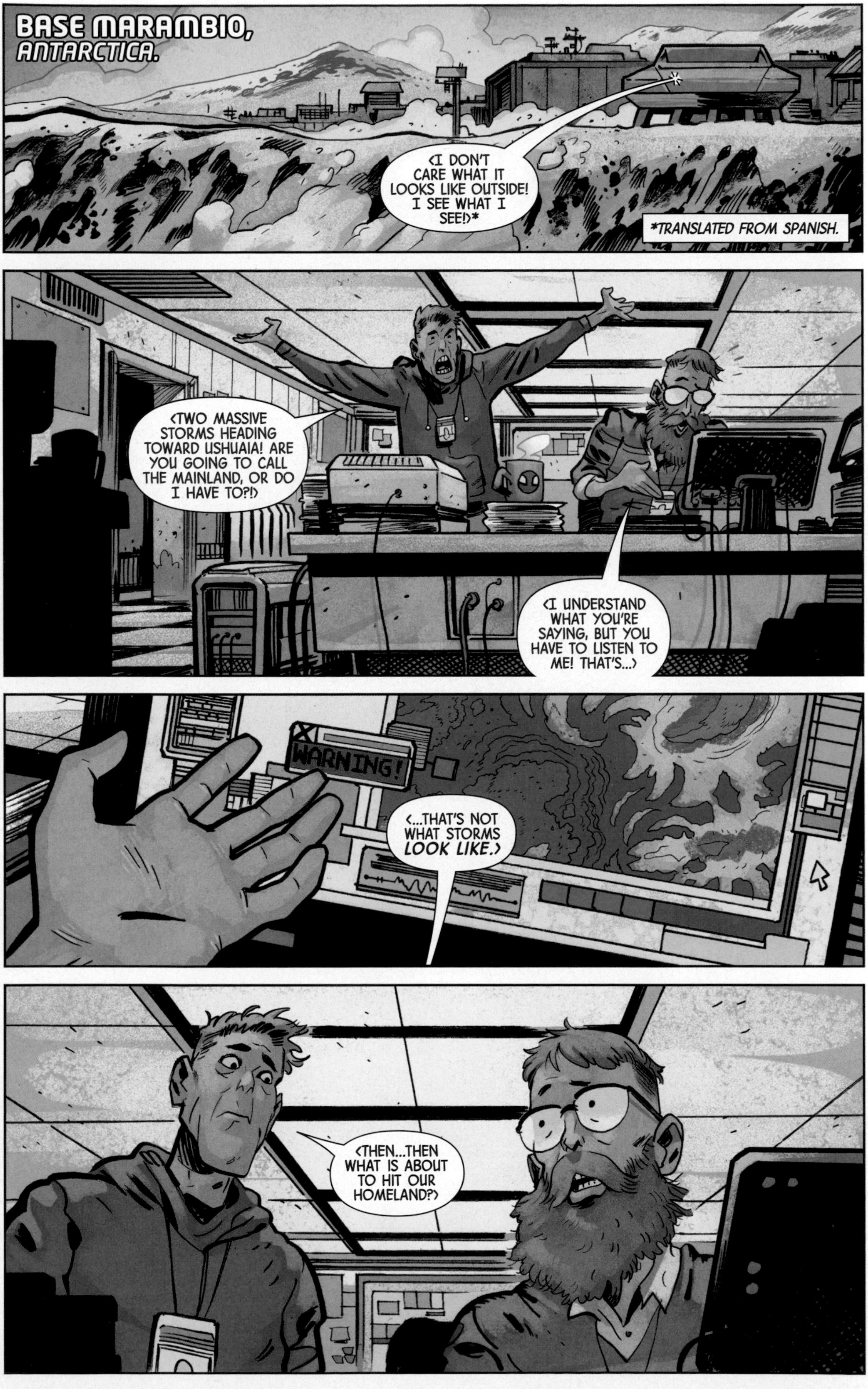
BASE MARAMBIO, ANTARCTICA.
<I DON'T CARE WHAT IT LOOKS LIKE OUTSIDE! I SEE WHAT I SEE!>*
*TRANSLATED FROM SPANISH.
<TWO MASSIVE STORMS HEADING TOWARD USHUAIA! ARE YOU GOING TO CALL THE MAINLAND, OR DO I HAVE TO?!>
<I UNDERSTAND WHAT YOU'RE SAYING, BUT YOU HAVE TO LISTEN TO ME! THAT'S...>
WARNING!
<...THAT'S NOT WHAT STORMS LOOK LIKE.>
<THEN...THEN WHAT IS ABOUT TO HIT OUR HOMELAND?>

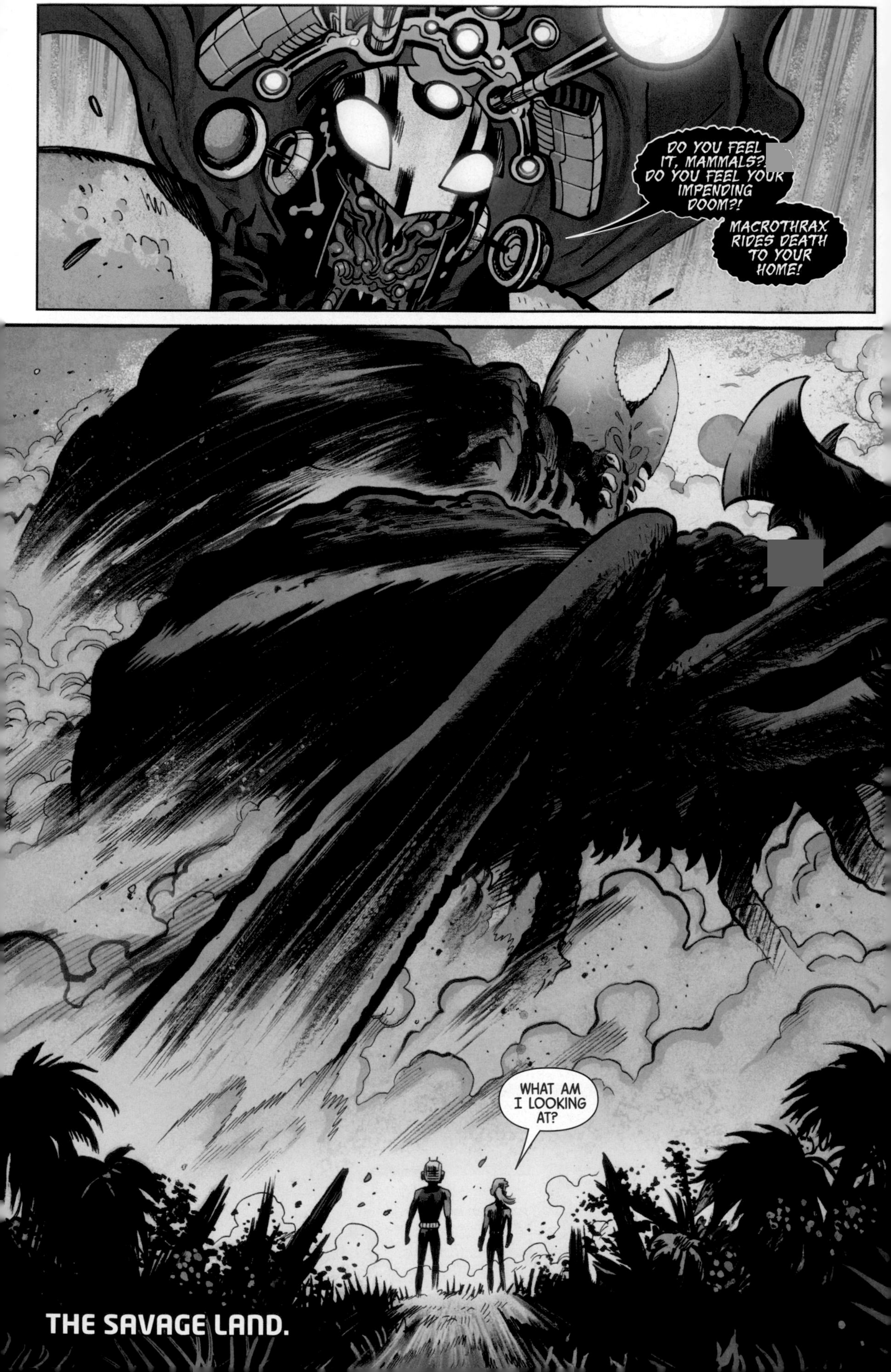
DO YOU FEEL IT, MAMMALS? DO YOU FEEL YOUR IMPENDING DOOM?!
MACROTHRAX RIDES DEATH TO YOUR HOME!
WHAT AM I LOOKING AT?
THE SAVAGE LAND.

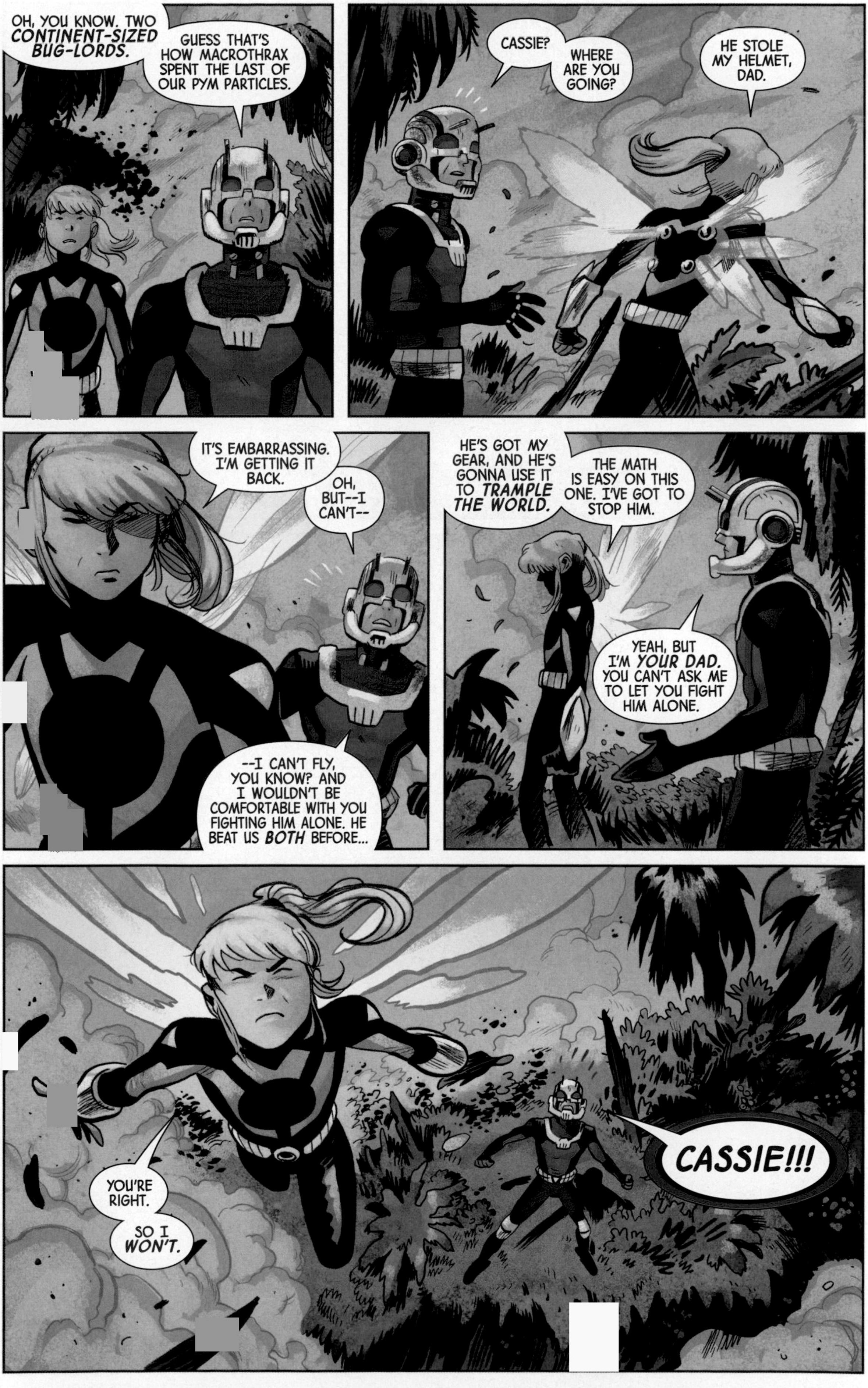
OH, YOU KNOW. TWO CONTINENT-SIZED BUG-LORDS.
GUESS THAT'S HOW MACROTHRAX SPENT THE LAST OF OUR PYM PARTICLES.
CASSIE?
WHERE ARE YOU GOING?
HE STOLE MY HELMET, DAD.
IT'S EMBARRASSING. I'M GETTING IT BACK.
OH, BUT--I CAN'T--
--I CAN'T FLY, YOU KNOW? AND I WOULDN'T BE COMFORTABLE WITH YOU FIGHTING HIM ALONE. HE BEAT US BOTH BEFORE...
HE'S GOT MY GEAR, AND HE'S GONNA USE IT TO TRAMPLE THE WORLD.
THE MATH IS EASY ON THIS ONE. I'VE GOT TO STOP HIM.
YEAH, BUT I'M YOUR DAD. YOU CAN'T ASK ME TO LET YOU FIGHT HIM ALONE.
YOU'RE RIGHT.
SO I WON'T.
CASSIE!!!

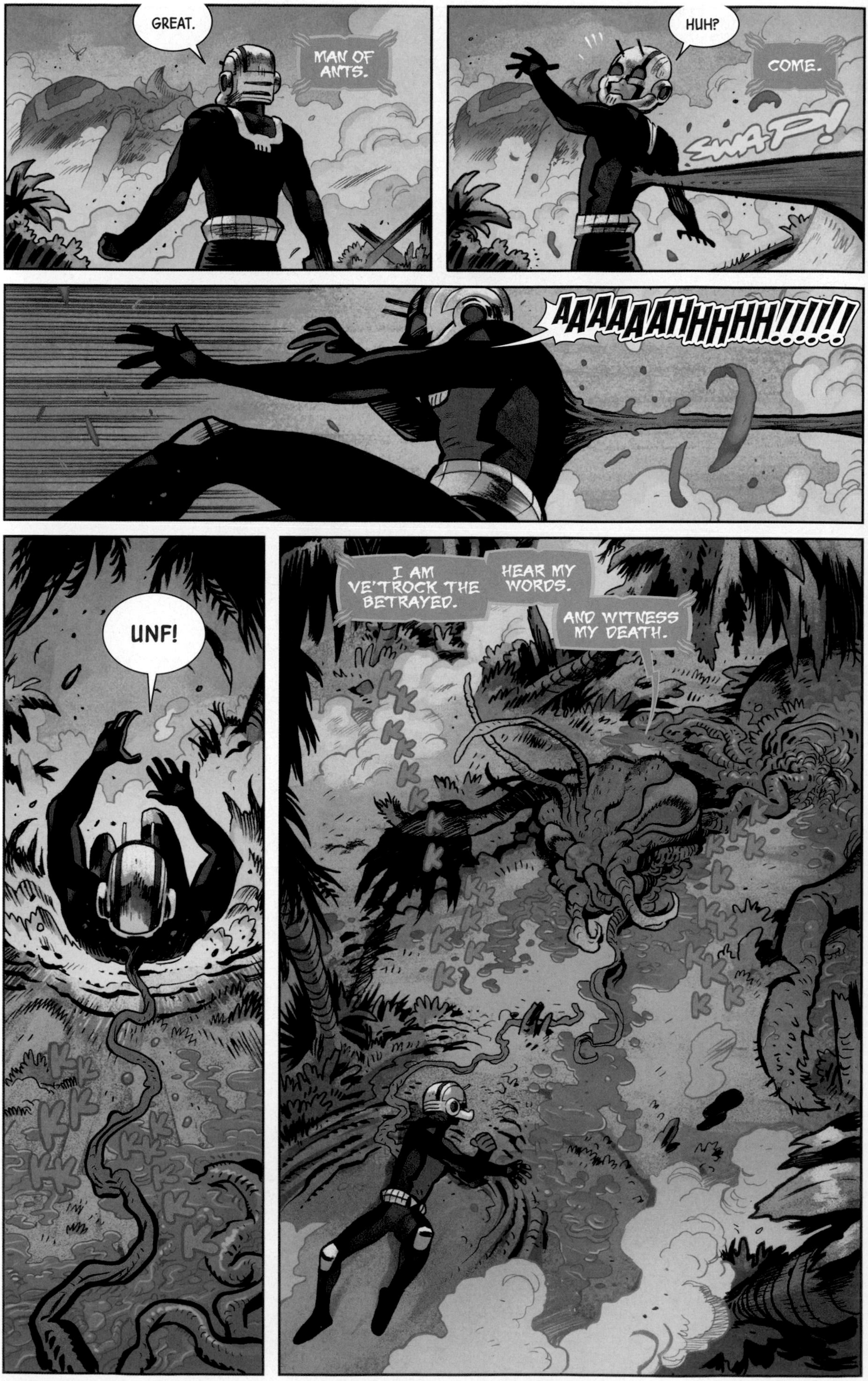
GREAT.
MAN OF ANTS.
HUH?
COME.
SWAP!
AAAAAHHHHH!!!!!!
UNF!
I AM VE'TROCK THE BETRAYED.
HEAR MY WORDS.
AND WITNESS MY DEATH.

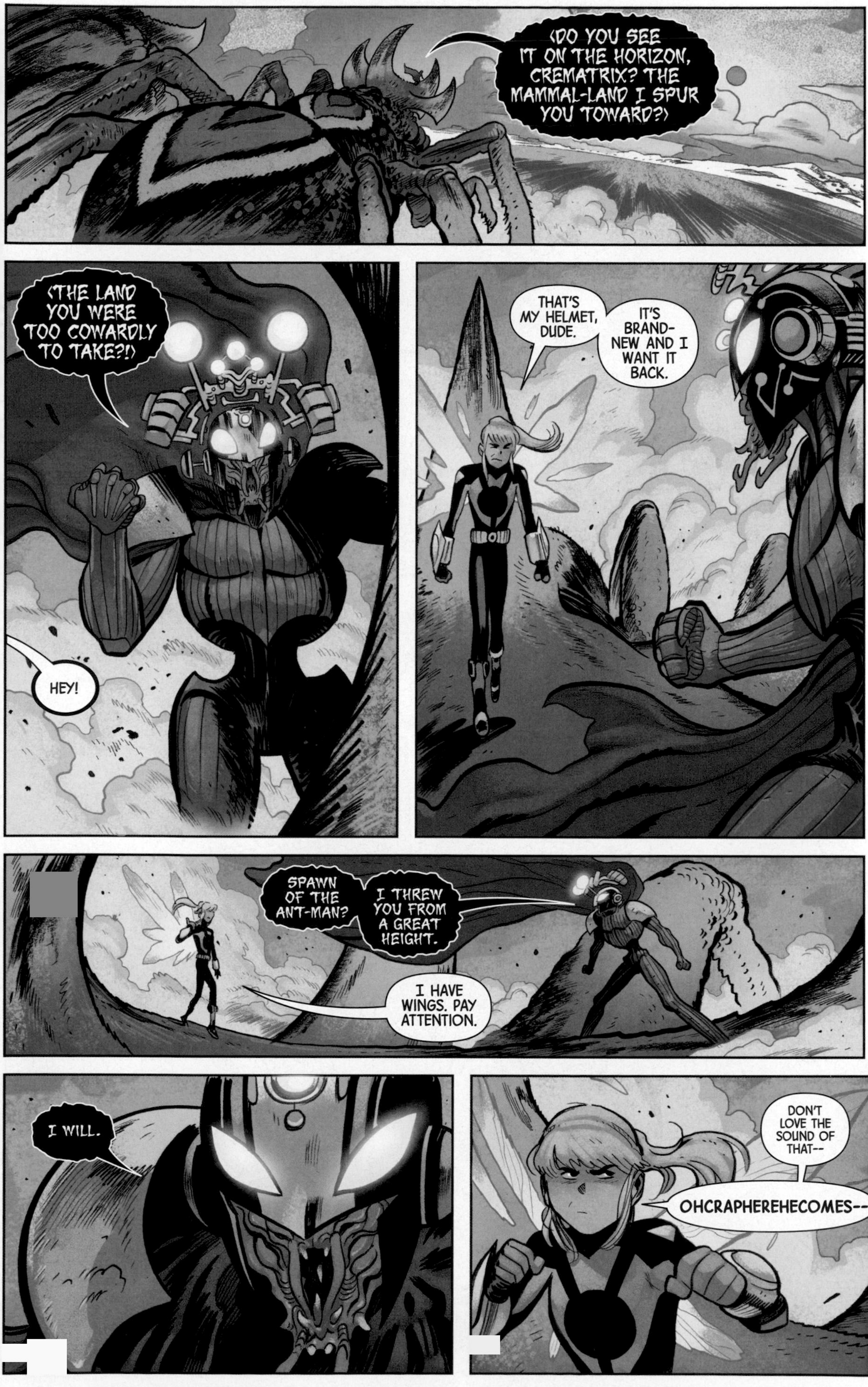
‹DO YOU SEE IT ON THE HORIZON, CREMATRIX? THE MAMMAL-LAND I SPUR YOU TOWARD?›
‹THE LAND YOU WERE TOO COWARDLY TO TAKE?!›
HEY!
THAT'S MY HELMET, DUDE.
IT'S BRAND-NEW AND I WANT IT BACK.
SPAWN OF THE ANT-MAN?
I THREW YOU FROM A GREAT HEIGHT.
I HAVE WINGS. PAY ATTENTION.
I WILL.
DON'T LOVE THE SOUND OF THAT--
OHCRAPHEREHECOMES--

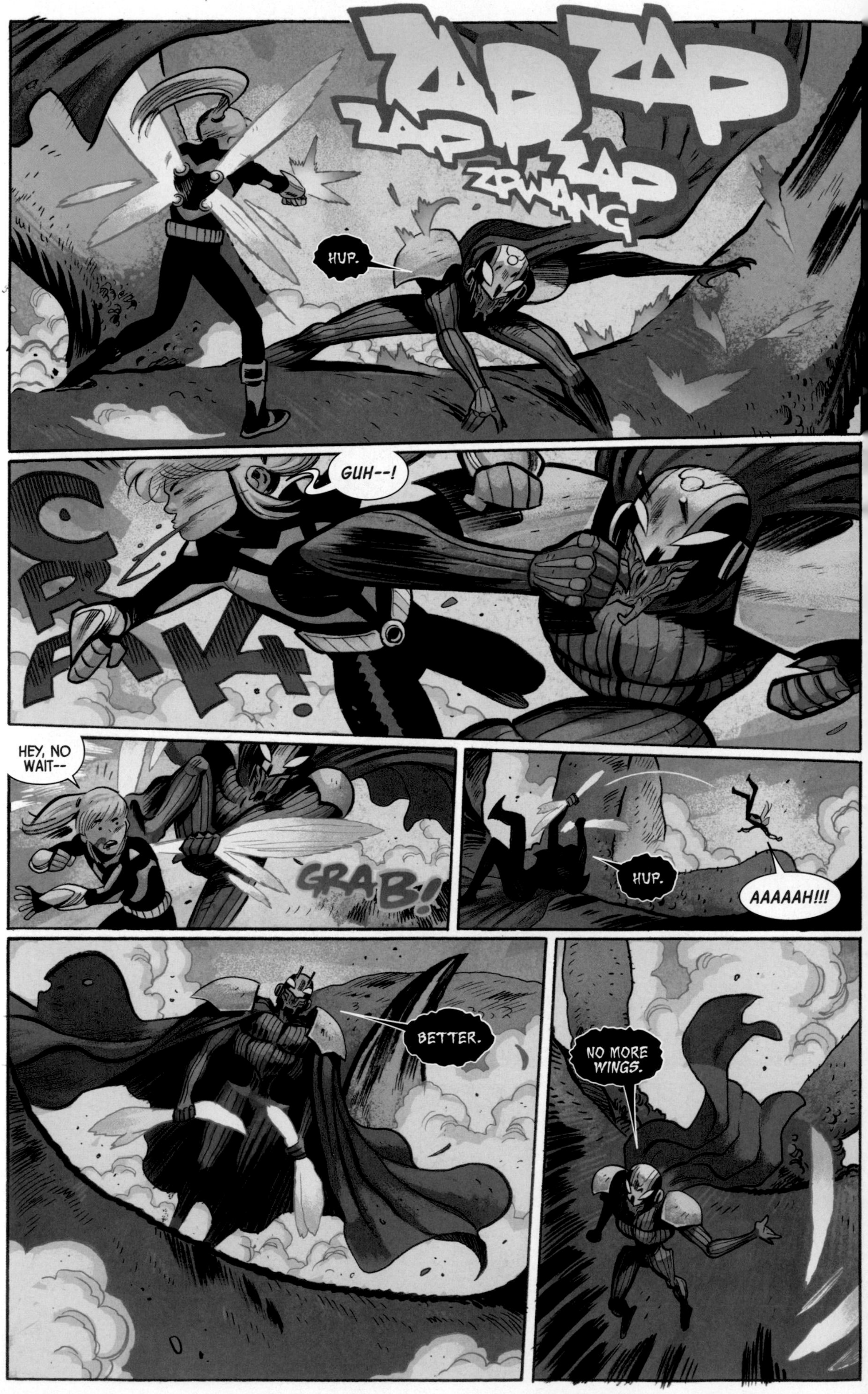
ZAP ZAP
ZAP ZAP
ZPWANG
HUP.
GUH--!
CRAK
HEY, NO WAIT--
GRAB!
HUP.
AAAAAH!!!
BETTER.
NO MORE WINGS.

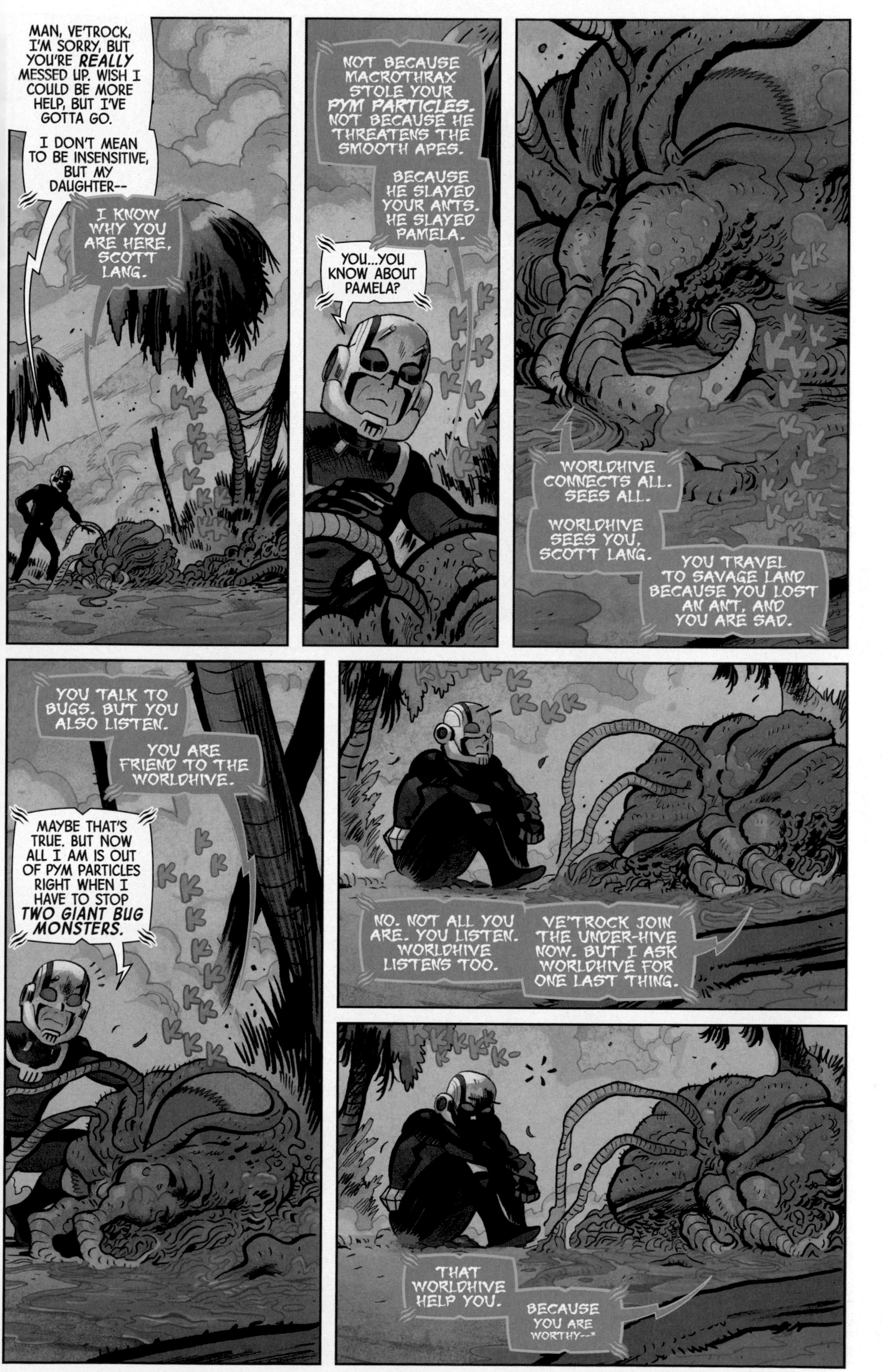
MAN, VE'TROCK, I'M SORRY, BUT YOU'RE *REALLY* MESSED UP. WISH I COULD BE MORE HELP, BUT I'VE GOTTA GO.
I DON'T MEAN TO BE INSENSITIVE, BUT MY DAUGHTER--
I KNOW WHY YOU ARE HERE, SCOTT LANG.
NOT BECAUSE MACROTHRAX STOLE YOUR *PYM PARTICLES.* NOT BECAUSE HE THREATENS THE SMOOTH APES.
BECAUSE HE SLAYED YOUR ANTS. HE SLAYED PAMELA.
YOU...YOU KNOW ABOUT PAMELA?
WORLDHIVE CONNECTS ALL. SEES ALL.
WORLDHIVE SEES YOU, SCOTT LANG.
YOU TRAVEL TO SAVAGE LAND BECAUSE YOU LOST AN ANT, AND YOU ARE SAD.
YOU TALK TO BUGS. BUT YOU ALSO LISTEN.
YOU ARE FRIEND TO THE WORLDHIVE.
MAYBE THAT'S TRUE. BUT NOW ALL I AM IS OUT OF PYM PARTICLES RIGHT WHEN I HAVE TO STOP *TWO GIANT BUG MONSTERS.*
NO. NOT ALL YOU ARE. YOU LISTEN. WORLDHIVE LISTENS TOO.
VE'TROCK JOIN THE UNDER-HIVE NOW. BUT I ASK WORLDHIVE FOR ONE LAST THING.
THAT WORLDHIVE HELP YOU.
BECAUSE YOU ARE WORTHY--*

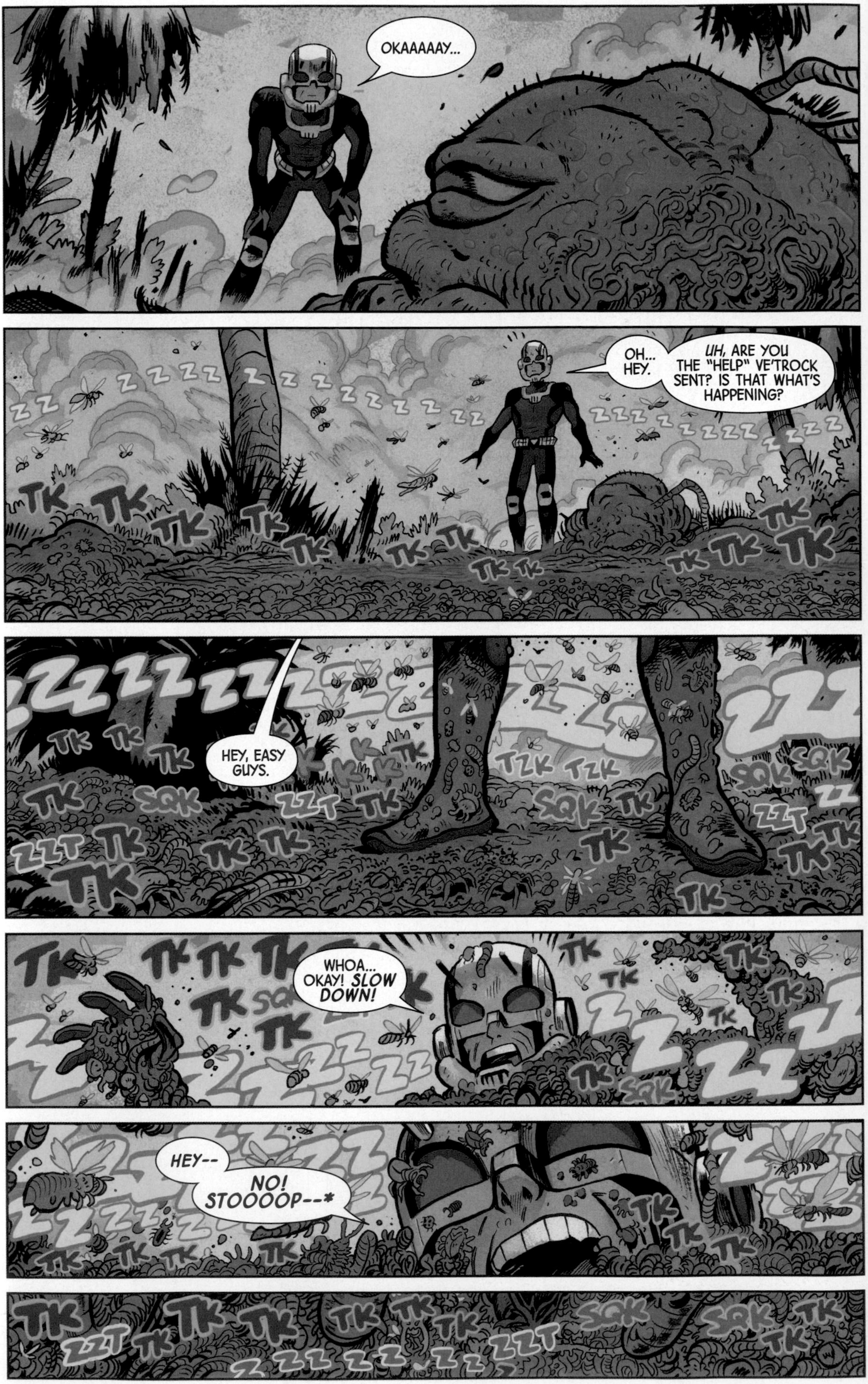
OKAAAAAY...
Z Z Z Z Z Z Z Z Z Z Z Z Z
TK TK TK TK TK TK TK TK
OH... HEY.
UH, ARE YOU THE "HELP" VE'TROCK SENT? IS THAT WHAT'S HAPPENING?
ZZZZZZ
TK TK TK
HEY, EASY GUYS.
TK SQK ZZT TK TZK TZK SQK SQK ZZT TK
TK TK TK TK SQK
WHOA... OKAY! *SLOW DOWN!*
Z ZZ ZZ TK SQK
HEY--
NO! STOOOOP--*
TK TK TK TK
TK ZZT TK TK TK TK TK SQK SQK TK TK ZZT
ZZZ ZZZ

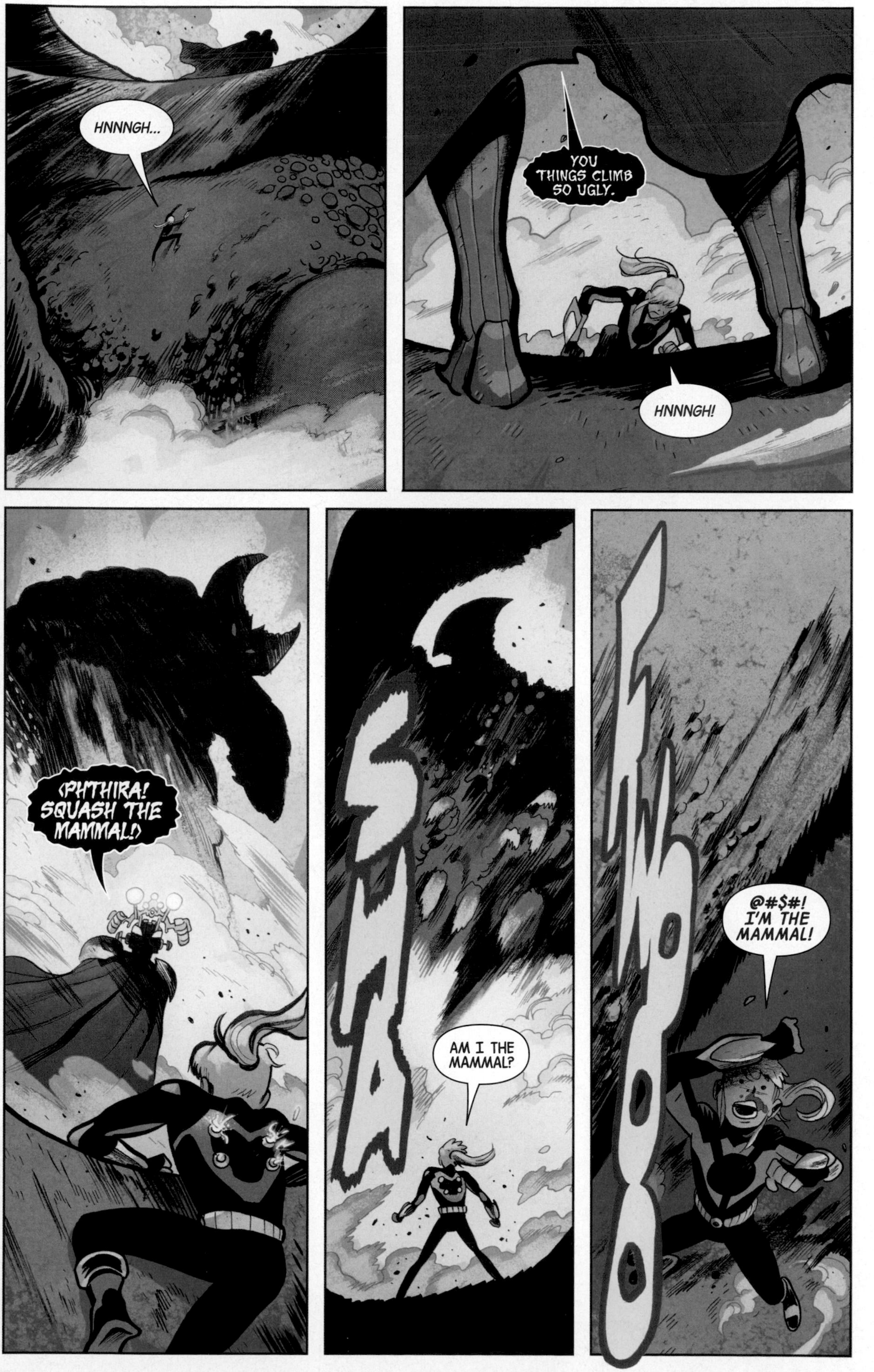
HNNNGH...
YOU THINGS CLIMB SO UGLY.
HNNNGH!
‹PHTHIRA! SQUASH THE MAMMAL!›
AM I THE MAMMAL?
@#$#! I'M THE MAMMAL!

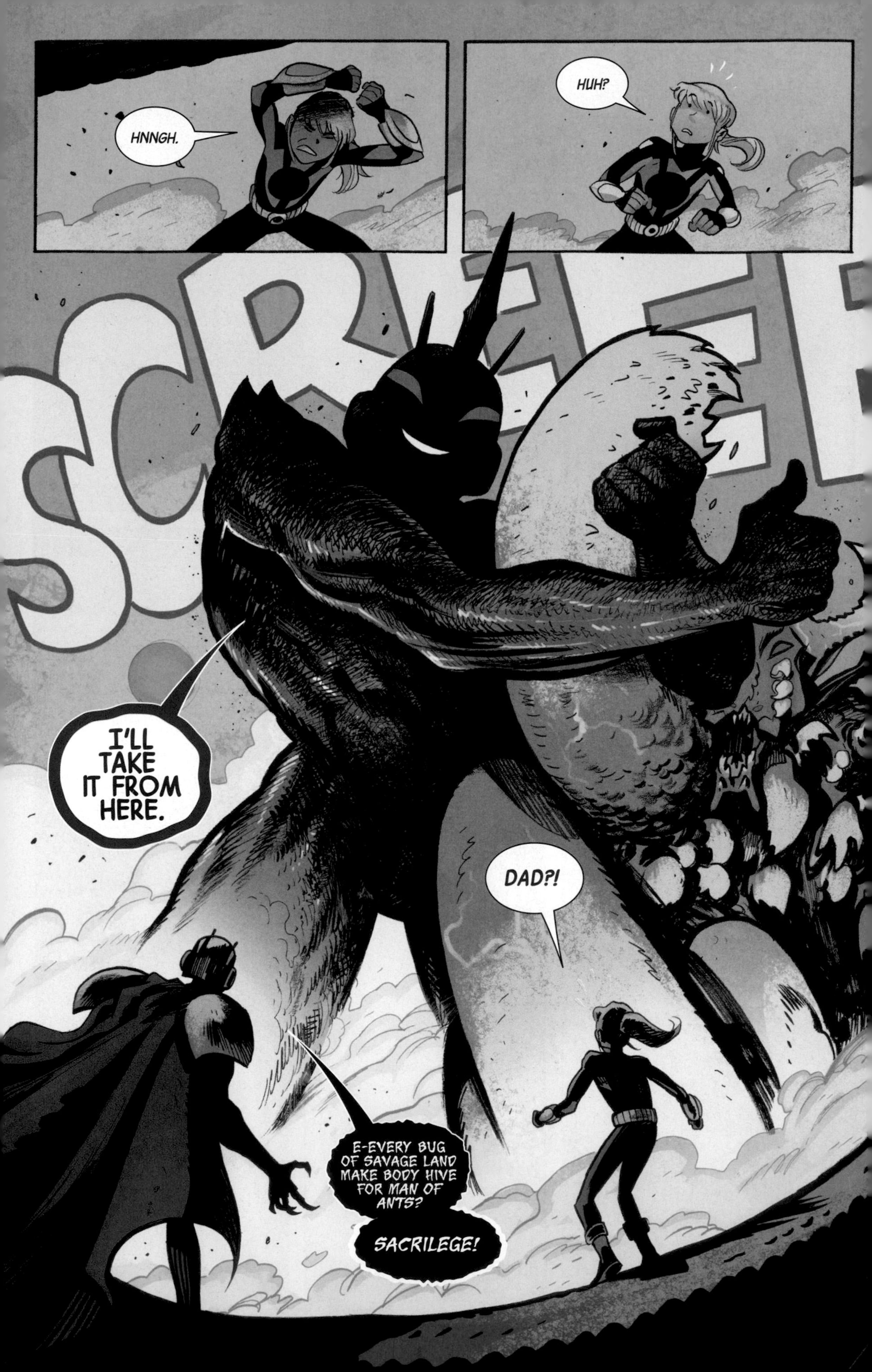
HNNGH.
HUH?
SCREEE
I'LL TAKE IT FROM HERE.
DAD?!
E-EVERY BUG OF SAVAGE LAND MAKE BODY HIVE FOR MAN OF ANTS?
SACRILEGE!

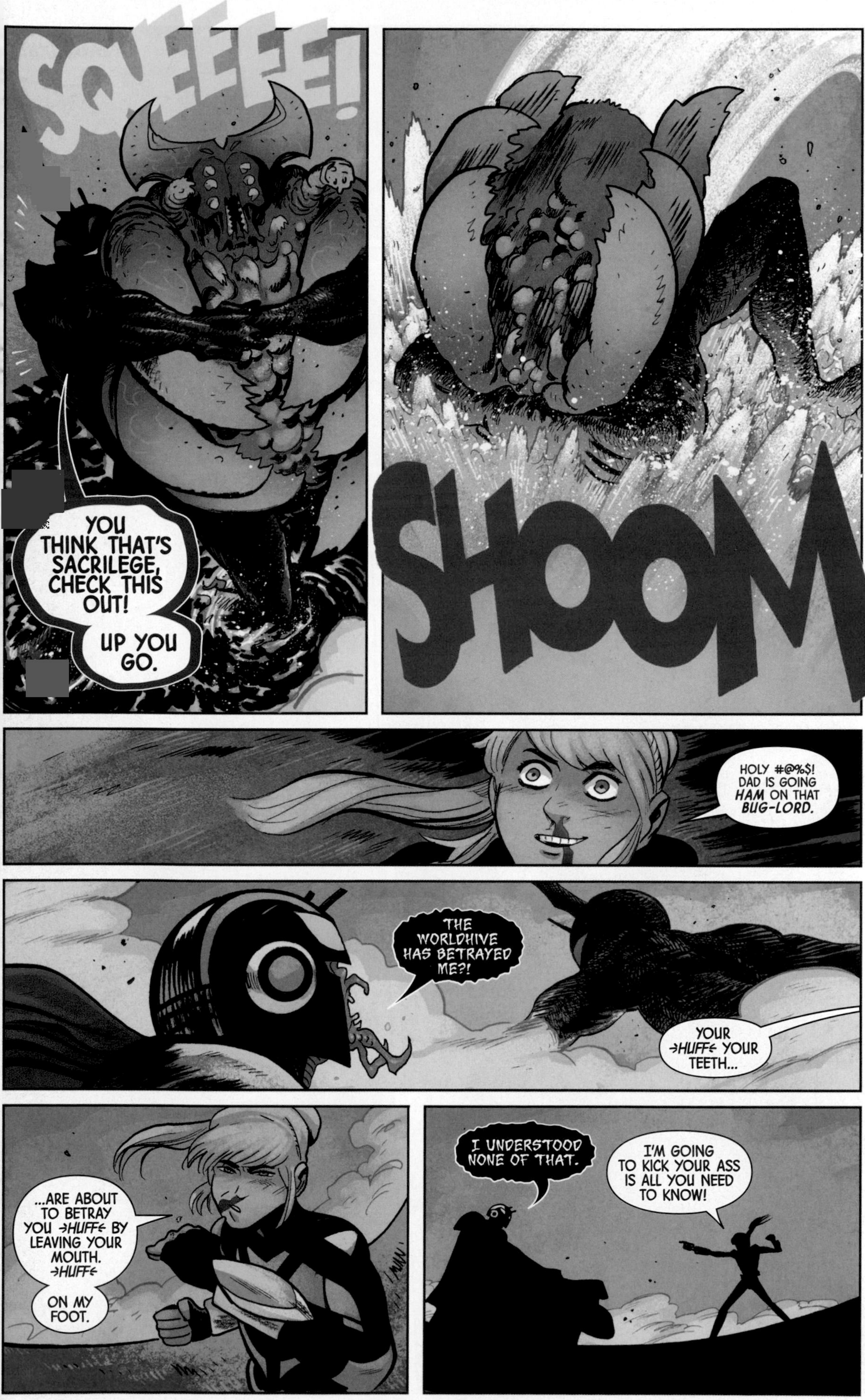
SQEEEE!
YOU THINK THAT'S SACRILEGE, CHECK THIS OUT!
UP YOU GO.
SHOOM
HOLY #@%$! DAD IS GOING HAM ON THAT BUG-LORD.
THE WORLDHIVE HAS BETRAYED ME?!
YOUR →HUFF← YOUR TEETH...
...ARE ABOUT TO BETRAY YOU →HUFF← BY LEAVING YOUR MOUTH. →HUFF←
ON MY FOOT.
I UNDERSTOOD NONE OF THAT.
I'M GOING TO KICK YOUR ASS IS ALL YOU NEED TO KNOW!

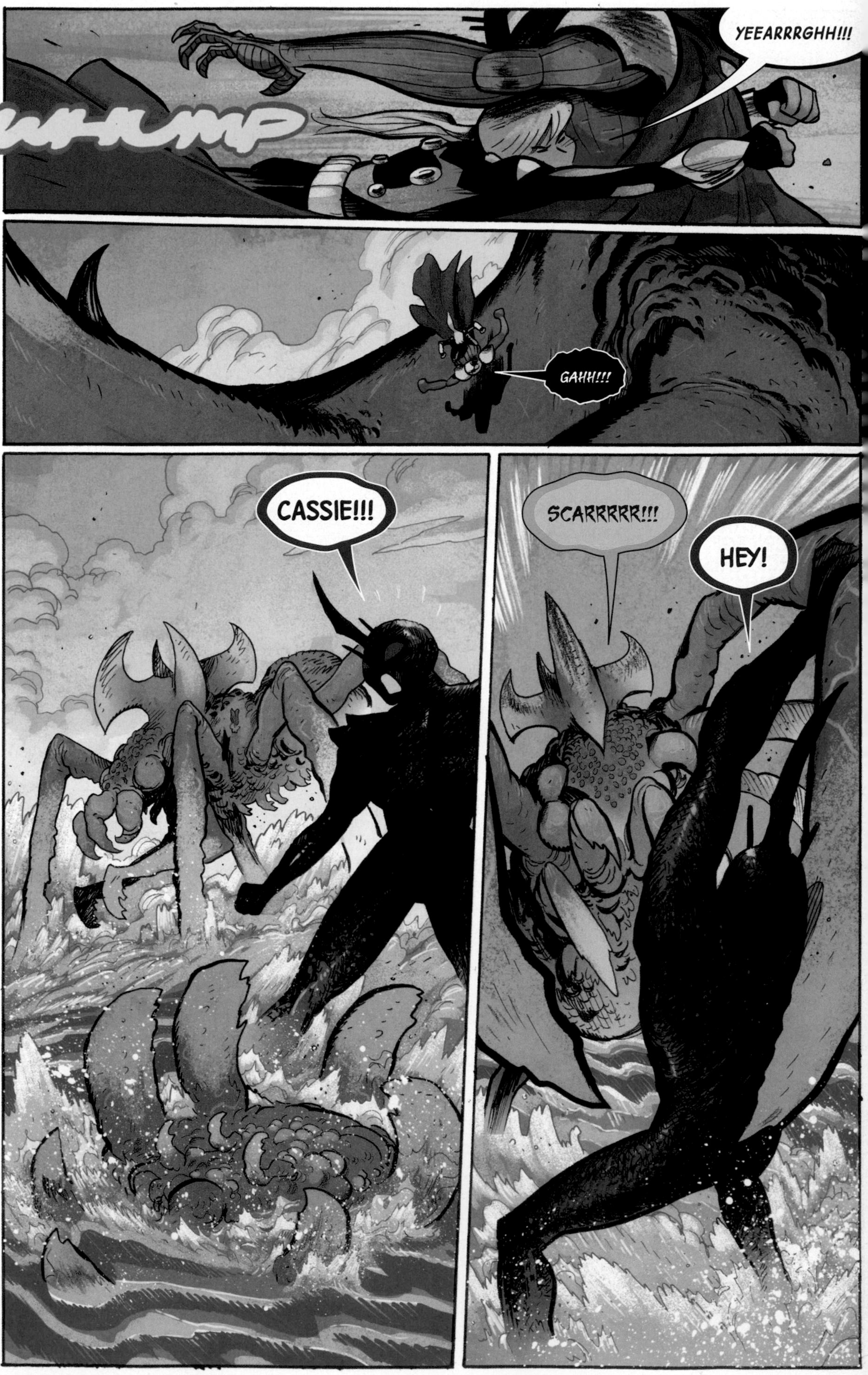
YEEARRRGHH!!!
WHUMP
GAHH!!!
CASSIE!!!
SCARRRRR!!!
HEY!

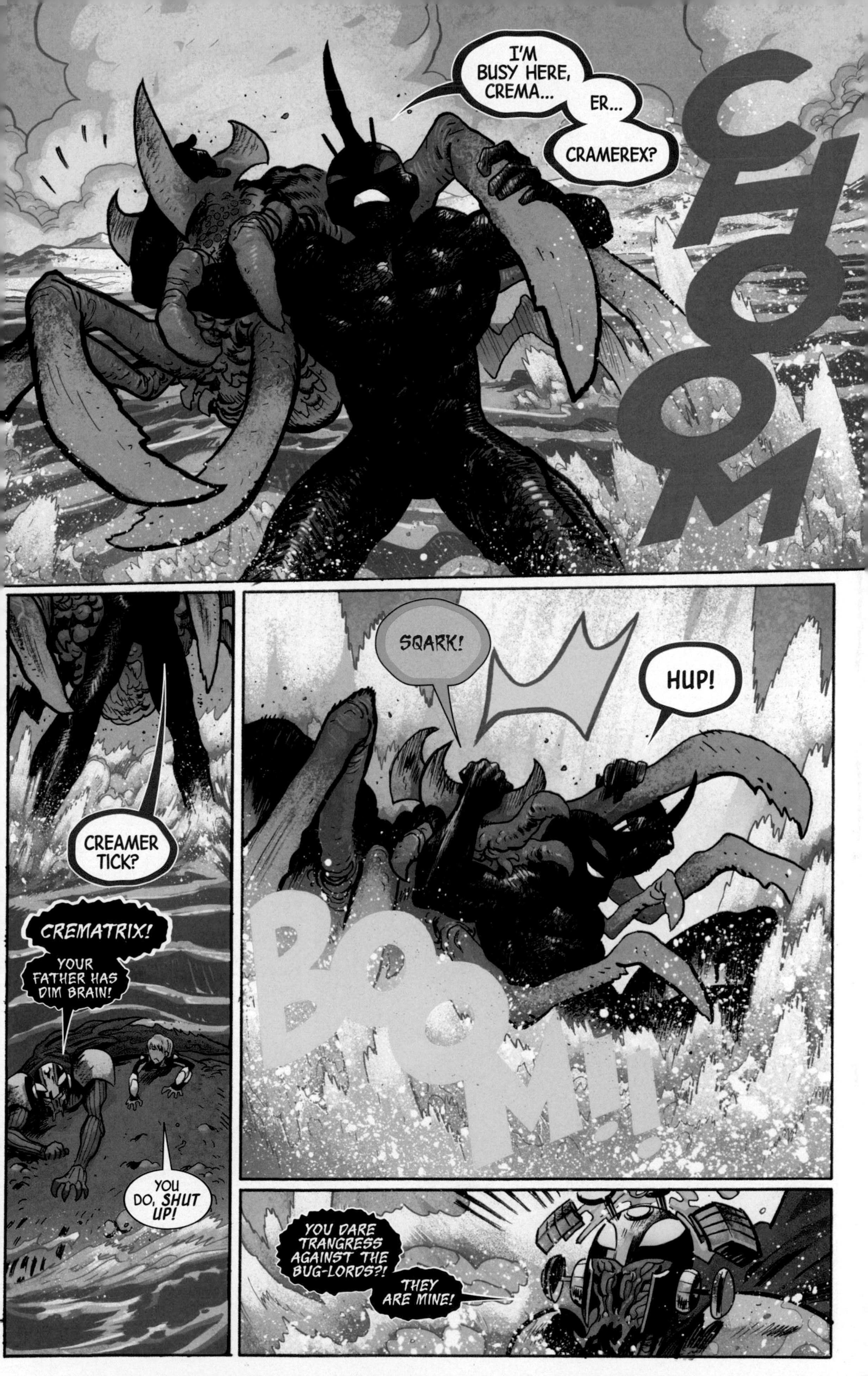
I'M BUSY HERE, CREMA...
ER...
CRAMEREX?
CHOOM
CREAMER TICK?
CREMATRIX!
YOUR FATHER HAS DIM BRAIN!
YOU DO, SHUT UP!
SQARK!
HUP!
BOOM!!
YOU DARE TRANGRESS AGAINST THE BUG-LORDS?!
THEY ARE MINE!

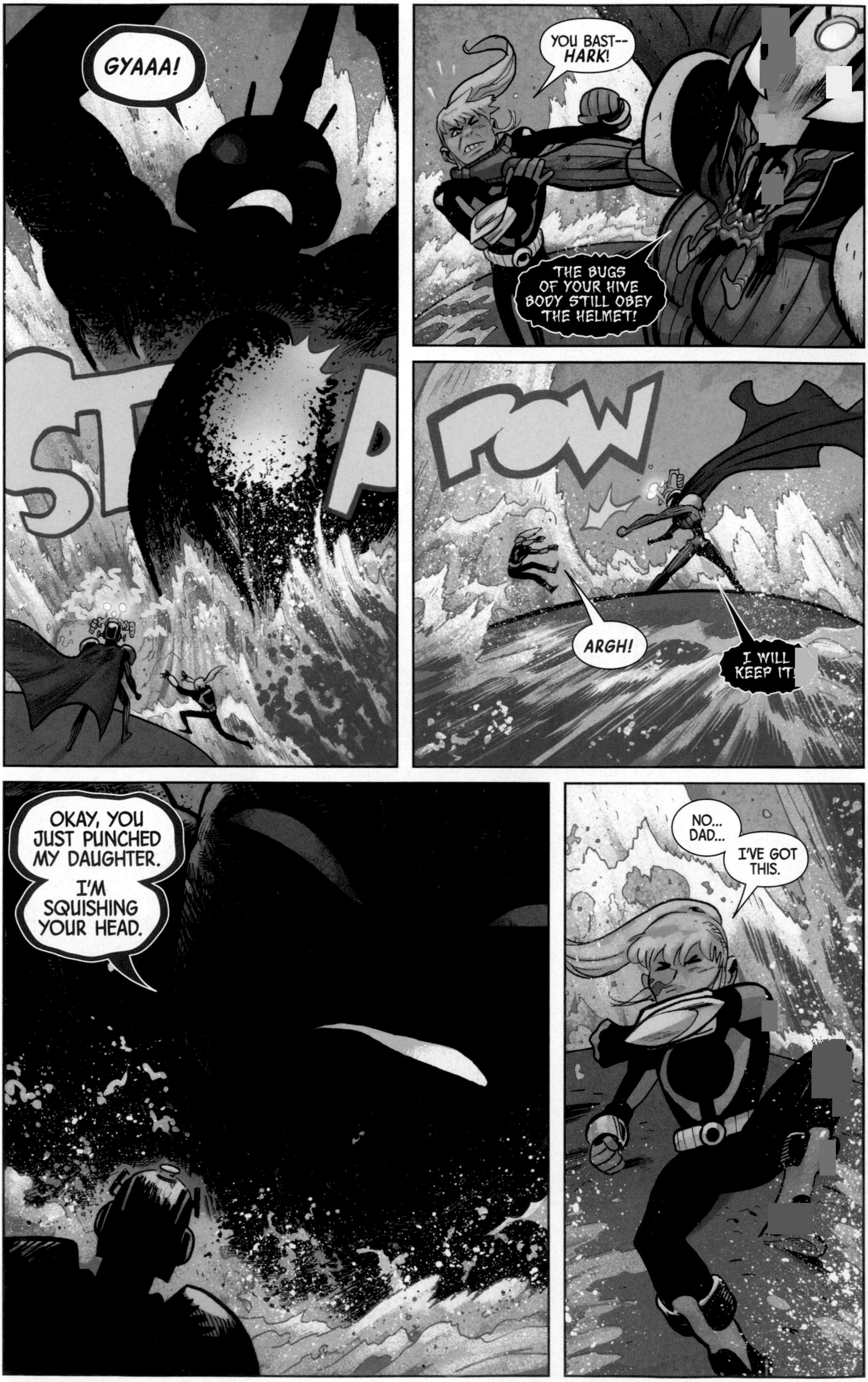
GYAAA!
ST P
YOU BAST-- HARK!
THE BUGS OF YOUR HIVE BODY STILL OBEY THE HELMET!
POW
ARGH!
I WILL KEEP IT!
OKAY, YOU JUST PUNCHED MY DAUGHTER.
I'M SQUISHING YOUR HEAD.
NO... DAD...
I'VE GOT THIS.

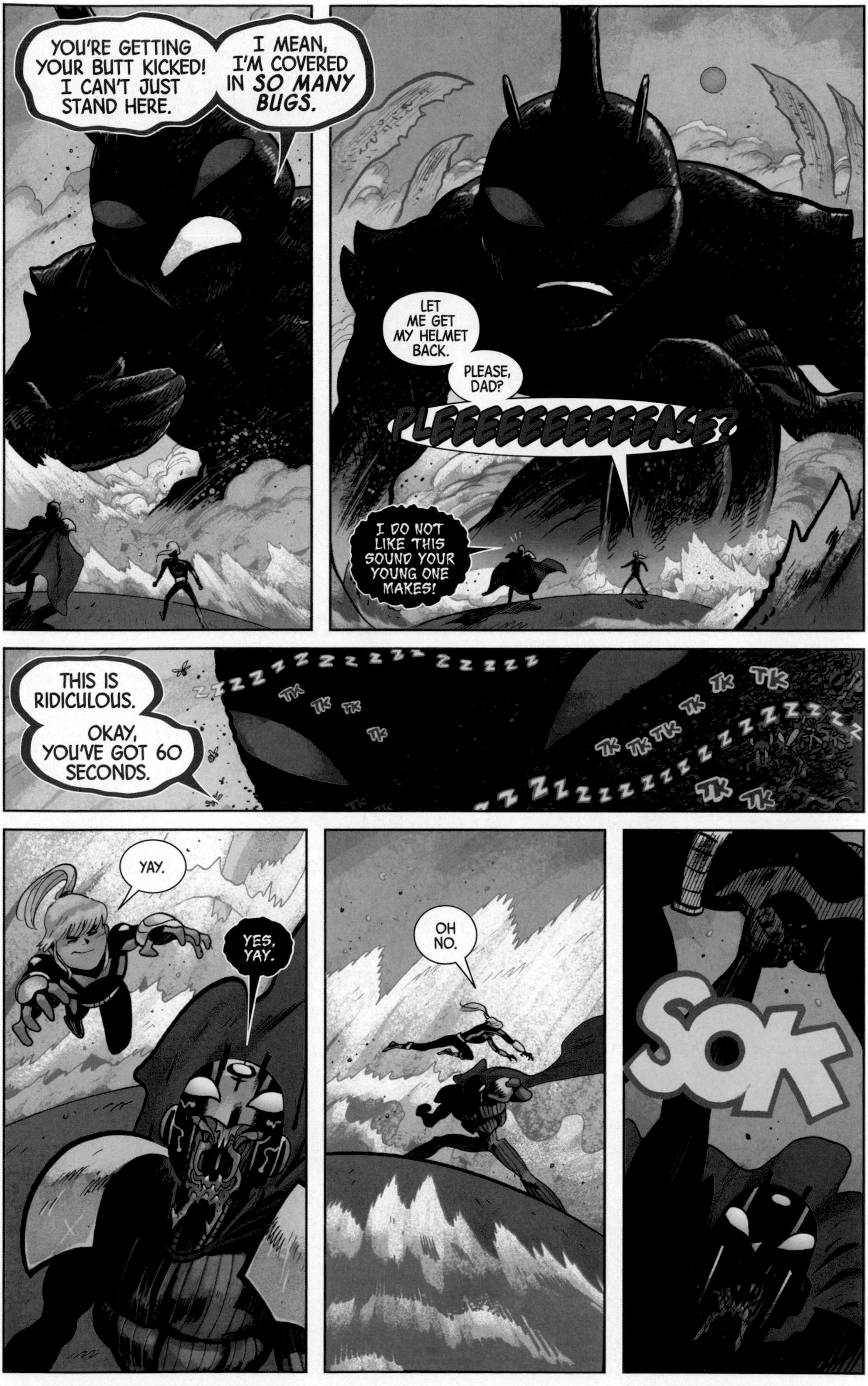
YOU'RE GETTING YOUR BUTT KICKED! I CAN'T JUST STAND HERE.
I MEAN, I'M COVERED IN SO MANY BUGS.
LET ME GET MY HELMET BACK.
PLEASE, DAD?
PLEEEEEEEEEEEASE?
I DO NOT LIKE THIS SOUND YOUR YOUNG ONE MAKES!
THIS IS RIDICULOUS.
OKAY, YOU'VE GOT 60 SECONDS.
YAY.
YES, YAY.
OH NO.
SOK

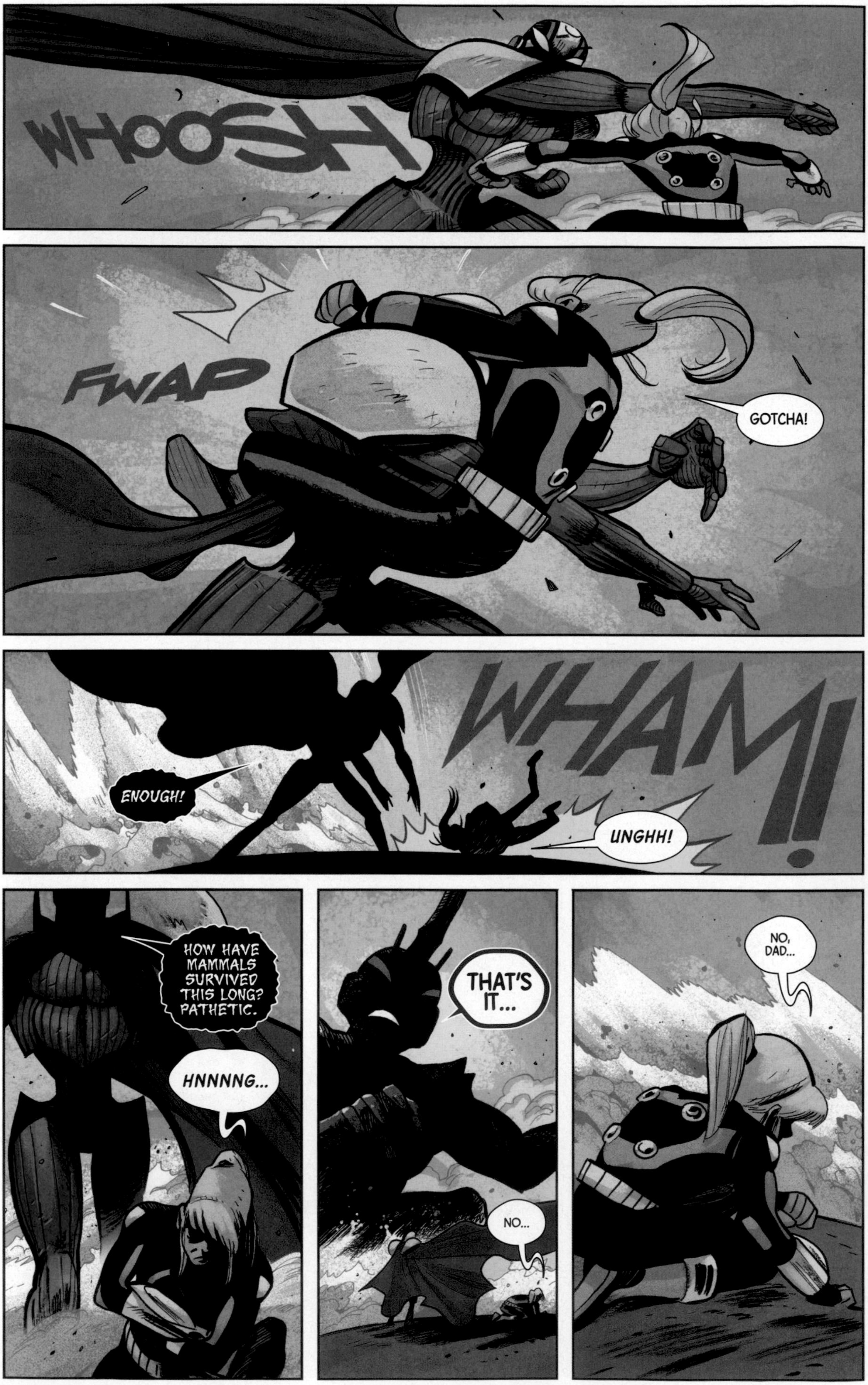
WHOOSH
FWAP
GOTCHA!
WHAM!
ENOUGH!
UNGHH!
HOW HAVE MAMMALS SURVIVED THIS LONG? PATHETIC.
HNNNNG...
THAT'S IT...
NO...
NO, DAD...

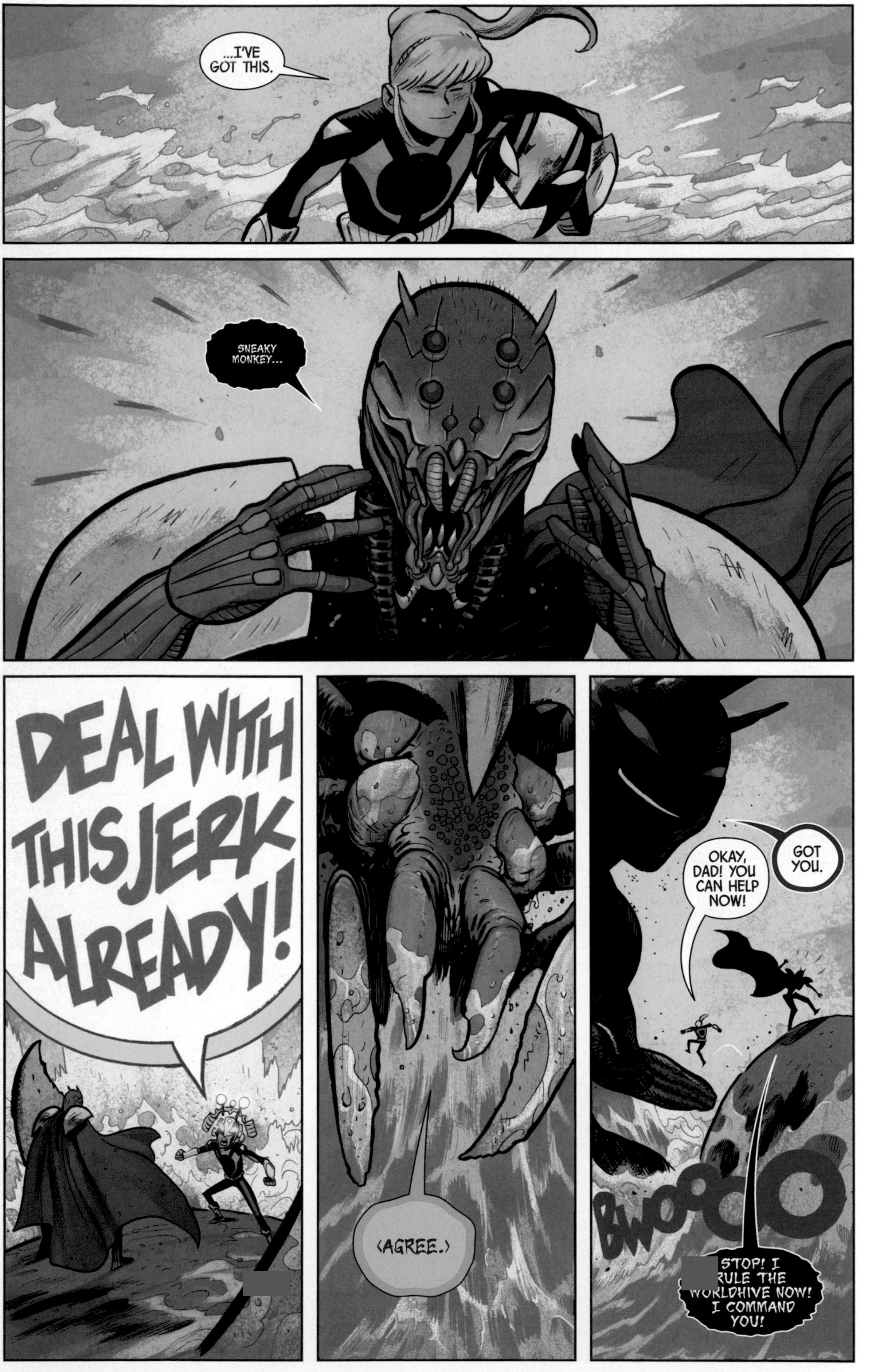
...I'VE GOT THIS.
SNEAKY MONKEY...
DEAL WITH THIS JERK ALREADY!
‹AGREE.›
OKAY, DAD! YOU CAN HELP NOW!
GOT YOU.
BWOOOOO
STOP! I RULE THE WORLDHIVE NOW! I COMMAND YOU!

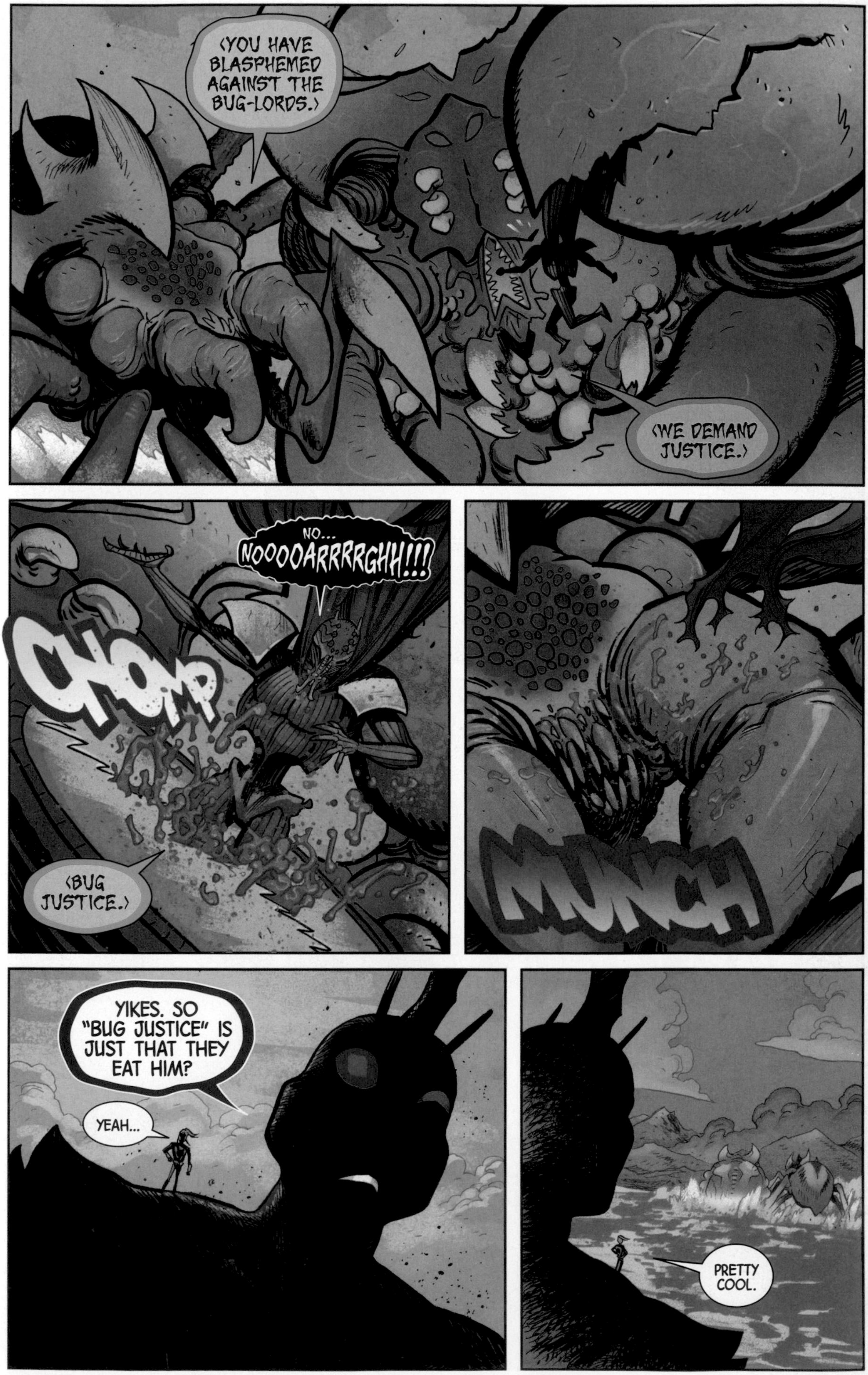
‹YOU HAVE BLASPHEMED AGAINST THE BUG-LORDS.›
‹WE DEMAND JUSTICE.›
NO... NOOOOARRRRGHH!!!!
CHOMP
‹BUG JUSTICE.›
MUNCH
YIKES. SO "BUG JUSTICE" IS JUST THAT THEY EAT HIM?
YEAH...
PRETTY COOL.

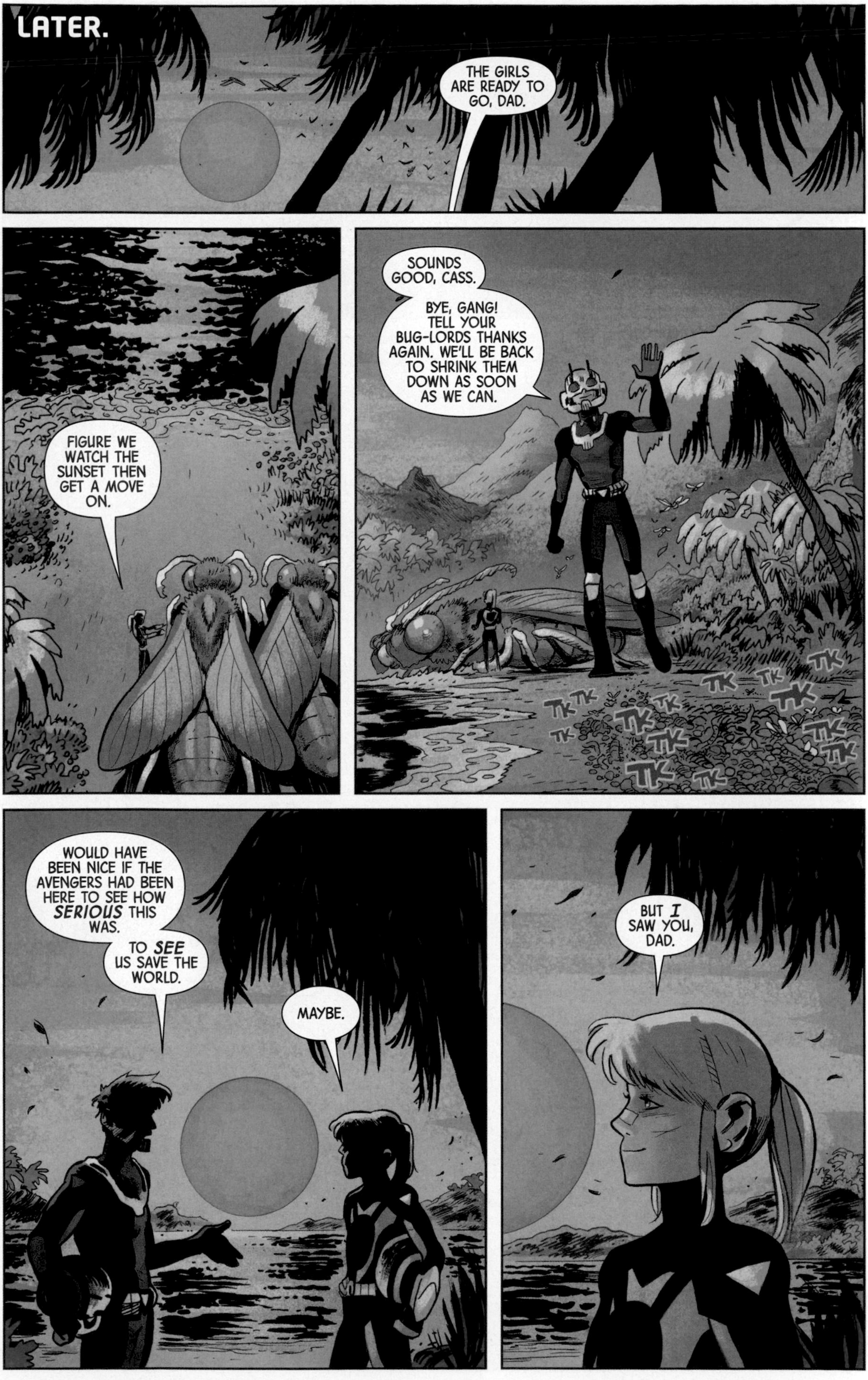
LATER.
THE GIRLS ARE READY TO GO, DAD.
FIGURE WE WATCH THE SUNSET THEN GET A MOVE ON.
SOUNDS GOOD, CASS.
BYE, GANG! TELL YOUR BUG-LORDS THANKS AGAIN. WE'LL BE BACK TO SHRINK THEM DOWN AS SOON AS WE CAN.
TK TK TK TK TK TK TK TK TK TK TK TK TK
WOULD HAVE BEEN NICE IF THE AVENGERS HAD BEEN HERE TO SEE HOW SERIOUS THIS WAS.
TO SEE US SAVE THE WORLD.
MAYBE.
BUT I SAW YOU, DAD.

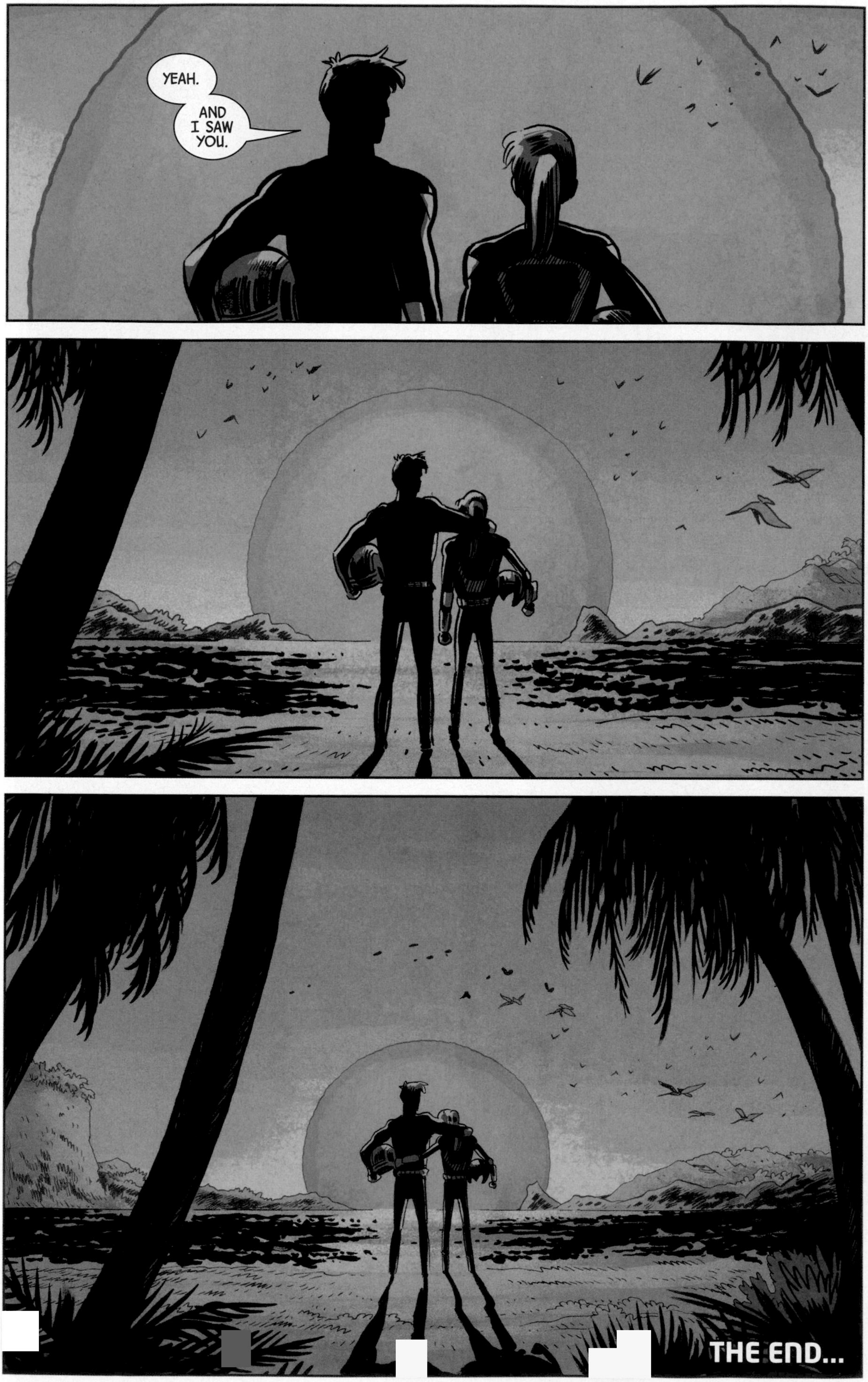
YEAH.
AND I SAW YOU.
THE END...

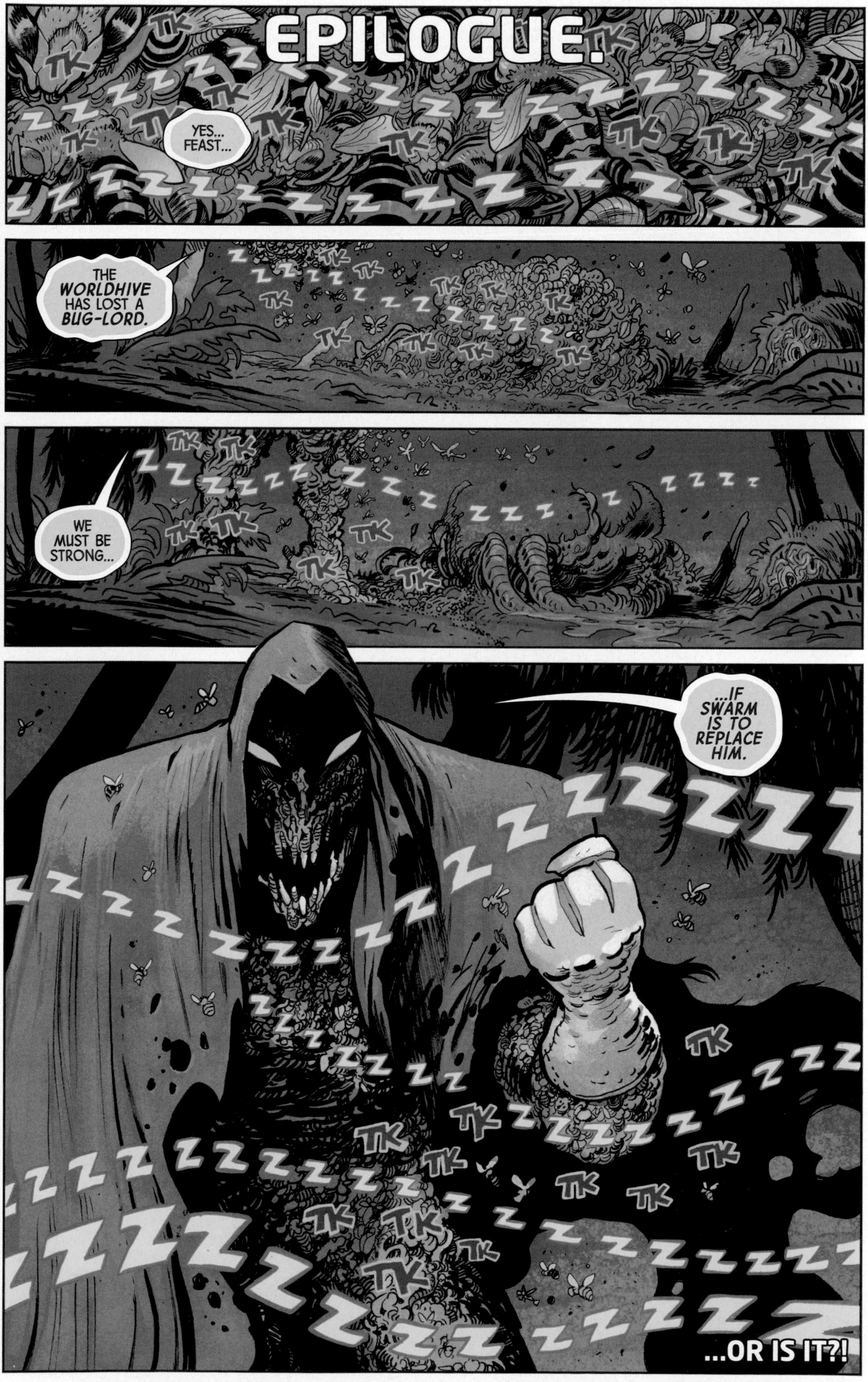
EPILOGUE.
YES... FEAST...
THE *WORLDHIVE* HAS LOST A *BUG-LORD.*
WE MUST BE STRONG...
...IF *SWARM* IS TO *REPLACE* HIM.
...OR IS IT?!

#1 VARIANT COVER BY
JOHN TYLER CHRISTOPHER

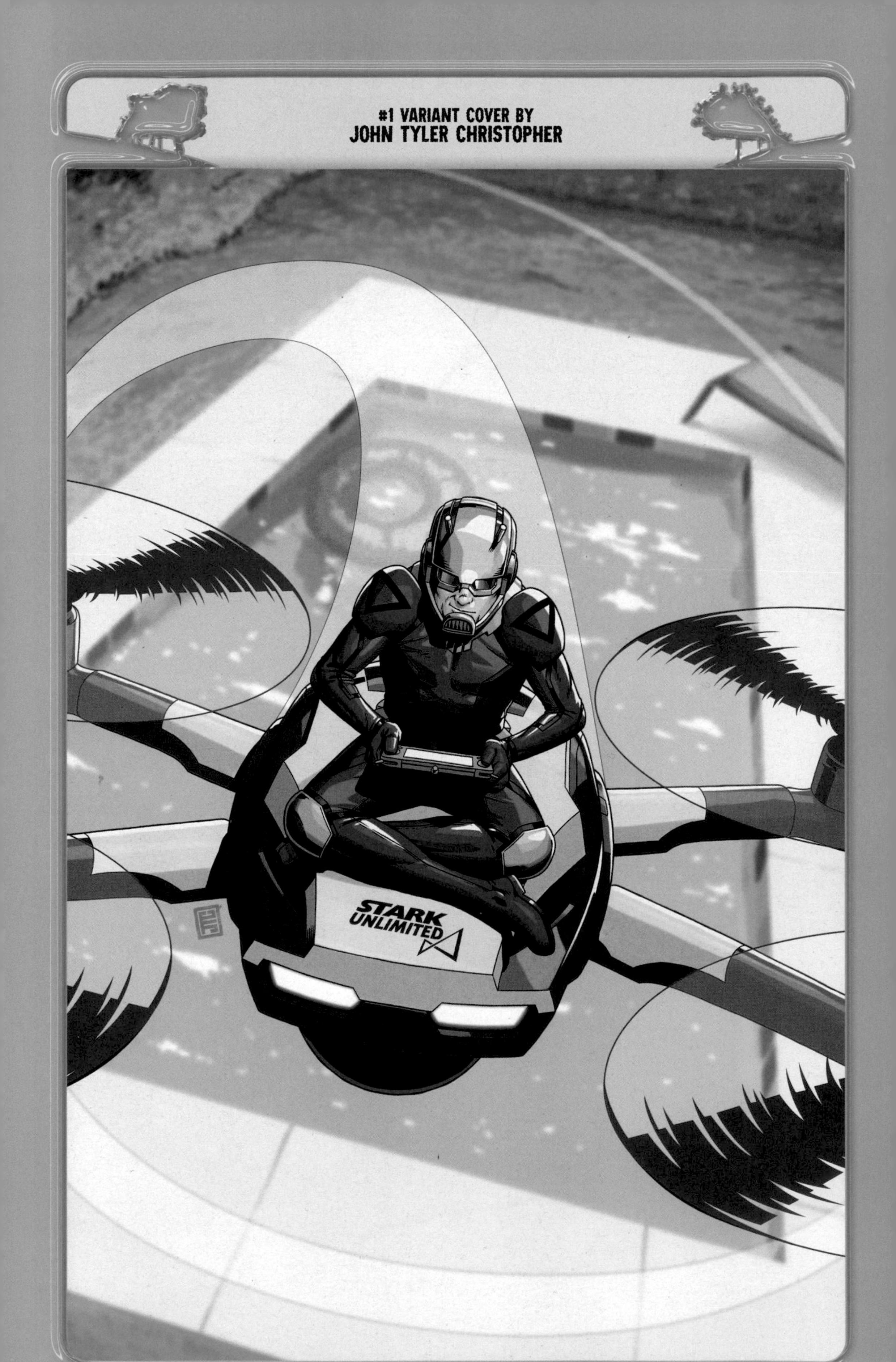
STARK
UNLIMITED

#1 HIDDEN GEM VARIANT COVER BY
HERB TRIMPE & MORRY HOLLOWELL

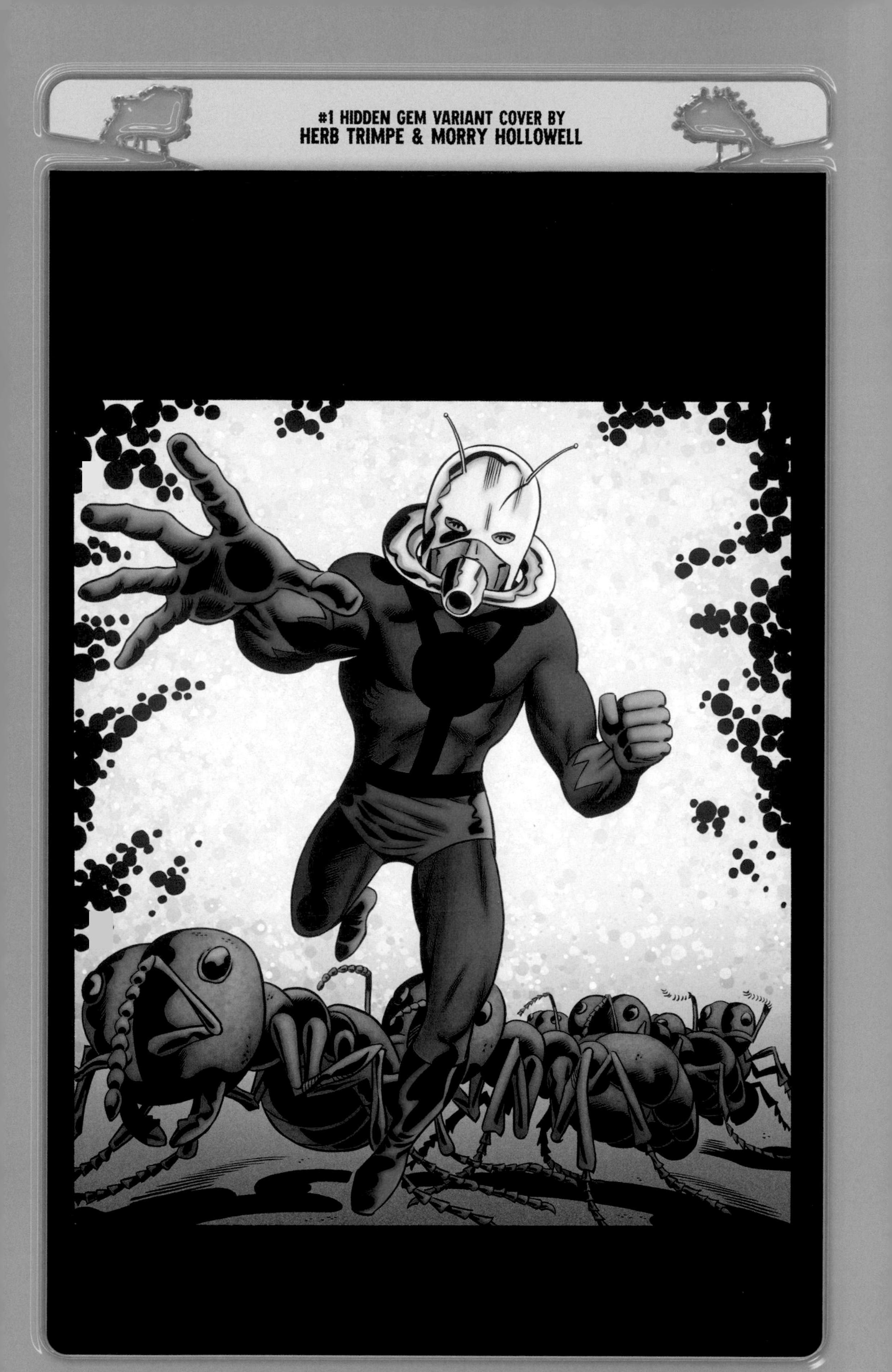

#1 VARIANT COVER BY
MARCOS MARTIN

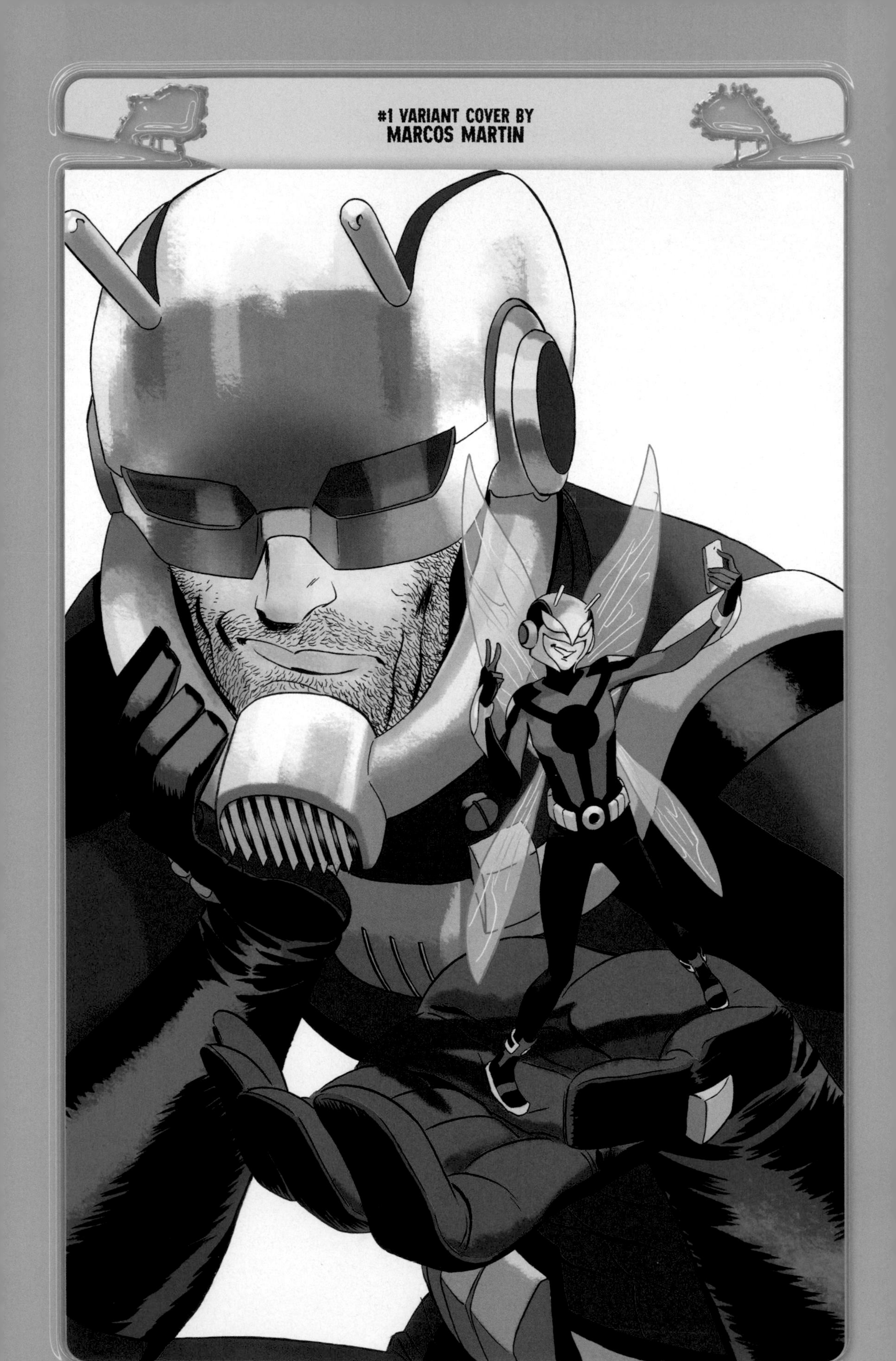

#2 VARIANT COVER BY
SUPERLOG

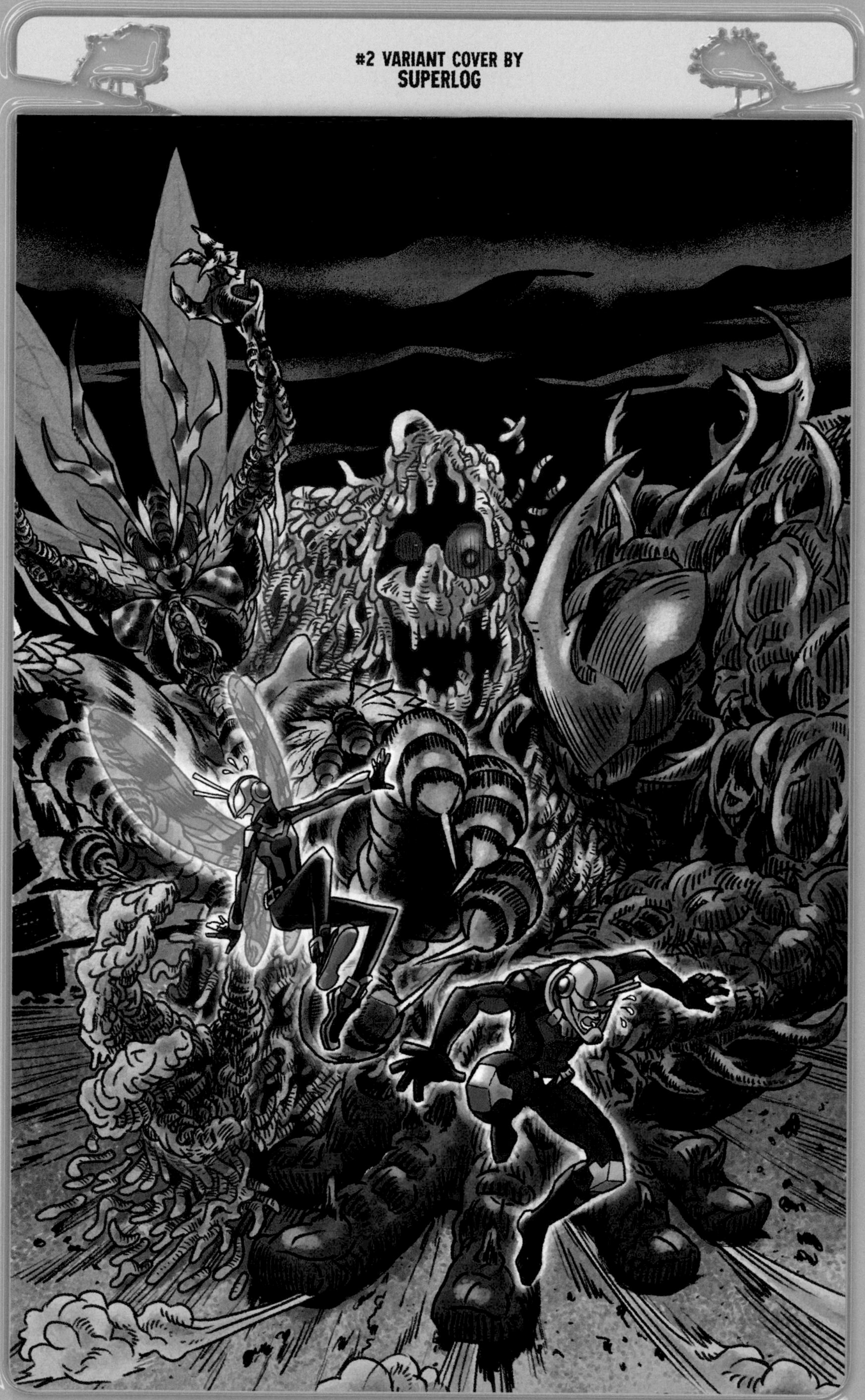

CHARACTER DESIGNS BY
DYLAN BURNETT

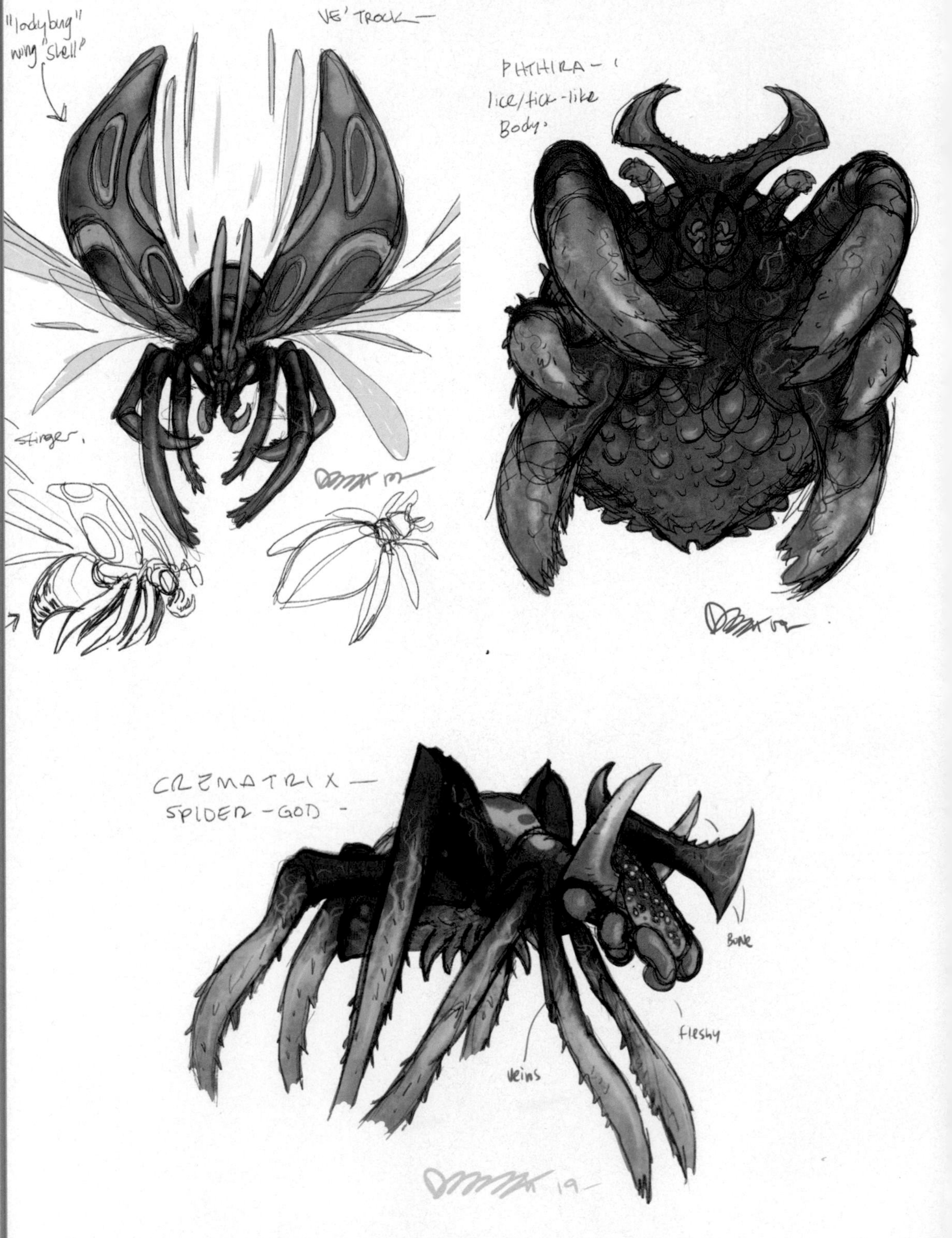
"ladybug" wing "shell"
VE'TROCK—
stinger.
PHTHIRA—
lice/tick-like Body.
CREMATRIX—
SPIDER-GOD-
Bone
Fleshy
Veins

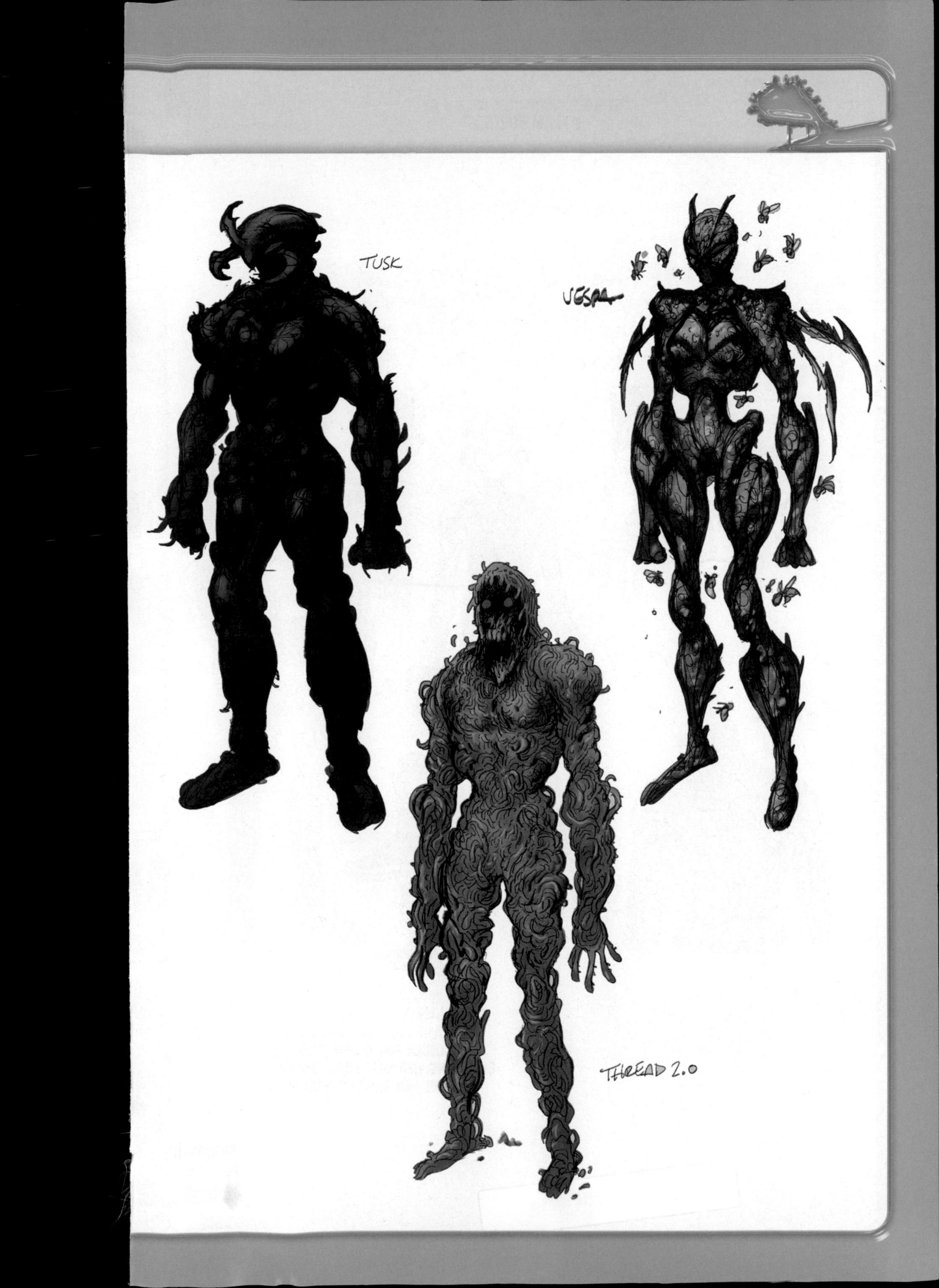
TUSK
VESPA
THREAD 2.0

STINGER CHARACTER DESIGN BY
DYLAN BURNETT

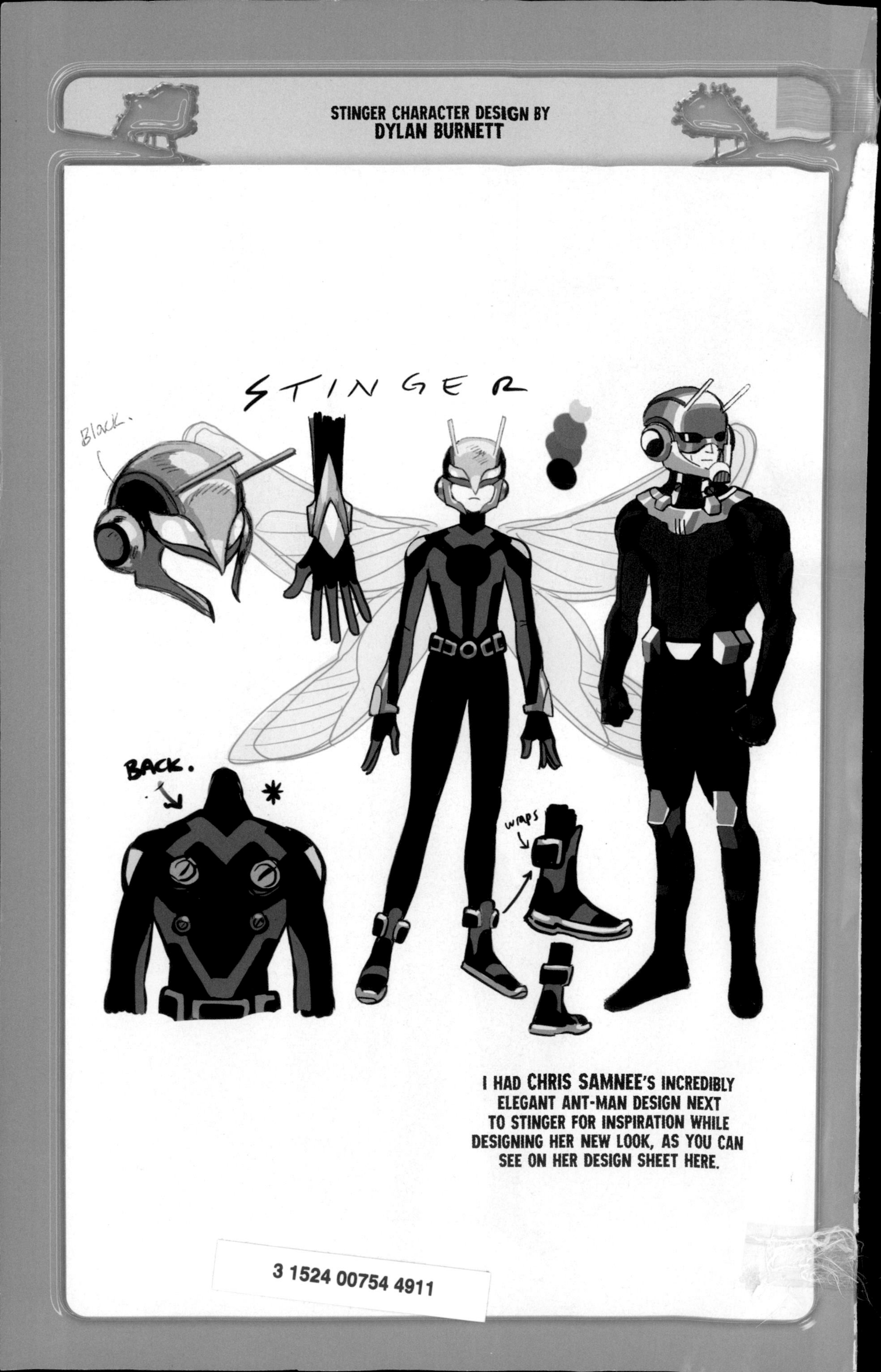
STINGER
BLACK.
BACK.
WRAPS

I HAD CHRIS SAMNEE'S INCREDIBLY ELEGANT ANT-MAN DESIGN NEXT TO STINGER FOR INSPIRATION WHILE DESIGNING HER NEW LOOK, AS YOU CAN SEE ON HER DESIGN SHEET HERE.